MAKING NORTH AMERICA

Trade, Security, and Integration

Much has been written about the trilateral relationship between Canada, the United States, and Mexico and the free trade agreements that this relationship has spawned. In *Making North America*, James Thompson uses the Canada–US Free Trade Agreement of 1988 and the North American Free Trade Agreement of 1994 to demonstrate that there has been an often-unrecognized impulse behind the process of North American integration – national security.

Featuring interviews with key decision-makers from all three countries, including Brian Mulroney, George H.W. Bush, and Carlos Salinas, *Making North America* is a rigorous analysis of the role national security has played in North American integration. Furthermore, Thompson's evidence suggests that the processes at work in North America are part of a global phenomenon where regions are progressively coalescing into larger-scale political entities.

JAMES THOMPSON is an assistant professor in the Department of Political Science at Hiram College.

Making North America

Trade, Security, and Integration

JAMES THOMPSON

UNIVERSITY OF TORONTO PRESS
Toronto Buffalo London

ISBN 978-1-4426-4620-9 (cloth)
ISBN 978-1-4426-1426-0 (paper)

A cataloguing record for this publication is available from Library and Archives Canada.

University of Toronto Press acknowledges the financial assistance to its
publishing program of the Canada Council for the Arts and the Ontario
Arts Council.

**Canada Council
for the Arts**   **Conseil des Arts
du Canada**

ONTARIO ARTS COUNCIL
CONSEIL DES ARTS DE L'ONTARIO

50 YEARS OF ONTARIO GOVERNMENT SUPPORT OF THE ARTS
50 ANS DE SOUTIEN DU GOUVERNEMENT DE L'ONTARIO AUX ARTS

University of Toronto Press acknowledges the financial support of the
Government of Canada through the Canada Book Fund for its publishing
activities.

Contents

Acknowledgments

Writing this book about international politics has caused me to incur an array of debts that is likewise international in its extent. The largest debts are owed to two Daniels: Lindley and Quinlan. Dr Daniel Lindley served as my advisor during my time in graduate school and played a crucial role in ensuring that my dissertation – which ultimately evolved into this book – was a focused and efficiently structured bit of scholarship. In the process, he bravely rode the rollercoaster of creation-destruction-creation which was the inevitable price to be paid for agreeing to work with me. Daniel Quinlan served as my editor at the University of Toronto Press and, in that capacity, exceeded all possible expectations in terms of providing guidance and support as I transitioned the manuscript into a more reader-friendly piece of prose. In addition to these two gentlemen, I would also like to thank Professors Jim McAdams, Daniel Philpott, and Kier Lieber for serving alongside Professor Lindley on my dissertation committee. More generally, I feel a real sense of gratitude to the Political Science Department at the University of Notre Dame, which provided the intellectual nest within which this project was hatched. Furthermore, I would like to thank all of those individuals who agreed to be interviewed for this research effort, as well as the many people who, in one form or another, facilitated my fieldwork. Special mention in this regard goes to Jean and Michelle Ducroux, who provided me with a place to stay during three weeks of research in Paris, and to Dr Albert Kersten, who, upon finding me trolling through the archives of the Netherlands Foreign Ministry, went out of his way to ensure that I was able to make the best possible use of my time while in his country. Finally, and most fundamentally, I would like to thank my family – Marylynne, Melissa, and Jim – for their full and unwavering support.

MAKING NORTH AMERICA

Trade, Security, and Integration

1 Core Concepts

Something seemingly unimportant occurred in Waco, Texas, on 23 March 2005. It was there on that day that the leaders of Canada, the United States, and Mexico met together and established the Security and Prosperity Partnership (SPP) of North America. This event went largely unnoticed by the general public, which is not surprising. The SPP, after all, was conceived of by its creators as an extension of the North American Free Trade Agreement (NAFTA) of 1994, which, in turn, is a vast document whose numerous details pertaining to cross-border trade might strike most people as rather arcane. Furthermore, several of the SPP's own programmatic concepts were somewhat vague. Worse still, certain analysts argued that the entire SPP agenda was flawed and therefore destined for failure. Even the choice of venue for launching the SPP was inauspicious, considering that the most famous event in Waco's history was the tragic episode in 1993 when members of a religious group known as the "Branch Davidians" were immolated in the course of fighting against US federal law enforcement officers.

And, as it turned out, the negative predictions and portents were confirmed. Although more SPP summits were subsequently held – one per year for the next few years – relatively little in the way of policy substance emerged from these gatherings. Then in 2009 the SPP agenda was effectively cancelled. As of this writing, more than four years later, it remains to be seen whether another continent-wide project akin to the SPP will come along any time soon.

In terms of what it actually accomplished, therefore, the SPP effort was fairly unimpressive. Yet when considered in light of what it represented, that effort appears less ineffectual. Via the holding of their yearly SPP meetings, for instance, the three leaders demonstrated a desire to think and act in a consistent, collective fashion on behalf of continental concerns. That might not seem like much of a feat, but the fact is that, despite the three states' obvious mutual interests as the members of a single continent, such trilateral summits prior to 2005 were relatively rare. Even more significantly, the SPP was the first substantial initiative undertaken by all three states for the purpose of pushing the boundaries of NAFTA-based relations into the realm of security policy. Although that push was tentative and ultimately unsuccessful, it is nonetheless noteworthy that the attempt was made at all. Indeed, as the following chapters will demonstrate, mutual trust has often been in short supply among these three states. It therefore represented an important, symbolic step forward when an ambition was expressed – much less in public, official form – to begin combining national security strategies via a NAFTA-related framework.

Of course in the end it is concrete results and not merely symbolic gestures that ultimately count. The question to consider, therefore, is what constitutes "ultimately" when it comes to North American integration? Is the NAFTA process, in other words, a limited project in terms of integrative developments, such that we should not expect many more building-on-NAFTA initiatives, or is NAFTA part of an integration effort that, despite setbacks, is likely to continue moving forward and involving the three states in ever-deeper levels of policy intermeshing? More specifically, is it plausible that a truly viable version of the SPP might someday be established such that comprehensive security goals will be directly and effectively connected to the trilateral integrative endeavour?

Anyone answering this question in the affirmative might point by way of comparison to the case of European integration, which has witnessed both setbacks and successes with integration in general and with security policy integration in particular. That process began in 1951 when six western European states signed a treaty establishing the European Coal and Steel Community (ECSC). Shortly thereafter, those states sought to add a military component to their integration effort, to be known as the European Defence Community (EDC). The EDC effort failed, yet in 1957 those same states managed to establish the European Economic Community (EEC), thereby extending the economic scope of their integration scheme. Following this, further attempts were made in the 1960s to incorporate security policy into the integration agenda, but these efforts fell flat. Indeed, for the next two decades European integration in general experienced a protracted lull. Nonetheless, during the early 1970s a tentative step was taken by these states to at least be-gin discussing foreign policy in the context of their integration-related meetings and to try coordinating – in a general way – their responses to international developments. This low-level approach to consultation was given the name of European Political Cooperation (EPC). Then in the mid-1980s, as European integration as a whole began to accelerate, so too did integration pertaining to foreign policy. In 1987 EPC was officially incorporated into the larger treaty structure of the integra-tion project, and in 1992, via the Treaty on European Union (TEU), EPC was transformed into the Common Foreign and Security Policy (CFSP), which gave the integrating states – now referred to collectively as the European Union (EU) – a new range of instruments and objectives with regard to crafting a unified position on foreign and security affairs. The creation of the CFSP thus constituted a significant step forward; it was followed, however, by the break-up of Yugoslavia and a decade of Bal-kan wars, during which the CFSP repeatedly came up short in terms of providing the EU states with an adequate foreign and security policy capacity. In response to these shortcomings, the CFSP was progres-sively strengthened during the 1990s, such that by the early 2000s the EU was prepared to field peacekeeping forces in trouble spots in Europe and Africa, and it has since done so on multiple occasions. In conjunc-tion with these activities, an enhanced position of High Representative of the Union for Foreign Affairs and Security Policy has been created, as has a more formalized position of European Council president. Mean-while, an ever-expanding range of goals and responsibilities are regu-larly attached to the CFSP.

Based upon the European example, therefore, a case might be made that, in the course of complex integration processes, setbacks – such as the lack of progress associated with the North American SPP – are part of the experience, that what matters is the long-range trajectory. On the other hand, those arguing against the likelihood of further NAFTA in-tegration and hence against such a comparison with the EU might reply that the differences between the EU and the NAFTA processes are many: the EU, after all, has far more states; its member states' economies are more akin to one another than those of, for instance, the United States and Mexico; the European process from the outset was accompanied by grander ambitions than those typically associated with NAFTA; and so forth. Yet it might then be argued in counterresponse that the similari-ties between the two projects are likewise noteworthy: both are made up entirely of democracies; all of the states involved in each project have accepted some basic tenets of free-market capitalism; and both processes have thus far displayed a "progressive" quality, insofar as the European project has evolved from the ECSC of 1951 into the highly complex EU of the twenty-first century, while in North America the process has also involved multiple steps, including the establishment of a free trade agreement (FTA) between Canada and the United States in 1988, known as CUFTA, which was then followed by the trilateral arrangement established via NAFTA.

The truly important point, however, in terms of this present attempt to determine where NAFTA-related integration is headed, pertains to the degree of similarity or difference between the two projects with respect to core motivations. After all, if the EU and NAFTA are driven by differing goals and aspirations, then their integrative trajectories will ultimately diverge regardless of whatever similarities they exhibit at any given historical moment; conversely, if their driving motivations are essentially the same, then they are much more likely to reach similar integrative end points regardless of "cosmetic" differences – that is, the number of member states, or the present level of integration on a given policy, and so forth – they might display at any one time. The fundamental question, therefore, in its simplest form, is what prompted and continues to prompt integration in Europe and in North America?

In the case of Europe, the evidence is persuasive that, among the variety of possible motives, a primary driver in persuading the six founding states to launch the ECSC in 1951 was security concerns. More specifically, and as is explained in detail in chapter 4, in the wake of World War II the six founding states feared a return to war-scale violence among themselves. To forestall that eventuality, they began to combine their respective realms of political authority into a supra-national political structure, with economic integration being viewed as the first step in that process. In subsequent years, the original fears were then paired with added fears of the Soviet Union and its East European allies, thereby prompting still further integration among the West Europeans, this time as a means to aggregate strength against the threats from the East. All of these threats lingered on at varying degrees of intensity throughout the following decades, until the security situation became exceptionally dangerous in the 1980s, at which point – not coincidently, I would argue – integration was reinvigorated, thereby initiating the phase of robust integrative activity that we are currently witnessing.

If security issues have indeed played such a central role in prompting European integration, then many readers will likely assume that the EU and NAFTA must be fated for differing end points, since NAFTA is typically conceived of as strictly an economics-focused affair, with security issues being of only marginal relevance – at most – to its creation and perpetuation. The argument offered here, however, is rather the opposite. The central claim of this book is that security concerns played an important role in the establishment of both CUFTA in 1988 and NAFTA in 1994. This is not to suggest that economic incentives were insignificant in prompting these FTAs' creations. Such incentives have clearly played a key part in the integration process. What is being proposed, however, it that security issues deserve far more attention than is typically accorded to them in the study of North American free trade negotiations.

To argue this point, an analysis is conducted in the following pages regarding the geostrategic circumstances that were in place when these two North American FTAs were established, as well as the manner in which statesmen responded to those circumstances by seeking to use trade techniques as a means to facilitate the achievement of security policy goals. So as to demonstrate the full validity of the argument, however, it is also essential to consider the larger, long-term historical context in which these events took place. Specifically, it is necessary to identify patterns that have played themselves out repeatedly during the course of US-Canadian and US-Mexican relations – patterns pertaining to interstate insecurity and to interstate trade. Time and again, similar security concerns have manifested themselves in the course of US-Canadian relations, and time and again these two states have sought to use trade techniques to help address their security issues. The same applies to US-Mexican relations. As such, if we wish to fully appreciate why CUFTA and NAFTA were signed, it is essential to recognize certain larger patterns of state behaviour. To understand such patterns, in turn, we need to grasp a few core concepts of international relations (IR) theory. With these core concepts in hand, we can comprehend not only the security motivations for creating the two North American FTAs but also why security concerns are likely to continue confronting these three states and hence why further integration is likely among them. We can also recognize the ways in which such patterns of trade-and-security-seeking behaviour operate in the context of European integration, and thus we can discern the core similarities between the European and North American processes. Finally, we can observe the similarities between these two integration projects and those that are currently transpiring in fledgling form in other regions of the world, such as in South America and Southeast Asia. Once we are armed, in other words, with a few IR theory ideas, we can appreciate a global pattern of state behaviour of which North American integration is a part.

Indeed, the larger rationale for examining the North American case is precisely that it provides a useful starting point for considering the widespread phenomenon of regional integration. Such usefulness derives from three features of the North American process. First, since relatively few people recognize that this process is part of a multiregional, integrative trend that is partially prompted by security concerns, the North American example can provide a tough test – arguably the toughest – of the claim that contemporary states are in fact caught up in security-seeking integrative undertakings. An argument that passes this specific test thus simultaneously provides strong evidence for the larger, global trend. Second, studying the North American process serves as an excellent entrée for examining the long-term, durational nature of global integrative patterns, because there are only two dyadic relationships involved in the North American scenario and hence the histories of Canadian-US and US-Mexican relations can be explored in some depth. Third, because this integration scheme involves the world's only current superpower, anything happening with this specific process has substantial significance for the rest of the world.

The first of these three features – the toughness of the test – is particularly noteworthy; thus it is useful to more specifically delineate how this present analysis differs from extant economics-focused studies of North American integration.[1] With regard to creation of CUFTA, for example, an influential explanation of Canadian motivations for the FTA emphasizes the economic downturn experienced by the United States during the early 1980s and the strain this placed on the Canadian economy.[2] The argument is that, due to a desire to obtain stronger guarantees of access to the US market during this troubled economic time, Canada's ruling Conservative Party agreed to a dramatic overhaul of the bilateral trading relationship. Furthermore, certain statesmen in Canada assumed that this opening-up of the Canadian market would have an energizing effect on Canadian industry, forcing Canadian firms to compete more aggressively with each other and with their US counterparts.[3] In addition to this, "the pressures of the 1981–82 recession in Canada and apprehension about a nationalist lurch in Canadian energy and investment policies had further convinced the traditionally cautious and suspicious business community of the need for a change in direction of Canada's commercial relations with the United States."[4] Scholars have also highlighted the fact that Canadian economic policies of the 1970s – which sought to diversify Canadian trade relations to reduce US dominance – had proven economically damaging and thus by the early 1980s Canada was ready to accept the economic logic of closer ties to the US market.[5] Finally, certain analysts have focused on how the Macdonald Commission, which was appointed in 1982 by Prime Minister Pierre Trudeau and tasked with assessing trade strategies with the United States, played an influential role at the time in focusing Canadian minds on the benefits of engaging in free trade with Canada's neighbour to the south.[6]

Explanations of why the United States sought an FTA with Canada have also typically focused on strictly economic incentives. The United States, as noted, was facing economic challenges at this time, and in that context the US regime began pursuing in-depth bilateral FTAs with certain states. The argument is that this trade strategy appeared particularly attractive because the General Agreement on Tariffs and Trade (GATT) – which was established following WWII to ensure a relative measure of liberalized trade between its many member states, and which was transformed in 1995 into the World Trade Organization (WTO) – seemed insufficient for meeting US trade needs. Although the United States had pursued an FTA with Canada many times in the past – including when GATT was in effect – the assumption of this scholarship is that GATT's limitations made the advocacy of the bilateral policy more pronounced at this time.[7] Concomitantly, the fact that both Canada and the United States experienced ideological shifts towards neoliberal economic theory during this period is presumed to have been conducive to the support of a free trade initiative.

A similar, economics-only analysis is often applied to the decision of the United States and Mexico to negotiate an FTA in the early 1990s, which then led to the creation of NAFTA. A prominent analysis of this FTA-creation process suggests that "the journey toward North American free trade began for Mexico, as it had for Canada, in the punishing recession of 1981–82 ... The recession and the collapse of oil prices decimated the Mexican economy and brought the country to the brink of default on its foreign debt." Indeed, "this economic crisis triggered the start of a prolonged policy shift by Mexican authorities as they attempted to deal with the profoundly changed economic world that emerged from the global recession."[8] One of Mexico's responses, according to this argument, was to gain accession to GATT in 1986 as a means of inserting itself into a global, multilateral trading framework.[9] Furthermore, by late 1989 Mexico also made the decision to pursue bilateral trade agreements with the United States, although these agreements were focused only on a few sectors of the two states' economies, not on general free trade. In early 1990, however, when the Mexican regime realized that hoped-for, large-scale investment from European states was not going to materialize, Mexico agreed to a full FTA with the United States, as the capstone of its efforts to revitalize and further enhance its economic strength.[10] Eventually Canada joined in these trade negotiations as well; the FTA then became regional and this ultimately resulted in NAFTA. Increased trade, however, was not the only economic benefit that Mexico sought via the FTA. By signing up to NAFTA, Mexico would bind itself more closely to the US economy and could thus present itself as a more attractive environment for foreign investment.[11] As for the American decision to pursue the FTA with Mexico, it is widely recognized as a continuation of the policy – initiated in the early 1980s – of seeking bilateral trade deals with various states.[12]

All of these foregoing economics-focused analyses do seem sound on their own terms. The logic of their claims is fundamentally clear, and, indeed, the very plausibility of such argumentation is partially responsible for the fact that scholars have seldom strayed from economics-only assessments in order to explain the creation of CUFTA and NAFTA. Besides this simple neglect of security issues, however, certain scholars have also made a specific point of arguing against analyses that conceive of a tight coupling of multiple policy areas, particularly in the context of US-Canadian relations. A fairly recent example of this perspective has been formulated, for instance, by Brian Bow in *The Politics of Linkage*. Furthermore, in those cases where analysts have indeed considered the role of security motivations in prompting the creation of the two North American FTAs, the security-focused approach has typically functioned as an analytical straw man, with scholars arguing that a security-based analysis does not allow for adequate treatment of the topic and thus an economics-focused approach is essentially all that is required.[13] Even in those rare instances where noneconomic rationales are given serious consideration, the analysis has still typically refrained from addressing specifically security-relevant issues.[14] A notable example in this regard is Lloyd Gruber's *Ruling the World: Power Politics and the Rise of Supranational Institutions*. Rather than focusing simply on the economic benefits of trade agreements, Gruber examines the manner in which institutionalized trade rules can enhance the power of the states that establish such institutions. Specifically, he observes that "institutionalized cooperation by one group of actors (the winners) can have the effect of restricting the options available to another group of actors (the losers), altering the rules of the game such that the members of the latter group are better off playing by the new rules despite their strong preference for the original, pre-cooperation status quo."[15] By establishing an FTA, for instance, certain states within a region can restrict the trade options of other states in that region that are not party to the FTA. Those other states will thus be induced to join that FTA, but on the terms of the FTA's founders. As a result, the founding states will be able to exercise power over the other states of the region. For example, Gruber argues that by establishing a bilateral FTA between themselves, the United States and Canada changed Mexico's set of preferred trading options. Mexico would ideally have liked to remain outside of a tight trading structure, but, after the US-Canadian FTA came into being, fear of exclusion from developing trade networks prompted Mexico to seek closer trade relations with its northern neighbours.[16] In this way, so the argument goes, the United States and Canada were able to exert significant power over Mexico. Gruber's analysis thus extends beyond issues of strict economics to consider the more purely power-based motivations of trade, although he does nonetheless remain focused on the economic relations between the participating states, without specifically analysing threat-related – and hence, ultimately, security – issues *per se*. Thus his work ultimately serves to reinforce the dominant trend in NAFTA scholarship.[17]

Yet, despite the paucity of arguments regarding the security motivations that lay behind the creation of CUFTA and NAFTA, there is in fact ample evidence to suggest that far more was involved in the establishment of the two FTAs than strictly economic considerations. An analysis of that evidence is provided in chapters 2 and 3. Before conducting that analysis, however, it is necessary to explain the IR theory concepts upon which that analysis is based. Specifically, the central claim of this book – that security motivations played an important role in prompting the creation of the two North American FTAs – rests upon the following two hypotheses: 1) Trading to Oppose: states can use trade agreements with each other to augment their power against a threatening third-party state, and 2) Trading to Control: states can use trade agreements with a threatening state to enhance their power vis-à-vis that state.

The idea that trade agreements can be used in such ways by states to help obtain security goals seems like a simple concept. There is nothing particularly complicated, for instance, about the idea that, by enhancing their reciprocal trade, states can potentially increase their overall economic strength and that such economic strength can then be translated into military power, which in turn can help the trading states to address threats posed by a third-party state. So too, it is easy to imagine that states that wish to influence the behaviour of a threatening state might seek to do so via the leverage gained by a close trading partnership with that threat-inducing state. Nonetheless, it is necessary to spend a few paragraphs precisely detailing the assumptions that are being made within the two hypotheses, so as to ensure clarity of analysis in the following chapters. First and foremost, it is essential to clarify exactly what is meant by "security," as well as the conditions under which states feel their security to be threatened, and then it is necessary to clarify the sort of cooperative/integrative relations in which states are engaging via FTAs.

For a state, security implies, fundamentally, the ability to ensure its continued existence. A state comes into existence in the first place by establishing a regime that can enforce laws within the state and that can protect the state against attacks from the outside. By establishing domestic legality and by preventing or fending off external attacks – in other words, by establishing sovereignty – a regime thus ensures the perpetuation of a stable order within the state, with all the attendant benefits that such order brings, including physical security, social justice, and so forth. Another way to say that a state wishes to exist, therefore, is to say that it wants to avoid having its internal order severely damaged. And such damage can be wrought by other states, given that 1) all states are ultimately free to attempt to do whatever they please, which is to say that, at the level of interstate relations, the world is anarchic, and 2) all states possess a certain amount of power. There are various ways to conceptualize a state's power; this study uses "the old and simple notion that an agent is powerful to the extent that he affects others more than they affect him."[18] Thanks to such factors as their economic strength, population size, and, most directly, military capacity, states have the power to impact and hence damage other states' internal order, and potentially to do so more than their own internal orders are impacted. States thus inherently pose a potential threat to one another, with the more powerful state posing the greater threat. Security for a state therefore implies, first and foremost, the mitigation of threats that are posed by other states' power.

Yet while there is assumed to be – for the purposes of this argument – a direct relationship between the amount of overall power that a state has and the sense of threat that it engenders in other states, other variables can add further complexity to this simple formula.[19] As the IR theorist Stephen Walt explains, "Although the distribution of power is an extremely important factor, the level of threat is also affected by geographic proximity, offensive capabilities, and perceived intentions."[20] For instance, a state will likely feel more threatened by a powerful state that is near to its borders than by a powerful state that is located far away; a state will likely feel more threatened by a powerful state that possesses more military capacity to launch an attack than by another powerful state with less readily-utilizable capacity; and a state will likely feel more threatened by a powerful state that, for one reason or another, is perceived as harbouring greater hostile intent than by another powerful state whose intentions appear more benign. Walt thus proposes a theory based upon states' responses to threat rather than to power, in which power – in a general sense – is the main ingredient of threat but is then either partially enhanced or partially mitigated by the intervening variables of proximity, military capacity, and apparent intent. That approach seems reasonable and as such is incorporated into this argument's hypotheses.

If states wish to preserve their internal order, and hence seek to mitigate the threats posed to that internal order by the power of other states, then the seemingly most obvious way to do that is for states to enhance their own power. This leads to the question of how much power states will want. The logical assumption is that states will want, if possible, to accumulate as much power as will be necessary not only to resist the impact of another state (or states) upon the internal order of one's own state but also, ideally, to have such power as to dissuade other states from attempting to impact that internal order. The question thus becomes how much power is necessary to achieve these objectives. Some IR scholars suggest that states will seek a finite amount of power to meet their security needs, and that a rough balance of power between states will therefore arise, while others argue that states will seek to obtain as much power as they can possibly get, since it is difficult to determine whether a balance exists, whether another state's clever strategy might disrupt an existing power balance, or whether the balance might change in the future.[21] For the purposes of the present ánalysis, it suffices to say that when faced with a threatening state, other states will wish to at least augment their own power and quite possibly to surpass that of the other state so as to guarantee their own security.

If states are in fact motivated to enhance their power for the sake of security, the next question to consider is how they might go about doing that. There are essentially two options, which are not mutually exclusive. States can either attempt to increase their power via internally focused means, such as developing their natural resources, increasing their populations, enhancing their military capacity, and so forth, or they can establish partnerships with other states in order to achieve a power increase. Although the first approach is a natural path to take, the finite nature of all states' internal capacities makes it logical for them to likewise attempt to establish power-enhancing partnerships with each other. Indeed, to the degree that states seek a preponderance and not merely a finite amount of power, the logic of power-accentuating partnerships would seem particularly compelling. Such power-enhancing relations between states, in turn, can take place in one of two ways. One way is via a strategy of combined opposition, whereby states work together against a third party. By agreeing to exercise their power jointly, partnering states can automatically and, in certain cases, dramatically augment their strength in relation to another powerful state, or to a group of other states.[22] The other power-enhancing strategy is that of partnering to control.[23] In this case, states seek to gain an edge vis-à-vis another state by binding themselves to that threatening state, thereby constraining that state's range of action and/or benefiting from that state's economic or military capacity.

One obvious means of facilitating and reinforcing such relations between states, in turn, is to use techniques of interstate trade. Trade agreements are natural tools for this purpose because they can serve to bind the interests of states together in a relatively concrete fashion and hence in a manner not always achieved by other sorts of interstate partnerships, such as peace treaties, alliances, and so forth. The second key point that needs to be clarified, therefore, is the nature of the cooperative/integrative relations that occur via a free trade agreement.

An FTA is one of a variety of economy-integrating arrangements that states can establish among themselves. Other such arrangements include, for instance, a common market or a monetary union. Among these types of arrangements, an FTA is one of the simplest. Essentially, an FTA establishes a free trade area wherein tariff barriers between the participating states are significantly reduced or eliminated altogether. This sort of agreement can operate in various ways. Most fundamentally, it can function as either a more or a less "institutionalized" arrangement, insofar as it can simply be a set of rules of behaviour – articulated perhaps in treaty form – by which states agree to abide, or it can result in a situation in which the rules of the FTA are buttressed by an institutional structure – possessing, in some cases, supranational authority – whose role is to ensure that the rules are indeed abided by.[24] The more institutionalized such arrangements become, of course, the more they impinge upon states' sovereign independence. Indeed, insofar as states actually give up aspects of that independence, those states are not simply cooperating with one another – that is, interacting with one another in a way that does not impact their sovereignty – but are rather "integrating" with one another to some degree.[25]

An FTA can function as either an institutionalized or noninstitutionalized arrangement because it can be a fairly limited agreement between member states who are seeking to enhance their trade relations, or it can be a more complex agreement that calls into creation new international institutions that are designed to facilitate still greater and/or more efficient trade. In the case of the two North American FTAs, for instance, the arrangements established between the member states can be classified as moderately institutionalized, insofar as institutional structures have been established that go beyond the sole authority of any of the participating states, yet those institutional structures are nonetheless quite limited in their policy purview. In line with this classification, the behaviour of the North American states in the context of their FTA creation can be viewed as "moderately integrative cooperation," insofar as their relations are still largely cooperative in nature, yet in certain ways they have agreed in principle to relinquish their independent authority over particular policy areas.

In light of this explanation of an FTA, and in light of the definition of state security articulated earlier, there would seem to be an array of fairly obvious functions that FTAs can perform on behalf of states' security-seeking strategies. Five such functions are considered here. Specifically, FTAs can presumably serve to 1) increase member states' economic and hence military strength, 2) provide member states with the ability to influence policymaking processes in the other member states, 3) help resolve disputes between the member states, 4) provide some insurance of a lasting relationship among the member states, and 5) lay the groundwork for still greater integration between the member states. All five of these functions, in turn, are applicable to both the trading-to-oppose and the trading-to-control hypotheses, although the ways in which these functions are utilized differ depending upon whether they are being employed on behalf of one or the other of the two strategies.

The Role of FTAs in States' Security-Seeking Strategies

An FTA can assist states' security-seeking efforts by:

Function 1: Increasing trade between the participating states, which in turn can potentially enhance their economic strength, and thereby enhance their military strength as well

Function 2: Providing voice opportunities, whereby member states can influence the other members' policy processes in various ways

Function 3: Providing an enhanced capacity to resolve trade disputes among the participating states

Function 4: Serving as a form of insurance by establishing a structure of restraint, via which the interests of the participating states are more closely bound together

Function 5: Providing a first step in a larger integration process

---

We can examine the applicability of these functions by first considering them in the context of a trading-to-oppose strategy, since the most obvious manner in which they operate is as trading-to-oppose mechanisms. As indicated, the first function that an FTA can serve, in terms of enhancing a trading-to-oppose strategy, is to increase trade relations between the participating states. By increasing trade, the participating states' economic strength is potentially enhanced; that enhancement then translates into increased material resources for each state and hence into the possible strengthening of the participating states' militaries. This increased military capacity, in turn, translates into a greater ability to mutually oppose the power of a threatening, third-party state.

The second function that an FTA can serve with regard to reinforcing a trading-to-oppose effort is to provide the potential for member states to influence policy within the other member states. When states engage together in a trading-to-oppose strategy, they naturally take an interest in the policy processes of the other partner states, insofar as those processes may have some bearing on the effectiveness of the trading-to-oppose strategy. As such, it is logical for these states to seek "voice opportunities" whereby they might be able to exert some influence on said processes. An FTA can provide a context for voice opportunities, insofar as it serves to coordinate or combine the authority of different states with regard to trade policies, with the concomitant result that states need to take into consideration the policies of other states before they act on certain trade issues, and that "need to consider" provides an opportunity for states to influence each other – to make their voices heard – in various ways.[26]

The third function that an FTA can serve on behalf of a trading-to-oppose strategy is to provide an increased capacity to resolve trade disputes among the participating states. This function is obviously tied closely to the first two functions, but is nonetheless distinct. Two states can increase their level of trade across any number of economic sectors, for instance, and also enjoy voice opportunities on an array of issues, while simultaneously leaving unaddressed certain contentious areas of the trading relationship. An FTA arrangement can potentially provide a means – via its tools and rules for enhanced coordination in general – to address and effectively resolve those outstanding and difficult issues. For instance, with regard to NAFTA, a dispute-resolution mechanism is built into the treaty. Thus it is possible to imagine a scenario wherein two states already have in-depth trade relations, but then establish an FTA to resolve remaining trade disputes. By facilitating the resolution of such disputes, in turn, an FTA allows for smoother relations overall between the participating states, and hence for a greater likelihood that their efforts to engage in effective strength aggregation against a third-party state will not be derailed by disagreements among themselves.

The fourth trading-to-oppose function that an FTA can serve is to provide a degree of insurance regarding the future behaviour of the states involved, by raising the price of defection from the overall power-opposing arrangement. If two states are engaged in complex trade relations with one another, then they are potentially more likely to remain committed to the larger interstate relationship – involving not only trade but also power-aggregating, and so forth – than they would be if such trade ties did not exist. Of course, states have a basic incentive to engage in that aggregative effort simply by virtue of the fact that they feel threatened by a third-party state, but there is always the possibility that states might decide that a more efficacious strategy would be to try to appease the threatening state, or to choose other trading partners for their trading-to-oppose strategy. The existence of the FTA thus offers a "structure of restraint" on the member states' behaviour.[27]

The fifth function that an FTA can serve on behalf of a trading-to-oppose effort is to provide a step in a larger integration process. It is logical for states to engage in such processes since 1) integration provides greater power-augmenting benefits than cooperation, insofar as the former not only is an enhanced version of the latter but also has the potential to end anarchic relations between participating states, and 2) the power-augmenting benefits of integration increase in proportion to the level of integration that is achieved; in other words, the more that states combine their authority regarding various realms of policy, the more effectively – that is to say efficiently, thoroughly, and rapidly – they will presumably be able to draw upon their combined resources. Nonetheless, as noted, states are also fundamentally concerned about preserving their own internal orders; thus any thoroughgoing integration between them would likely need to proceed very cautiously so as to ensure that the relevant states could preserve those specific aspects of internal order that are most important to them. And of course, more generally, there is the issue of nationalism to consider, insofar as people tend to value various cultural attributes pertaining to their particular national identity. National identity, in turn, is often twined rather closely – although not necessarily – to the structure of a particular state's political regime, thereby lending that much more resistance to any interstate integrative enterprise.[28] Indeed, as is explained further in chapter 4, only certain circumstances actually allow for in-depth integration between regimes to transpire at all. Where such integration can in fact occur, furthermore, it is logical for the integration process to begin at the "low" level of economic policy, since states are typically assumed to be more willing to surrender sovereignty over economic issues than over issues pertaining directly to security policy – for instance, issues pertaining to the military – given that the ability to wield large-scale coercive force is the fundamental *raison d'être* of a state's existence. It is therefore plausible that states that are engaged in an integrative, power-opposing effort, while potentially seeking to integrate to a high degree – perhaps even to a level that encompasses security policy – will nonetheless begin their intermeshing of authority in the relatively less controversial realm of economics. Once a substantial degree of economic integration has been achieved and the states' respective members have grown accustomed to the situation, next steps might then be taken regarding the high politics of national security.[29] Thus, although it is not essential for a thoroughgoing integration process to begin in the economic realm – for instance, a great deal of integration occurred in US-Canadian relations before those states' establishment of free trade – an FTA does provide a first possible step in such a process. This function of an FTA, in turn, can operate in tandem with the other functions noted earlier, or it can take place largely on its own. Regarding the former option, it is plausible that two states whose trade is already largely unfettered by tariffs and that do not have outstanding trade-related disputes that need to be resolved might nonetheless establish an FTA for the primary reason of launching a long-term integration effort.

In sum, these are at least five of the functions that an FTA can serve with regard to reinforcing a power-opposing effort among states. I assume that these five functions can come into play in any number of scenarios, among any set of states, regardless of their power-quotients. For example, I assume that two states might establish an FTA – and one that may require in-depth integration, not simply cooperation – even if the two states possess vastly different levels of power, and even if those states are not threatened by a major hegemonic power, but merely by a credible military threat.[30]

As for the strategy of trading-to-control, it is, as noted, fundamentally different from the trading-to-oppose strategy because it involves states working with rather than against a particularly threatening state. The manner in which the five security-facilitating functions of an FTA operate is likewise somewhat different in a trading-to-control context. Furthermore, in a trading-to-control strategy, there are three different scenarios in which closer cooperation and/or integration – and hence an FTA – with a threatening state makes sense. The first scenario is when the threatening state is more powerful than the other state or states engaged in a cooperative/integrative venture. The second scenario is when the threatening state is less powerful than the other state or states. The third scenario is when the threatening state has a level of power roughly equal to the other states involved.

In the context of a trading-to-control strategy engaged in by a state vis-à-vis a more powerful state, the first listed function of an FTA – to increase the member states' economic strength, and thus by extension their military strength – obviously operates in a different manner than in a trading-to-oppose strategy. Whereas there is a clear logic in states wishing to increase their coalition's overall strength in opposition to another threatening state or states, in a trading-to-control strategy the rationale for a weaker state to seek the enhancement of both its and its partner states' economic strength is less straightforward. On the one hand, a weaker state may want to increase its own economic – and hence, potentially, military – strength via an FTA, insofar as that strength amplifies its ability to exert some level of influence vis-à-vis a threatening state. On the other hand, if the FTA also serves to increase the more powerful, threatening FTA member's strength, then the weaker state will need to weigh carefully whether the benefits of this particular function outweigh the costs. When such benefits are indeed presumed to outweigh the costs, then not only this function but also the subsequent four functions can plausibly come into play.

As for function 2, regarding voice opportunities, it is easy to see that in an FTA-based, trading-to-control approach, an FTA offers voice opportunities for the weaker states such that they might be able to exert some level of influence over what the more powerful state chooses to do with regard to certain policies. For instance, in the case of Europe after World War II, certain European states agreed to enhance their integration with West Germany, which was still viewed as potentially threatening, since they anticipated having an effective voice – via the institutions of the European Economic Community – on various economic policies that would pertain to the EEC member states as a whole. This is because West Germany, in crafting some of its own economic policies, would be obliged to abide by the decisions of the EEC – decisions arrived at collectively by the member states – with regard to such policies. There would thus be a means by which these weaker states could potentially influence some of West Germany's economic decisions.[31]

The third function that an FTA can serve, in terms of helping a weaker member of an FTA to address threats posed by a more powerful member, is to facilitate the resolution of disputes between the two states. Just as in the trading-to-oppose hypothesis, it is assumed that, due to FTAs' ability to enhance productive behaviour between states, the member states will find it easier to resolve trade disputes than if the FTA had not existed. In the trading-to-oppose hypothesis, the purpose of resolving such disputes is to improve the overall relationship between the member states so that their efforts to oppose a threatening third-party state will be amplified. In the trading-to-control hypothesis, however, the purpose of resolving such disputes is to provide the weaker state with a greater sense of security vis-à-vis its stronger FTA partner.

As with the trading-to-oppose hypothesis, so too in the context of trading-to-control, an FTA can also offer a general sort of insurance – function

4 – that can limit states' behaviour in less direct ways than is done via voice opportunities, dispute resolution mechanisms, and so forth. For instance, if two states establish an FTA, and through that FTA their trading relationship becomes highly interdependent, such that a breakdown in the relationship would be damaging to both economies, then that arrangement places constraints on the power of both states. For instance, the stronger state will presumably – though not inevitably – be more reticent to engage in threatening behaviour towards the weaker state due to the potential damage to the stronger state's economy. The FTA thus serves as a structure of restraint upon the stronger state, even if the weaker state is not regularly presented with voice opportunities to directly influence the stronger state's behaviour. It is logical to assume, of course, that a weaker state will have more influence over the stronger state with both a structure of restraint and an institutionalized setting in place that allows for abundant voice opportunities, than with just a structure of restraint, but such a structure by itself can still provide a desirable degree of insurance against unwanted behaviour by a more powerful state that poses a potential threat.

The fifth function that an FTA can serve, in terms of helping a weaker member of an FTA to address threats posed by a more powerful member, is to provide a starting point for much more complex integration between the FTA states. Whereas in the trading-to-oppose hypothesis it is assumed that two states might launch an FTA to begin a more involved integrative process so as to more effectively resist a threatening third-party state, in the trading-to-control hypothesis it is assumed that such a progressively integrative process could serve to more effectively constrain the behaviour of the more powerful, FTA-member state. In light of this potential function, therefore, an FTA might be initiated by the weaker state even if it already has largely unfettered trade relations with the more powerful state. Of course, depending upon the severity of threat posed, the weaker state may not wish the integration to proceed beyond a fairly low level, lest the benefits of trading-to-control be cancelled out by the threat of being dominated. Furthermore, as noted with the trading-to-oppose hypothesis, states are likely to proceed warily along the integration track regardless of who their partners might be, given their concern for maintaining their own internal orders, and that wariness is likely to be all the more pronounced when integrating with a more powerful and highly threatening state.

These, then, are five functions that an FTA can serve in the case of a weaker state attempting to address a threat posed by a more powerful state. In the second scenario relevant to the trading-to-control hypothesis – where a more powerful state is seeking to influence the behaviour of a weaker state – the security-relevant functions of an FTA are essentially the same. The question to be addressed, however, is why a more powerful state would bother trying to influence the behaviour of a weaker state. The answer is not simply that the more powerful state – State A – fears the power of the weaker state – State B – although presumably State B's power might be of some concern. Rather, State A fears that State B may intend to ally itself with another powerful state, or with a group of other states, and that such an alliance will pose a serious threat to the security of State A. For instance, in the post-WWII period, West Germany was willing to commit to the creation of the EEC, and to the EEC's subsequent enhancement over time, in part because the Germans feared that the other states of Europe might decide to band together against West Germany. Indeed, even when the disparity between states is far greater than that between the various states of Europe, the strategic logic of wanting to influence a weaker power is still relevant. Throughout much of its history, for example, the United States has consistently been concerned that Mexico might ally with a powerful European state and thereby provide that European state with a launching pad for potentially attacking the United States. At the same time, it was precisely because of the power disparities between the United States and Mexico that Mexico sought so consistently to rely upon European assistance against the United States – hence all the more reason for the United States to seek to influence Mexico's behaviour.

A stronger state thus has good reasons for wanting to impact the behaviour of the weaker state, and an FTA can help facilitate that impact. First, an FTA can provide the stronger state with the opportunity to increase its economic strength, and hence its military strength, and thereby to more effectively exert influence over the weaker state. Second, an FTA can allow the stronger state to capitalize upon increased voice opportunities vis-à-vis the weaker state. Third, an FTA can also be initiated to enhance the ability of the member states to resolve trade disputes that might flare into greater conflict. Whereas a weaker state's incentive in this regard is to ensure that the stronger state does not try to use its greater power to threaten and potentially attack the weaker state, the stronger state's incentive is to ensure that trade disputes with the weaker state do not prompt that weaker state to seek allies with which to aggregate power in opposition to the more powerful state. Thus an FTA might be promoted by the more powerful state even if its trade relations with the weaker state are already largely unfettered. Fourth, an FTA can help establish a structure of restraint that can influence the behaviour of the weaker state. For instance, just as an FTA can restrain the behaviour of the more powerful partner by intermeshing the two states' economies, and hence by increasing the costs to the more powerful state if it engages in aggressive behaviour towards the weaker state, so too an FTA can restrain the weaker state for the same reason, although that weaker state might be more likely to first seek out other partners before engaging in such aggression. Finally, in terms of a stronger state seeking to constrain the behaviour of a weaker state, an FTA can serve as a first step in a much more involved integration process. Even if an FTA is very limited, and hence offers only limited opportunities to influence the weaker state's behaviour, it can still be viewed by the stronger state as essential to its long-term security agenda, insofar as it offers a starting point for a more complex, and hence secure, relationship. Indeed, precisely because the weaker state is likely to be particularly wary of the stronger state, the stronger state has an incentive in moving very cautiously – that is, beginning at a low economic level – towards integration.

In addition to serving the trading-to-control goals of weaker and/or stronger states, an FTA can also, as noted, be used by states that possess relatively equal levels of power. In this scenario, any of the five functions that apply in the case of a weaker state attempting to influence a stronger state, or in the case of a stronger state attempting to influence a weaker state, can apply to the motivations of the states whose power is relatively equal.

Now that the logic of the trading-to-oppose and the trading-to-control hypotheses has been explained, the next step is to specify the observable implications of those hypotheses. Observable implications are those forms of state behaviour that we would expect to see occurring were states to behave in the manner that the hypotheses indicate. The concept of "observable implication" is thus closely related to that of "prediction." A prediction, however, is a statement about the future, whereas the events that are to be examined in this book have, of course, already transpired. In reviewing the cases that are presented in the following chapters, therefore, we are looking for state behaviour that corresponded to the hypotheses at the time that it occurred.[32] An understanding of the hypotheses' observable implications, in turn, then provides a basis for projecting those implications into the future so as to make predictions.[33]

For the first of the five functions, insofar as it pertains to the trading-to-oppose hypothesis – that is, an FTA can be used to increase the mutual trade, and hence the collective economic and military strength of states that are engaged in a power-aggregating effort against a third-party state – we should observe 1) statesmen in the relevant states identifying a genuine threat to their state; 2) those statesmen indicating that the establishment of an FTA will help them to address a specific threat, by facilitating a power-augmenting effort against the threatening state; specifically, that an FTA will increase trade between the FTA member states, thereby increasing their overall economic and military capacity; and 3) those statesmen attempting to establish an FTA. Similar sorts of observable implications, in turn, should likewise be looked for with regard to functions 2 through 5, insofar as they pertain to the trading-to-oppose hypothesis, and with regard to the same functions as they pertain to the trading-to-control hypothesis, with the only difference being that the second observable implication – that is, the strategy pursued via the FTA – will be different for each function.

Although I am presenting a series of observable implications that correspond to the five functions of the two hypotheses, I am not suggesting that any particular test case of these hypotheses needs to contain examples of all of the observable implications in order for the logic of the hypotheses to be proved sound. All that is being examined is whether any of these observable implications are manifested in the following cases. In fact, if none of these observable implications were manifested in the two North American cases then that would not necessarily imply that the hypotheses are inherently without merit, although it would suggest that those hypotheses might possibly be flawed. I am not, in other words, arguing that wherever there is an FTA, security concerns must be playing a prominent role in its formation and that the functions of the two hypotheses must be operative. Rather, I am arguing that security concerns can and sometimes do play such a role in FTA creation and that some such role was played in the cases of the two North American FTAs as well as in certain other instances of regional integration.[34]

With the core elements of the analytical approach thus clarified, we can now turn to the case studies themselves, with an analysis of CUFTA in chapter 2 and NAFTA in chapter 3, to determine the manner in which security-seeking behaviour influenced the FTAs' creation and hence the degree to which the five functions of the two hypotheses are observable within the data.[35] Furthermore, insofar as North America's free trade project has been bound up with security motivations, it is important to consider the extent to which the integrative endeavour might eventually extend beyond trade-related issues. The analyses of the two FTAs' creation are therefore followed – at the end of chapter 2 and the end of chapter 3 – by some thoughts on the manner in which security policy integration is likely to develop further between the relevant states. Exploration of this topic, in turn, leads to an examination in chapter 4 of how the North American project as a whole relates to a more globalized pattern of security-driven integration. Not only Europe, with its comparatively advanced integrative project, but likewise other regions with their fledgling projects provide evidence that what is happening in North America is part of a widespread phenomenon whereby states are combining themselves into security-seeking, trade-policy-using, regional groupings. A pattern of that sort, of course, could hardly hold greater significance for the structure of global politics. The next question to consider, therefore, is why it is that certain states are able to partake of that integrative pattern while others are not. Such an inquiry then inevitably leads to further contemplations regarding the political end point towards which all of this integrative activity appears to be heading.

2 CUFTA

At first glance it might appear challenging to determine what – if any – security issues could have prompted the United States and Canada to create an FTA in 1988. The North American region, after all, is presumed to enjoy one of the most benign security environments in the world, with the US-Canadian relationship in particular serving as an apparent paragon of peaceful interstate behaviour. Yet, despite this appearance of an untroubled security environment, patterns of reciprocal insecurity for the United States and Canada have manifested themselves repeatedly throughout the last two hundred-plus years, as have particular patterns of trade; indeed, these various patterns have often overlapped in significant ways. In the 1980s, most notably, such overlapping patterns asserted themselves with vigour and thereby prompted the creation of CUFTA. Recognition of the multiple historical patterns, therefore, and of how they have interacted, allows for a much enhanced appreciation of the security and trade policies of the two states during the 1980s, thus it is essential to place this case study within the larger historical context by first considering the time period stretching from the 1770s to the 1970s.

US-Canadian Relations, 1770s–1970s

US-Canadian relations before the 1980s went through three phases. In the first phase the two states viewed each other primarily as threats; in the second phase those mutual suspicions were partially alleviated as the relationship became less antagonistic; in the third phase, positive bilateral relations increased dramatically, thereby setting the stage for the eventual creation of the 1988 Canadian-US FTA.

1770s–1890s: Reciprocal Fear

The first phase of US-Canadian relations lasted from the 1770s to the 1890s. During this period the bilateral relationship was consistently characterized by reciprocal fear, with the United States fearing the intentions, proximity, and military capacity of Britain, which controlled the Canadian territory, while Canada feared the intentions, proximity, and military capacity of the United States.

These threat dynamics were present at the very founding of the United States as an independent state, due to the fact that, when the thirteen American colonies rebelled against Britain in the 1770s, the Canadian territory remained loyal to the crown. The rebels' primary enemy – Britain – was thus able to retain a firm foothold on the rebelling colonies' northern border, stationing as many troops and as much military capacity there as it liked. In response to this threatening situation, General George Washington sent two of his commanders into Canada in 1775 to attempt to persuade the Canadians to join the colonial bid for independence. When the Canadians resisted, the Continental Congress raised a force of several thousand troops and sent them to invade Quebec City.[1] That invasion, however, likewise failed to persuade the Canadians to join in the independence effort, such that when the United States and Britain agreed – via the Treaty of Paris in 1783 – to officially acknowledge the end of the war and the independence of the new North American state, Canada still belonged to the United Kingdom.

Tensions between the United States and the United Kingdom persisted following the signing of the 1783 treaty. Britain, for instance, insisted upon maintaining several forts along the northwestern edge of US territory, to be fully staffed with military contingents as insurance against another US incursion into Canada, thus causing serious concern in the United States regarding the lingering British threat. Anti-British sentiment in the United States was then amplified in the early 1790s when the United Kingdom and France went to war, as a result of which Britain began seizing US ships suspected of trading with the French. Meanwhile, British resentment towards the United States had persisted since the early 1780s due to US violations of the Treaty of Paris. To stem mounting momentum towards war between the United States and United Kingdom, therefore, the two sides agreed to the terms of the Jay Treaty of 1794. As would so often be the case with future such agreements, this treaty wove together new trading arrangements with initiatives pertaining to security policy. For instance, not only did the two sides reach agreement regarding British basing practices in the American northwest and British naval activity vis-à-vis US ships, but they also established reciprocity with regard to various aspects of their commercial relations. "Reciprocity" is a term used to describe a trade arrangement somewhat approximating what is known as "free trade." In a reciprocal trade agreement, states agree to either eliminate or reduce to a very low level the tariffs, quotas, and other restrictions applied to certain types of goods and commercial activities. Building upon the reciprocity agreement with the British, the United States also took the step of granting most-favoured-nation status to the United Kingdom, which meant that any favourable terms of trade that were established between the United States and another state would also be applied to British trade with the United States. Britain, in turn, agreed to grant, among other things, the access of US ships to lucrative trading opportunities in the British West Indies.[2]

Yet notwithstanding the Jay Treaty – which took effect in 1796 – another US/UK war nearly erupted in the first decade of the 1800s, this time as a result of the British practice of forcibly searching US ships for deserters from the British navy. Widespread American indignation at British behaviour appeared primed to produce a war resolution in Congress, and thus, in anticipation of war, the US administration drafted plans for a new invasion of Canada, which was a course of action viewed as inevitable should another US-British war break out. Ultimately, however, the decision was made to enact a punitive embargo against Britain instead, and war was thereby temporarily avoided.[3]

In 1812 a war nonetheless broke out between the two sides, due to an array of causes; from the US point of view, the most prominent issue was the British practice of impressing American sailors into the British navy. In the course of this new war the United States launched multiple invasions into Canada, for various strategic reasons. On the one hand, attacking and seizing Canadian territory was viewed as a means of preventing the British navy from using Canadian ports. At the same time, a successful invasion was also considered an effective way to defeat the Indian confederacies that menaced the United States' western regions and that depended upon their alliance with Canada for support.[4] Furthermore, US possession of Canada would presumably put pressure on Britain to sue for peace on American terms, so that Britain could then retrieve its territories.[5] Whatever the logic was for these new incursions into Canadian territory, when the war ended in 1814 the British remained firmly ensconced on the United States' northern border.

To solidify this hold, and to protect its Canadian territories, Britain next proceeded to increase the number of its warships on the Great Lakes, which, in turn, alarmed the United States and precipitated a naval arms race on the lakes. Ultimately, however, this naval competition was prevented from escalating into yet another armed conflict by the ratification of the Rush-Bagot Treaty of 1818, which limited the number of naval ships allowed in the region.[6] At the same time, in addition to this Great Lakes naval agreement, the US regime – particularly President James Monroe's secretary of state, John Quincy Adams – sought to reach a wider-ranging settlement with the British, addressing all outstanding issues between the two states. A chief goal of this larger agreement was the attainment of a reciprocal trade treaty between the United States and Britain's Canadian territories.[7] Along with the economic benefits that might accrue from reciprocal trade with Canada, the US desire for the trade deal had two important security rationales behind it. First, the United States at the time was engaged in a potentially dangerous attempt to forcibly acquire the territory of Florida from Spain. That effort could easily lead to war with the Spanish, and the US administration wished to ensure that problems with Britain did not erupt into military conflicts at the same time as the potential for war with Spain was ripe. Since the primary issue between the United States and Britain that had the potential to lead to conflict – once the Great Lakes naval arms race was settled – was the restrictive nature of trade relations between the United States and the Canadian territories, settling the trade issue became a key security priority.[8] A second security rationale for a trade agreement pertained to longer-term US strategy – in particular, to the policy known as the "Monroe Doctrine," the principal architect of which was John Quincy Adams. This doctrine insisted that European states should refrain from extending their efforts at political domination into the region of the Americas, since such behaviour was threatening to the United States. Continued British efforts to not only control the Canadian territories but also to prevent US trade relations with those territories thus ran counter to the basic premise of the Monroe Doctrine. Reciprocity with Canada, in turn, was viewed as serving to help weaken the colonial hold that Britain had over Canada, and to allow the United States' northern neighbour to move more easily into the US sphere of influence, thereby contributing to US security.[9]

This attempt at establishing freer trade between the United States and Canada was thus bound up with a set of security motivations. The United States and Britain, however, could not agree to terms of trade, and reciprocity was not enacted at this time, although a general treaty was reached that addressed other issues, such as fishing rights and the US-Canada boundary line.[10] Yet, notwithstanding this agreement, reciprocal insecurities persisted. British efforts to build a military road near the Canada-US border – as part of anti-US defences – inflamed tensions in the 1820s. Further border incidents then occurred in the late 1830s and early 1840s, nearly leading to armed conflict between the United States and UK-Canada on three separate occasions.[11] To address these simmering tensions, therefore, in 1842 the two sides agreed to another broad settlement of their differences and signed the Webster-Ashburton Treaty.[12]

This treaty was timely, allowing as it did for the United States to focus on threats along its southern border, where war broke out with Mexico in 1846. That war, however, raised new US-British/Canadian security problems, since through its defeat of Mexico the United States acquired California, which bordered the Oregon region, over which the United States and the United Kingdom had competing claims.[13] Long negotiations thus ensued to determine where the Oregon boundary should run, but to no effect. The issue was eventually resolved when Britain dispatched warships to North America in preparation for hostilities regarding the Oregon claims. The US regime, which was still unsure whether hostilities would resume with Mexico, and not wanting to fight Mexico in the South and Britain in the North simultaneously, agreed to settle the boundary question largely on British terms.[14]

No sooner had this issue been addressed, however, than serious disputes arose between the United States and Canada regarding US fishing rights in waters near Canadian shores. By 1852 these disputes had become sufficiently tense to prompt a British naval force to be sent to the Gulf of St Lawrence, in response to which the United States sent a naval force to the coast of Nova Scotia.[15] In order to prevent all of this activity from escalating into yet another war, the US regime then suggested to the British that the United States and Canada sign a reciprocal trade agreement on duties and fishing rights, but the British refused the offer.[16]

Their refusal was temporary. By 1854 Britain was engaged in the Crimean War against Russia and was disinclined to simultaneously take on the United States in North America.[17] For its part, the United

States was engaged in a struggle to acquire Cuba from Spain – a course of action that appeared likely to lead to war – and was simultaneously working to prevent war from breaking out again with Mexico over an array of different issues.[18] Both the United States and Britain, as such, were susceptible to the attractions of a trade agreement for the sake of resolving US-Canadian tensions and thereby maintaining peace between the United States and the United Kingdom. For US president Franklin Pierce, however, the short-term goal of using reciprocal trade to prevent the immediate outbreak of war ran parallel to a longer-term security strategy. Pierce had arrived in office championing the idea of expanding American borders for the sake of ensuring American security. In his inaugural address he declared that his administration would "not be controlled by timid forebodings of evil from expansion. Indeed, it is not to be disguised that our attitude as a nation and our position on the globe render the acquisition of certain possessions not within our jurisdiction eminently important to our protection."[19] Although Pierce's acquisitive actions focused most overtly on Cuba, he also clearly indicated – in private – that his reciprocity program with Canada was meant to eventually sever the connection between Britain and Canada, draw Canada permanently into the United States' sphere, and thereby rid the United States of a powerful presence on its northern border.[20] As a result of Pierce's motivations, as well as those of the British regime – combined with many Canadians' own interest in the deal, due to their current financial difficulties, and the desire of some Canadians for annexation to the United States – a treaty of reciprocal trade between the United States and Canada was signed on 5 June 1854.[21]

The cooperative relations did not last long. In 1861 the United States descended into civil war, in the course of which the Union states nearly became embroiled in a simultaneous war against Britain, stemming from Britain's practice of maintaining relatively cordial relations with the Confederacy. The Union regime under Abraham Lincoln demanded that such relations cease, the British regime insisted they would not, and tensions reached a dangerous pitch when, in the context of this disagreement, the British sent several thousand troops into Canada in anticipation of a possible war against the Union.[22] As in previous instances, however, the US regime bowed to the need to avoid a two-front war and agreed to allow the British to continue their trade with the Confederacy. Although military hostilities with Britain were thereby avoided, anger at Britain and Canada nonetheless ran high in the United States following the Civil War's conclusion in 1865, and this animosity played an important part in compelling the US Congress to subsequently abrogate the reciprocity treaty with Canada, which it did in 1866. Such animosity also set the stage for a series of raids into Canada by American groups that sought to punish Britain by attacking Canada, and this more isolated activity was paralleled in the general US population by widespread sentiment for punitive annexation of the Canadian territories.[23] The sense of threat that this engendered among Canadians thus helped prompt, in turn, the Canadian territories to form the single, integrated state of Canada, as a defensive power-aggregating measure against potential US aggression.

Following the abrogation of the trade treaty, only three years passed before Canada suggested to the United States that reciprocal trade be re-established. This Canadian action was prompted by what Canadians viewed as the economic benefits that they had reaped through reciprocity and the desire to secure them again, as well as by rising tensions between the United States and Canada over US fishing rights in northern waters and the fear that this issue might once again lead the United States and Canada towards military conflict.[24] On the American side, President Ulysses Grant was in fact inclined to invade Canada, while his secretary of state, Hamilton Fish, was interested in promoting trade reciprocity, not simply as a means of easing tensions between the United States and Canada-Britain – at a time when the Grant administration was seeking to acquire Santo Domingo (the Dominican Republic), and in the process was severely straining relations with Spain – but also because Fish wanted to break the ties that bound Canada to Britain.[25] Once these ties were broken, Fish reasoned, threats to the United States from the north would be reduced and the way would be paved for the eventual peaceful annexation of Canada, which Fish and Grant both viewed as essential to the long-term goals of US security. The US Congress, however, which was still in a belligerent mood regarding Canada, refused to allow for a renewal of reciprocity and thereby prompted Fish to comment that "where Congress might have sown flowers of union, it had scattered the tares of distrust."[26]

Undeterred, Canada tried again in 1874 for a reciprocity treaty with the United States. In this instance the motivations of Canada appear – interestingly enough – to have been strictly economic in nature.[27] The US administration was not overly enthusiastic about the idea, however, perhaps because Congress was still unwilling to support it, and thus this initiative likewise did not succeed. Another attempt, mutually sought by the United States and Canada, was made in 1888, motivated both by security concerns – in particular, fear of an impending military confrontation between the United States and United Kingdom over fishing rights – and economic interests. A trade treaty was therefore drafted, but was then rejected by the US Congress.[28]

The potential for war, however, and hence a new trade agreement, re-arose after the election of Benjamin Harrison to the US presidency in 1888. This time the dispute was over competing claims to seal hunting in the Bering Strait, which served to exacerbate already existing tensions between the two sides. Seeking to prevent Canadian sealing efforts, the United States captured eight Canadian ships in the Bering Strait region in 1889, in response to which the United Kingdom sent a group of naval ships to the Bering Sea in 1891.[29] With the potential for war thus very real, the Canadian regime agreed to explore the possibility of a new trade deal with the United States. Although the Canadians at this time were opposed to full reciprocity with the United States – concerned as they were that the goal of US free trade policy was to split Canada from Britain, and then to annex Canada into the United States – they were also convinced that the US secretary of state, James Blaine, whom the Canadians believed to control US policy, was likely to jump on any opportunity to go to war against Canada.[30] As such, while resisting Blaine's call for full US-Canadian reciprocity, yet wanting to placate Blaine sufficiently so as to preclude a US invasion, Canada offered to explore a trade deal with the United States. Blaine, for his part, was indeed interested in extending US influence over Canada to the degree possible. Although a champion of high tariffs early in his political career, he eventually embraced the technique of reciprocal trade precisely because it allowed the United States a means of influencing non-US territories and thereby effectively addressing long-term security threats near US borders.[31] Nonetheless, the trade deal, like many others, fell through. The fact that this did not lead automatically to war can perhaps be attributed to the fact that by this time Blaine had become seriously ill and could no longer carry out many of his official functions.[32]

1898–1944: Shifting Sources of Threat

At the end of the 1800s the strategic context pertaining to the United States and Canada began to change. Whereas prior to this point Canada's relationship with Britain gave the United States cause for concern, and the Canadians reciprocally feared the United States, now Canada's sense of threat shifted as the United Kingdom, rather than the United

States, began to appear more inimical to Canadian interests; this shift corresponded with Canada's progress towards full *de jure* autonomy, which eventually occurred in 1931. Similarly, US fears regarding Britain underwent an alteration during the early decades of the twentieth century, as other European powers began posing a greater threat to US security. What did not change during this period, however, was the attempted use of trade agreements to assist in the attainment of security policy goals.

The key actor in initiating this second phase was Sir Wilfrid Laurier, who served as Canadian prime minister from 1896 to 1911. Laurier hailed from a tradition of French-Canadian political activists who sought to loosen and potentially sever the connection between Canada and Britain.[33] The desire to disconnect Canada from its colonial master was heightened in 1897 when Britain began tightening its colonial network – in part, via free trade agreements with its colonies – in order to increase British power in light of rising US and German power, and it was then heightened again in 1898 when Britain participated in the Boer War in South Africa. The result of these events was that Britain now sought not only to establish firmer control over Canada but also to more comprehensively involve Canadian troops in its African war, both of which efforts Laurier strongly resisted.[34] The tightening of Britain's colonial control was a significant threat to Canada's budding sovereignty, while participation in Britain's African adventures threatened to draw Canada into extended military confrontations.[35]

A natural component of Laurier's resistance to British policy was to promote the idea of Canadian trade reciprocity with the United States. Just as the British were seeking to more tightly centralize their empire by establishing a free trade zone between Britain and its colonies, so too Laurier's counterattempt to establish free trade with the United States served as a means to block this British effort.[36] Yet, at the same time, Laurier did not want to establish too-close relations with the United States, given the continuingly strained nature of that bilateral relationship, and he apparently believed that an enhanced trade relationship with the United States could be engaged in without leading inevitably to US dominance over Canada.[37] On the American side, meanwhile, President William McKinley was receptive to this trade idea. McKinley had been instructed in the security-strategy importance of trade reciprocity by James Blaine and was sympathetic to the idea even before Laurier suggested it.[38] In 1898 a joint high commission was thus established between the United States, Canada, and Britain in order to address a range of issues, including the possibility of US-Canadian reciprocity. Eventually, however, these negotiations became bogged down over disputes regarding the Alaskan border with Canada – President Theodore Roosevelt, who succeeded McKinley after the latter's assassination, threatened to attack Canada if the border issue was not resolved to his liking – and the trade talks broke off.[39]

Before long, the talks were back on. Responding to the difficulties of the Boer War, and all the more concerned about growing US and German power, Britain renewed pressure during the first decade of the 1900s for a tighter imperial trading system while also calling for definite pledges from the colonies for army and navy contributions. Demands for Canadian contributions to Britain's naval power, in particular, reached a high pitch in 1909 when it became clear that Germany's shipbuilding program was overtaking that of the British.[40] Laurier was less disturbed than many by the portents of German naval power, yet he also recognized that Canada was going to need to build its own navy, if only a modest one.[41] Once built, however, it would be difficult to prevent the Canadian navy from being incorporated into the British naval structure and thereby dragged into British military endeavours.

It was thus in this political climate that Laurier began negotiating with the United States for a new reciprocity agreement, and in 1911 he dissolved the Canadian parliament and called for a general election, which would serve as a referendum on the issue of reciprocity.[42] Throughout the ensuing election campaign Laurier insisted that the purpose of such reciprocity was not to drive a wedge between Canada and Britain, but if he actually believed this then he was one of the only ones who did. French Canadians supported his reciprocity proposal precisely because of the manner in which it would split Canada from Britain, while a large segment of British Canadians, as well as the majority of manufacturers and industrialists and the major banking houses opposed reciprocity for precisely this reason.[43] Given the interests and the numbers arrayed against him in the election, Laurier not surprisingly went down to defeat and thus so too did his plan for reciprocal trade.[44]

On the American side, motivations for free trade in 1911 were likewise not strictly or even primarily economic in nature. Campaigning to promote US-Canadian reciprocity, President William Taft declared, "Before Canada is irrevocably fixed in a policy leading to consolidation and strengthening of the British empire we must turn her from her course."[45] The economic rationale for reciprocity at this time was dubious, given the fact that Congress had recently passed the Payne-Aldrich tariff, the most generous American tariff to apply to Canada since the US-Canadian reciprocity agreement had been abrogated in 1866. Further tariff lowering, in turn, was widely viewed as potentially detrimental to the US economy. When presented with this critique of reciprocity, Taft responded, "It may be economically rotten. But I regard it as good statesmanship."[46] Nor were there good electoral reasons to promote the policy. Taft's Republican Party had historically been opposed to tariff reductions, and intraparty debate over the Payne-Aldrich bill had already strained relations among republicans.[47] To then move ahead with promoting full reciprocity was a recipe for political disaster, and Taft knew it. He stated, with regard to pushing forward this policy, "I think it may well break the Republican party for a while," and "My judgment before I sent the message, was that it would blow me up politically, but ultimately it will help the country; and the question of parties is not quite so important, and still less the question of personal political fortunes."[48]

Yet, despite the great risks taken for reciprocity by both Taft and Laurier, Laurier's electoral defeat ensured that reciprocity between the two states would not take place. Through his efforts, nonetheless, Laurier did manage to set US-Canadian relations on a new course, with Canada henceforth using its relationship with the United States primarily as a means to address security threats posed by other states rather than vice versa. Furthermore, as the twentieth century entered its second decade, the sources of threat for both Canada and the United States shifted away from Britain and towards other European states. During World War I, the primary source of threat for both states was Germany and its allies, against whom the United States and Canada fought together.[49] After the war ended, the British enacted the Statute of Westminster in 1931, which gave Canada official control over its own foreign policy, which until then had still technically been under the authority of the British regime. Canada thus had that much more room for diplomatic manoeuvre when the storm clouds of World War II began to gather, and it was in preparation for and during that new round of conflict that Canada's orientation towards the United States became stronger still. Indeed, following President Franklin Roosevelt's Kingston Proclamation in August 1938, in which he declared that the United States "would not stand idly by" if Canada were threatened by another empire, the United States and Canada began substantially increasing their military relations.[50] During the war, in turn, particularly close military relations were established. Most notable in this regard was the Ogdensburg Agreement of 1940, which created the Permanent Joint Board of Defence (PJBD), a senior advisory body on continental security that is composed of diplomatic and military representatives from each country.

Notwithstanding this reorientation in US-Canadian military relations, the establishment of free trade between the two countries still remained elusive. In the wake of Laurier's 1911 electoral defeat, free trade had ceased to be a pressing issue between the two states, and throughout the subsequent two decades Canadian leaders remained averse to the idea. Likewise, after WWI the United States experienced a period of isolationism that coincided with worldwide high tariffs in the 1920s. By the mid-1930s, however, free trade was back on the agenda. Just as Canada had responded to economic strains in the past, so too during the depression of the 1930s it began viewing the idea of free trade with the United States as a possible solution to its economic problems. Concurrently, on the US side, President Franklin Roosevelt's administration began an ambitious effort – in response to the growing German threat, and in anticipation of an eventual confrontation with the Germans – to bind the states of the western hemisphere more closely to the United States, and to use free trade agreements as a means to accomplish this goal, a course of action – explored more fully in chapter 3 – that came to be known as the Good Neighbor Policy. This mutual interest in freer trade on the part of the United States and Canada thus led, in 1935, to Canadian prime minister William Lyon Mackenzie King and President Roosevelt signing the Canadian-US Reciprocal Trade Agreement, the purpose of which was to lower tariffs for a range of goods. Following upon this agreement, Mackenzie King signed another preliminary treaty with the United States in 1938, so as to demonstrate his willingness to further explore the possibility of reciprocal trade.[51]

The US ambassador to Canada at the time, Norman Armour, pointed out that the importance of the Reciprocal Trade Agreement was to be understood "not so much from an economic standpoint as from, well let us say, a political or international viewpoint if you will."[52] The agreement would have "the long range effect of bringing Canada not only within our economic but our political orbit." By making Canadian industry complementary to, rather than competitive with, American industry, economic gains would be reaped and, more importantly still, Canada would become bound to the United States in a cooperative manner. As Armour argued, "Is it not vitally important for our political future that we have next to us Canada ... supporting our policies in regard to Latin America ... the Far East and elsewhere."[53] Yet this program of free trade was never taken to fruition, since Canada entered the war against Germany less than a year later and the United States entered the war not long thereafter. Normal trade relations were suspended during this war period and thus so too was the possibility of reciprocity.

1945–1979: The Cold War Context

The third phase in US-Canadian relations began in the 1940s with the onset of the Cold War. In response to the rising power of the Soviet Union, the United States and Canada moved from merely being allies against a distant, dangerous state – in the case of Germany – to being vitally important strategic partners against a third-party state that possessed all the elements of threat: proximity, military capacity, and hostile intent. More specifically, enhanced US-Canadian relations during the Cold War resulted from two facets of the new, global military stand-off. First, one of the most direct lines of attack between the United States and USSR was across the North Pole. Thus whichever superpower attacked the other would likely overfly Canada to reach its targets. Second, the development of new weaponry – such as long-range bombers and missiles – in this period meant that rapidly covering the distance between the two superpowers and then delivering a devastating attack was well within the capacity of both states. As a result, the need to control Canadian airspace, and to utilize Canadian territory and Canadian waters for military purposes, took on urgent significance for the United States.

In recognition of the growing threat to the US mainland posed by increasing Soviet military capacity, George Kennan, the State Department official who prominently played an early role in alerting the American regime to the dangers of Soviet power, was sent to Ottawa in 1948 to persuade Mackenzie King "to agree to a further development of the defense arrangements under the Ogdensburg Agreement."[54] That same year, Undersecretary of State Dean Acheson noted, "Our military authorities are naturally intent on closing the gap between Alaska and Greenland"[55] – that is to say, the gap represented by a very modestly defended Canada. Around the same time, President Harry Truman approved a recommendation of the PJBD that called for personnel exchanges between the armed forces of the two states, standardization of military-related equipment, provision of military facilities by each state to the armed forces of the other, and other types of coordination.[56] In conjunction with this, Truman explained to Mackenzie King that within five years the two states "must be prepared to meet major enemy capabilities," and to do so together.[57] This was then followed in 1950 by a State Department memo declaring that, in regard to relations with Canada, "our commitments and risks are so extensive and important that Canada in a military sense must be considered as if it were an integral part of the United States. It is as important to our security to protect Canada as it is to protect California. Canada is the most logical avenue of attack on the United States."[58] Reinforcing the sense of urgency, in 1951 the US National Security Council predicted that after 1954 the Soviet Union would have the ability to carry out a devastating nuclear attack upon US and Canadian targets.[59]

During these early Cold War years, therefore, surveillance outposts were placed in Canada, the United States was allowed to establish military bases on Canadian territory, and greater coordination transpired between the surveillance gathering agencies of the two states.[60] For instance, the Pine Tree network of radar stations, which was completed in 1954, was built just north of major Canadian population centres and was operated jointly by the Canadian and US military. The Mid-Canada Line, in turn, which consisted of a string of radar stations located even further north, was built in 1957. This was subsequently considered insufficient by the US National Security Council, however, and that same year work began on the Distant Early Warning (DEW) System, comprising a string of radar stations stretching along Canada's northernmost coast from Alaska to Greenland, which was paid for by the United States and manned primarily by US military personnel. Thanks to these and other cooperative ventures between the two states – including the use of a major base at Goose Bay in Labrador by the US Air Force – in the mid-1950s there were roughly fifteen thousand US service personnel stationed throughout Canada.[61]

Canada also played an active role in establishing the North Atlantic Treaty Organization (NATO) in 1949, thereby committing itself to coordinating general defence policy with the United States and the European allies in response to the Soviet threat. Furthermore, it is worth noting that the Canadians from the outset viewed the NATO alliance as a means of not only coordinating defence policies but also as a framework for building a more comprehensive partnership between the member states. Lester Pearson, who at the time was Canada's foreign minister, notes that on Canadian insistence "it was agreed that a paragraph should be included in the text of any [NATO-creating] treaty to the effect that the signatories would make every effort, individually and collectively, to promote the economic well-being of their peoples and to achieve social justice." As Pearson points out, this insistence was "the genesis of the famous Article 2 of the [NATO-creating] treaty, which came to be known as the Canadian Article."[62] In 1958 the two states then established still closer bilateral military relations via the North American Air Defense Command (NORAD). Headquartered at Colorado Springs, NORAD brought about an unprecedented level of intermilitary coordination between the two states' air forces, with a system of integrated operational control, in which NORAD's American commander-in-chief and a second-in-command Canadian deputy coordinated "mutual self-defense" of "the Canada-United States region."[63]

While these various forms of military coordination were underway between the two states, the United States simultaneously sought once again to establish free trade with Canada. This time the task of negotiating an FTA with Canada was given to one of the State Department's more famous diplomats, Paul Nitze.[64] Nitze's talks with the Canadian regime lasted throughout 1947 and 1948, but in the end Mackenzie King decided to back away from the free trade effort. As he put it, "I felt sure that the long objective of the Americans was to control this continent. They would want to get Canada under their aegis. If I was an American, I would have the same view, especially considering Russia's position."[65] Thus while the Canadians were interested in general economic coordination with the United States in the context of a multilateral partnership such as NATO, they were not yet ready for something more in-depth and involving only themselves and the United States. As such, when another US push for free trade was made in 1953, this time at the suggestion of the US secretary of defense, it also came to naught.[66]

The evolving military partnership between the United States and Canada eventually ran into difficulties as well. Despite general improvements in the relationship since the early 1900s, Canadian politicians and the Canadian public were still wary of establishing too close of a partnership with their historic antagonist. To take just one example: in 1957 John Diefenbaker was elected Canadian prime minister, and although at first he supported many of the military coordination initiatives proposed by the United States, he quickly modified this stance. This shift was in response to a strong public backlash in Canada following Diefenbaker's announcement in 1959 that he had agreed to allow nuclear weapons to be stationed in Canada. In the wake of this public outcry, Diefenbaker decided to retract his acceptance of the US nuclear request.[67] This larger source of tension then combined with a very poor personal rapport between Diefenbaker and the Kennedy administration in Washington, resulting in a period of particularly strained US-Canadian relations.[68]

Another reason for the lack of progress in the bilateral relationship was based upon strategic developments. Most notably, in the 1960s intercontinental ballistic missile (ICBM) technology rendered the utility of US-Canadian military relations less relevant. An ICBM is launched – as the name implies – from one continent and lands on the target in another, although similarly constructed ballistic missiles can also be launched from submarines or dropped from planes. And since the capacity to shoot down missiles in mid-flight was not yet developed, guaranteed defence against ICBMs was considered infeasible. At the same time, because many ICBMs were stored in underground bunkers and on hard-to-target submarines, it was assumed that a certain percentage of the attacked state's ICBMs would survive a first strike, all the more so since ICBMs were less than ideal as first-strike weapons because they were not always accurate. Furthermore, because of these missiles' typically long flight times, it was possible to develop early warning systems to detect an impending ICBM strike and thus retaliate against the attacking state before the initiating attack was completed. It was therefore irrational for either side to initiate an attack since whoever did so would likewise be destroyed. These factors thus fed into the larger strategic situation known as mutually assured destruction (MAD).[69] In this context the strategic role of Canadian territory was naturally diminished, and hence so too were US efforts to pressure Canada on issues pertaining to both security and trade relations.[70]

The Security Context of the 1980s

If we want to understand why a particular foreign policy decision was made, then it is necessary to understand the relevant context of that decision. With regard to the decision to create the US-Canadian FTA of 1988, the relevant context was the US-Canadian bilateral relationship of the 1980s. That relationship was characterized – at least in part – by a particular security environment, and it is essential to consider the nature of that environment since, as the foregoing demonstrates, security and trade relations between the two states have often overlapped in the past. Indeed, the historical record prior to the late 1970s demonstrates that the

United States has repeatedly been concerned that a powerful state – first Britain, then Germany, then the Soviet Union – might utilize Canadian territory in some fashion for a potential attack on the United States, and the United States has often resorted to free trade agreements as a means to ally itself with Canada more closely in response to that threat.

The influence of such noneconomic issues on US trade policy towards Canada was noted with particular clarity by Simon Reisman, the chief Canadian negotiator of the 1988 US-Canadian FTA and the most prominent Canadian trade official during the latter half of the twentieth century. As Reisman observed, "With its vast home market and much smaller dependence on trade, there is much less advantage in free trade for the United States in immediate economic terms. US interest in free trade with Canada has usually been inspired by considerations not confined to a search for gains in trade."[71] As he further explained, "Indeed, if one looked at trade gains alone it would be hard to raise much enthusiasm in the United States for the free-trade option. But there are advantages, albeit less tangible, in such an arrangement. Not least of these would be the removal of recurrent grievances on both sides of the border that constantly threaten to sour relationships in related economic and noneconomic spheres."[72]

In another format, Reisman noted,

On those occasions when the United States did get interested in free trade with Canada there were considerations in play that went well beyond the calculus of economics or the profits to be made from trade. The successful negotiation of the 1854 Reciprocity Treaty, and its rude abrogation in 1866, confirm the importance of non-trade issues in making and breaking trade agreements by the United States. In the American mind, if not in ours, there has always been, to a greater or lesser degree, "linkage" between trade issues and other interests.[73]

That potential for linkage, however, had not – as of the early 1980s – led to a lasting, comprehensive trade deal between the two states. Nor was Reisman hopeful that such could be attained in the near future. As he noted at the time, "May we expect early progress to establish free trade between the United States and Canada? I do not think it will happen, certainly not now [1984]. Conditions are not bad enough in Canada nor are they good enough in the United States to provide just the right mixture required to ignite the political leaders on both sides of the border. That is what history tells us, and history is usually right."[74]

The best hope for a new trade deal, he concluded, was to offer something extraordinary to the United States by way of inducement.

> We will never know, of course, unless we try and see what we can achieve through negotiations. A major difficulty, I fear, is that in economic terms the benefits from free trade are likely to be asymmetrical ... It is this thought – the need to find some major attractions for the US side in other areas – which has led me to a rather bold and controversial proposal. Given the extreme sensitivity of the subject that I am about to raise, some of you may think that I have taken complete leave of my senses ... The subject is water. For some years now, a group of Canadian engineers ... have been developing the concept of harnessing the flow of fresh water into James Bay to provide a new, large, reliable source to meet the requirements of both Canada and the United States.[75]

Thus while Reisman recognized that the United States had historically been motivated by more than simply economic concerns in its efforts to pursue free trade with its northern neighbour, and although he also appreciated the weakness of any economic incentives that could prompt the United States to consider an FTA in the early 1980s, he does not appear to have appreciated the security situation that the United States – and Canada – began to face as the 1970s drew to a close and hence why access to Canadian water supplies – or similar such inducements – were unnecessary to bring the United States to the free trade negotiating table. This new security context reflected two dynamics that came into play in the late 1970s and continued into the 1980s. The first dynamic was the partial weakening of Canada – economically and militarily – during Pierre Trudeau's tenure as prime minister. The second dynamic was the commencement of an Arctic arms race.

In 1968 Pierre Trudeau became Canadian prime minister and retained this post – save for a short interlude during 1979–80 – until 1984. During that long tenure of Trudeau's leadership, Canada attempted to disengage from the United States both commercially and militarily. Taking advantage of the decreased Cold War tensions of the détente period – which lasted from the late 1960s to mid-1970s – Trudeau advocated a reduction in military spending and a recall of significant numbers of Canadian troops from Europe. Likewise, since many of the early warning systems that had been put in place in Canada during the 1950s were now viewed as less relevant, the DEW line and the other facilities that had been manned jointly by the United States and Canada were allowed to go unused and fell into disrepair. Trudeau simultaneously sought to diversify Canadian economic activities by promoting trade with countries other than the United States, as well as by erecting tariff walls and enacting laws that limited the foreign ownership of Canadian companies, with the hope being to thereby gain greater leverage vis-à-vis Canada's dominating southern neighbour. The results – given Canada's geographic position – were predictable. With Trudeau's long reign in office and his continued commitment throughout this period to such policies, Canada arrived at the final years of Trudeau's term with a defence budget that ranked near the bottom among the NATO allies.[76] More generally, by the latter years of the Trudeau administration Canada had significant economic problems.[77] And it was against this backdrop of a weakened Canadian economy and a poorly defended Canadian territory that Cold War tensions re-escalated in the late 1970s.

Although the Cold War security environment was always dangerous, in the late 1970s and early 1980s the threat level became amplified by a series of US and Soviet foreign policy initiatives. On the Soviet side, these included the invasion of Afghanistan in 1979, the placement of nuclear missiles within close proximity to the Iron Curtain in Europe in the early 1980s, the support of communist forces and regimes in Central America and the Caribbean during the late 1970s and early 1980s, and a massive military build-up in the Arctic region. The United States responded to these activities by arming Afghan rebels against the Soviet army, by placing its own intermediate-range nuclear missiles in western Europe, by arming right-wing forces in Central America, by toppling left-leaning regimes in the Caribbean, and by likewise participating in an Arctic arms race. This latter issue, not surprisingly, was of particular significance for US-Canadian relations.

There were several strategic factors that fed into the Arctic arms race of the late 1970s and 1980s; for the purposes of this study, the most significant is arguably the development of cruise missile technology. Whereas ICBMs are launched in the expectation that they will fall near and possibly on the intended target, cruise missiles can be directed to fly at low altitudes – under the radar – and then land directly on the target with pinpoint accuracy. This new level of accuracy, combined with cruise missiles' ability to avoid radar detection, thus had a destabilizing aspect to it in terms of Cold War strategy. The rationale of MAD, after all, is that the target state will be able to see via radar that an ICBM attack is coming, and that a significant number of the target state's nuclear missiles should be capable of surviving a nuclear first strike. The attacked state, as such, can counter-attack and thereby ensure that both states are mutually destroyed. Given this rationale, no state should seek to precipitate a nuclear war. A key part of the survivability of missile forces, however, depends upon the fact that some of the incoming ICBMs that are aimed at the target state's nuclear silos will not fall directly on those silos, and that those silos can be sufficiently hardened to ensure the survivability of some of the stored missiles against a nearby nuclear strike. It also depends upon the fact that other missile launch platforms – such as submarines and planes – can potentially avoid an impending attack, insofar as submarines can conceal themselves from enemy detection systems, thus rendering themselves difficult to target, while aircraft can avoid attack due to speed – that is, mobility – and/or stealth. Cruise missiles, however, can be programmed to impact directly on the targets themselves, thereby making sufficient protection of the stored missiles far more difficult. Likewise, given the ability of cruise missiles to fly below the radar, the targeted state will have much less – if any – warning of the impending attack, and evasive manoeuvres will be that much more difficult to execute.

Guided missiles came online in a major way in the late 1970s, although efforts to develop such weaponry had been underway long before then. Indeed, by some accounts the history of cruise missiles stretches back to the second decade of the 1900s, when the United States and other countries sought to create bombs of various sorts that could be programmed with precision in terms of target impact.[78] Early efforts in this regard were fairly rudimentary, but over time the technology progressively improved, although it did so slowly. "The American military made numerous efforts with winged missiles during the quarter century following World War II, albeit with only meager success. Because of the cruise missile's inherent technical limitations (inaccurate and unreliable operation), more effective weapons pushed aside winged vehicles."[79] Such was the case until 1970, when "two technological breakthroughs transformed the cruise missile."[80] First, rapid technological advances significantly reduced the size, weight, and cost of computers, while also dramatically increasing computer capabilities. As a result, the computer-based guidance systems that were built into the cruise missiles were now smaller and more useful. When these advances were paired with satellite mapping, they allowed for the creation of "a small, practically autonomous, reliable, long-range and highly accurate guidance system called TERCOM. The computer also enabled the vehicle to fly very, very low, making it difficult to detect and destroy."[81] The second development in 1970 was the creation of a small, efficient turbofan jet engine that could be paired with a smaller missile airframe, which in turn meant that less power and fuel would be needed to propel the missile towards its target. "The smaller size also reduced radar cross section (RCS) and costs, and increased both the number of weapons that could be carried aboard aircraft or submarines and the relative ease with which the land-launched version could be handled and concealed."[82] As such, in 1970 cruise missiles suddenly became potentially much more accurate, much harder to detect, and much easier to deploy in large numbers.

Yet, while the essential technological innovations occurred in 1970, the complex process of developing and building the missiles, as well as the fact of competing political agendas within the armed services, meant that the US Navy and Air Force did not actually begin flying and testing cruise missiles until 1976. The key step was then taken the following year when Defense Secretary Donald Rumsfeld ordered a full-scale effort to build up US cruise missile capabilities. This was "probably the most important decision point in the evolution of the weapon." As a result, in the final years of the 1970s and into the 1980s the US cruise missile program got underway in earnest.[83] And not surprisingly, the Soviet Union's own cruise missile program's progress correlated with the program in the United States.[84]

The important point for present purposes is that, to make best use of their cruise missiles, neither the United States nor the USSR could be expected to remain content with simply launching those missiles from their own territory. Rather, the most strategic approach would be to launch them from planes or submarines flying or floating close to the other state's territory, thereby conducting a strike that was both accurate and rapid. The role of Canadian territory, airspace, and sea-space, in turn, could hardly have been more central to this new strategic situation. Canada's northern territories were ideal locations for the establishment of early warning systems to detect Soviet ALCM – air-launched cruise missile – bombers that were flying near or over Canadian territory in order to get close to US targets. These territories would also be ideal base locations from which to launch GLCMs – ground-launched cruise missiles – as well as interceptor missiles and jets at Soviet aircraft. Arctic waters off northern Canada would likewise be crucial for use by US nuclear attack submarines, which could carry SLCMs – sea-launched cruise missiles. Conversely, such territory and sea-space would be logical first targets of acquisition in a major Soviet offensive against the United States. It is hardly surprising, therefore, that in the late 1970s and early 1980s an Arctic arms race involving both cruise missile and advanced ICBM technology transpired between the two superpowers.

The Soviet Union, for instance, began substantially increasing its Arctic forces in the late 1970s. The result was that by mid-1983 the USSR's Northern Fleet, which was headquartered at Murmansk and was already the largest fleet in the Soviet Navy, had come to possess 405 warships, 200 auxiliary ships, 430 aircraft, and 118,000 soldiers. It also had over half of the Soviet Union's SLCM-carrying nuclear submarines. The port city of Severodvinsk, located south of Murmansk, possessed the world's largest submarine building yard, and the city of Plesetsk, also south of Murmansk, was the site of a missile base housing sixty-five ICBMs. As was noted at the time, "The Kola Peninsula [which is where Murmansk and Plesetsk are located] may be the single greatest concentration of military power anywhere in the world. It is certainly the world's largest naval complex, supporting more ships than all the United States' Atlantic ports combined."[85]

The United States participated with equal vigour in the enhancement of its Arctic arsenal. In the late 1970s, for instance, a joint Canadian-US air defence study was undertaken. The report was completed in 1979 and pointed out that NORAD's air defence system had significant gaps in terms of providing warning for Canadian airspace and that NORAD had ignored "airspace integrity problems." In response, Congress directed the Defense Department to develop a strategy for improving North American air defences. The US Air Force responded, in turn, with the Air Defense Master Plan, and this plan then served as the basis for the further US-Canadian efforts to modernize NORAD.[86] Among its key proposals was the assignment of at least six airborne warning and control (AWAC) planes to patrol northern Canada, as well as further development of Arctic intercept capabilities and ground-based warning systems to counter the threat from Soviet ALCMs.[87]

In terms of ground-based warning systems, the out-of-date early warning systems that were set up in the 1950s would need to be replaced with more modern, functioning radar stations. In 1985 an agreement was therefore reached to replace the old system with the new North Warning System (NWS) at a cost of $7 billion.[88] The NWS was to consist of thirteen long-range and thirty-nine short-range radar stations running along the northern limits of Canada from its border with Alaska to its eastern province of Newfoundland and Labrador.[89] These stations, in turn, would complement the US radar capabilities that already existed in Alaska. In addition to these efforts, the United States also worked out an agreement with Iceland in 1985 to build two new radar stations on that island in order to monitor Soviet sea and air activity in the Arctic. The United States simultaneously sought to strengthen relations with Norway and Greenland, both of which played important roles in monitoring Soviet activity in the region.[90]

Along with the "passive" activities of radar surveillance, the United States began engaging in more active military efforts in the Arctic during this period. A key area of US action pertained to submarine patrols in Arctic waters. US submarines, often preceded by US icebreakers, began regularly trolling the seas surrounding the Canadian Arctic archipelago without requesting Canadian permission to do so, which generated much anger in Canada. Canadian concern was enhanced, in particular, by certain specific instances of American trespassing, such as the voyage of the US icebreaker *Polar Sea*, which sailed through the Canadian waters of the Northwest Passage in 1985 without asking leave from the Canadians. The outcry this aroused was then amplified in 1987 when the public learned that several US nuclear attack submarines had held a rendezvous at the North Pole, thereby demonstrating that US submarine activity in Canada's Arctic waters was occurring on a large scale.[91]

US military activity in Canada's northern expanse also increased during this period in the form of missile testing. Although the Trudeau administration had long sought to distance itself from close association with US military activities, in the early 1980s it bowed to US pressure – and, more fundamentally, to the pressure of a renewed sense of threat from the USSR – and allowed the US military to commence testing cruise missiles in Canada's northern region. This activity likewise triggered major protests throughout Canada, but Trudeau allowed the testing to take place nonetheless.[92]

Meanwhile, the United States continued to seek even more fundamental and comprehensive military relations with Canada. The range of US ambitions in this regard can be appreciated by noting, for instance, the manner in which military coordination with the Canadians fit into the major defence project of the Reagan administration – the Strategic Defense Initiative (SDI), which acquired the nickname "Star Wars." SDI was, fundamentally, a repudiation of the doctrine of MAD, and although the concept was evidently conceived of by members of Reagan's staff during his 1979 presidential campaign, it was officially announced by President Reagan in March 1983. The core goal of SDI was to develop a system by which incoming nuclear missiles could be destroyed far in advance of reaching their target. The appellation "Star Wars" was derived from the fact that the envisioned means of destroying incoming missiles was a system that relied, in part, on space-based lasers to shoot down the missiles in-flight. The space-based aspect of the program, however, was only one feature of the general strategic concept. Accompanying SDI was the Air Defense Initiative (ADI), which was focused on developing air-based and air-directed defences that would also protect against a nuclear strike. Thus whereas SDI was conceived of as the defensive "roof," ADI was to form the defensive "walls." These walls were necessary because, were SDI in fact feasible, the USSR would naturally attempt to compensate for this impediment to its use of high-altitude missiles by increasing its use of bombers and low-flying cruise missiles. The goal of ADI, therefore, was to "develop technologies appropriate to surveillance, interception and battle management in regard to hostile bombers and cruise missiles."[93] And naturally, if the idea was to locate, intercept, and destroy these planes and missiles before they came within close range of their targets, then much of the surveillance equipment would need to be stationed in northern Canada, as would the anti-aircraft surface-to-air-missile (SAM) sites and the bases housing US fighter aircraft and battle management capabilities.

For example, among the proposed defense measures were super, remote-controlled AWAC planes, equipped with giant telescopes to detect incoming warheads, which would patrol Canadian skies for multiple days at a time, and the most logical basing site for these planes would be Canada's far north. The images picked up by these planes would then be transmitted to Terminal Imaging Radar (TIR), also based in Canada, which would refine the images to distinguish actual incoming warheads from decoys. This information, in turn, would then be programmed into US interceptor missiles, which would be launched to shoot down the incoming Soviet missiles. Although these interceptor missiles would be useful if based in either the United States or Canada, if based only in the United States they would be obliged to intercept the incoming missiles during the last 500–2,000 kilometres of the Soviet missile's flight, thereby giving the US missile only 100–600 seconds of flight time between launch and impact. If these missiles were stationed in northern Canada, however, then the United States would have the option of attempting to shoot down the Soviet missiles at an earlier phase of the flight, which would naturally be the preferable option.[94]

Around the same time as the United States was pushing for this closer ADI-based military coordination with Canada, the role of NORAD was also modified. In 1981 it was decided that, instead of "North American Air Defense," the NORAD acronym was now to stand for "North American Air Defense and Aerospace Surveillance Command." The name change reflected the strategic reorientation that was currently underway, with NORAD forces now tasked with defence against cruise missile and bomber attacks. In the same year, Canada also agreed to let drop a clause in the NORAD treaty – which had been put into the treaty at Canadian insistence in 1968 – which restricted NORAD's participation in antiballistic missile (ABM) defence. Thus although NORAD was not yet engaged in ABM defence, it was being prepared for that role. Then in 1982 the US Defense Department initiated an effort "to develop a concept for integrated defense against bombers, cruise and ballistic missiles through the year 2000." This study, known as Strategic Defense Architecture 2000, was to be undertaken by the commander-in-chief of NORAD. Canada agreed to participate in Phase I of the study, which dealt mainly with air defence.[95]

When it became public knowledge in 1984 that Canada was considering joining the United States in these various efforts, however, protests broke out in Canada as they had in the past. In response to this protest, and to the debate it engendered in the Canadian House of Commons – all of which was then coupled with internal administration misgivings – the Canadian regime eventually decided not to participate in SDI.[96] Yet, while it would not be directly involved in SDI, Canada did continue to participate in ADI. Indeed, the determination to do so received a crucial impetus in 1984 when Brian Mulroney became Canadian prime minister and proceeded to reorient Canadian foreign policy in a far more US-friendly direction. The essence of this new Canadian strategic perspective was expressed when the Mulroney administration issued a defence white paper in 1987, which essentially repudiated Canadian security policy under the Trudeau administration.[97] The white paper stressed that "much of the equipment of most elements of the Canadian forces is in an advanced state of obsolescence or is already obsolete." After outlining a plan to address this problem, the white paper explained that this rebuilding was necessary because "the West is faced with an ideological, political and economic adversary whose explicit long-term goal is to mould the world in its own image." This enemy "has at its disposal massive military forces and a proven willingness to use force, both at home and abroad, to achieve political objectives." The white paper "rejects as naïve and self-serving the arguments of those who promote neutrality or unilateral disarmament," and it also pointed out that failure to participate in the effort of military defence would simply make Canadian dependence upon other states – that is to say, the United States – all the more complete.[98]

The white paper thus called for a strategic reorientation of Canada's military along with a general rebuilding of its material assets. This included a recognition of the need to enhance Canada's ability to patrol the waters off its Pacific Coast, where Soviet naval activity had been steadily increasing, as well as the need to patrol the Arctic region and to address the threat of Soviet technologies such as cruise missiles, which were once again making Canadian territory the central focus of North American defence.[99] To meet the sea-born challenge, therefore, a major enhancement of Canadian naval capabilities was envisioned, including the building of ten or twelve nuclear-powered attack submarines, twelve new frigates, an under-ice surveillance system in the Arctic, six additional long-range maritime patrol aircraft, the modernization of medium-range aircraft, and more minesweepers.[100] To meet the various other military challenges facing North America, the white paper pointed out that, while Canada would not be participating in SDI, it would be actively participating in ADI efforts under NORAD. And such active participation in the sorts of ADI projects noted earlier would require, in turn, a level of interstate military cooperation/integration that went far beyond the levels of interoperability that the two states had heretofore experienced.

Thus, by the mid-1980s we see both the Canadian and US regimes actively promoting a dramatic increase in their bilateral efforts to secure the northernmost portions of North America, and not coincidentally it was also at that time that the two states launched their most recent – and most successful – effort at establishing bilateral free trade.

The Decision to Establish an FTA

In light of a historical record that indicates that the United States and Canada have often sought to use trade agreements to address security issues that involved one another, it would be unsurprising if security and trade policy overlapped in the context of the 1988 US-Canadian FTA, since the threat faced by the United States and Canada in the 1980s was as intense as any they had ever confronted. One obvious means, in turn, of determining why the FTA was established between the two states, and hence whether an overlap occurred, is to examine the statements of the individuals who were influential in the FTA policymaking processes in each state.

The first piece of data to examine in this regard is a statement made by Ronald Reagan when he was running for the presidency in 1979. In the speech announcing his candidacy that November, Reagan presented his primary foreign policy idea, which he referred to as a "North American Accord." As he explained,

> The world has become a place where, in order to survive, our country needs more than just allies – it needs real friends. Yet, in recent times we often seem not to have recognized who our friends are. This must change. It is now time to take stock of our own house and to resupply its strength ... We live on a continent whose three countries possess the assets to make it the strongest, most prosperous and self-sufficient on Earth ... A developing closeness among Canada, Mexico and the United States – a North American accord – would permit achievement of the potential in each country beyond that which I believe any of them – strong as they are – could accomplish in the absence of such cooperation. In fact, the key to our own future security may lie in both Mexico and Canada becoming much stronger countries than they are today.[101]

The Accord, as initially articulated, called in broad terms for closer relations between the United States and its two neighbours. Its immediate purpose was to create an environment in North America "in which the peoples and the commerce of its three strong countries flow more freely than they do today."[102] But, as Reagan clearly indicated in his speech, the "future security" of the United States was the ultimate objective of this policy. Such security was being called into question at a time when détente was breaking down and when the Canadian regime was led by a prime minister who could not always be counted upon to support major US initiatives. Thus a new, more "proactive" approach to securing North American territory was evidently required – an approach that did not simply rely upon NORAD-based arrangements but that gave greater assurance that the sorts of assets made available via NORAD would be used as the United States wished. The Accord fit squarely into this new strategic orientation. Indeed, an even greater depth for the possible relationship was hinted at when, in the same speech, Reagan called for Puerto Rico to be made a full US state. As he put it, "It is time to stop thinking of our nearest neighbors as foreigners."

After subsequently assuming the presidency, the first trips that Reagan took abroad were to his counterparts in Mexico and Canada, the purpose of these trips being to follow up on the North American Accord idea. When he met with the Mexican and Canadian heads of state, however, Reagan found them wary of his Accord agenda, fearing as they did that, among other things, Reagan's proposals might mask a US intention to gain greater access to its neighbours' natural resources. In light of this evident wariness, therefore, Reagan's aides stressed that the Accord would be somewhat informal in nature. As one aide put it, "The accord is more of a state of mind than it is a programmatic approach ... We understand that both Canada and Mexico have become cynical after years of neglect of their interests by the United States, and both leaders are understandably hesitant about our intentions."[103] Yet despite US attempts to ease suspicions, both the Mexican and Canadian regimes continued to resist the Accord concept, with the result that Reagan was obliged to temporarily set it aside.

This early lack of progress with the North American Accord has caused the policy concept – as well as the motivations that lay behind it – to remain underexamined in the scholarly literature. Indeed, various scholars treat it as only marginally relevant to the integration process, which is understandable given the policy's initial nonrealization, as well as the fact that most scholars focus on the economic aspects of the CUFTA case and consider security issues to be largely irrelevant to it in general. Nonetheless, the Accord concept was of some importance, because it constituted an early step in a longer process of policy advocacy that ultimately resulted in the 1988 FTA. Determining what the exact motivations for the Accord were is therefore useful if we wish to understand the purpose of the larger US-Canadian free trade effort.

Aside from Reagan – who was fairly clear about the security-focused purposes of the Accord concept in his November 1979 campaign speech, but who was no longer able to be interviewed at the time this study was conducted – the most relevant people to address this topic are those Reagan advisors who dealt with issues of economic, foreign, and security policy. More specifically, the most useful interviewees are those who served in influential roles during both the Reagan presidential campaign – and thus were present when the North American Accord concept was initially formulated as a policy goal – as well as during the Reagan presidency and hence could observe the implementation of that policy first-hand. Three individuals fit these criteria ideally. The first is Martin Anderson. Anderson was a presidential campaign advisor to Reagan and was also one of the original crafters of the North American Accord. After Reagan's election, Anderson then became one of Reagan's primary economic advisors, retaining that position during the first two years of Reagan's presidency. He was therefore in a good position to understand the purpose of the Accord concept, particularly from an economics-focused point of view. When asked by the author what the Accord agenda was about, however, Anderson stressed first and foremost that, while economics was "part of" the overall Accord concept, it nonetheless went "way beyond economics" and included issues pertaining to US national defence. With regard to defence, he pointed out that US-Canadian relations were crucial for US security. More specifically, he noted that, at the time the Accord idea was floated, the United States was facing the Soviet nuclear arsenal in the Arctic, that it needed to counter that threat by placing greater military capacity in the North American Arctic region, and that as such it needed to develop closer relations with Canada. The northern Canadian territory, he observed, was "the first line of defence" against a Soviet nuclear attack. Anderson also suggested that he, along with other Reagan aides such as Reagan's campaign manager Richard Sears – who, like Anderson, is also credited with being one of the key crafters of the SDI concept – developed the idea for the Accord in the period before and during Reagan's 1979 presidential campaign.[104]

A second person who was well placed to articulate the purpose of the Accord was George Shultz. Shultz was, like Anderson, a member of Reagan's presidential campaign team. He then served as chairman of President Reagan's Economic Policy Advisory Board until he became secretary of state in 1982, a post that he held for the remainder of Reagan's presidency. He was thus in an ideal position to appreciate whether there was an overlap between the economic and noneconomic goals of the Accord agenda. When asked by the author whether he was in consonance with Anderson's claim that the Accord went "way beyond economics," Shultz agreed and noted that "obviously there were security concerns."[105] With regard to those concerns, "the main things of course were ... our agreements with Canada, which included all sorts of things beyond the Canadian participation in NATO." When asked whether the North American Accord was therefore intertwined with the general US-Canadian effort to enhance their security relations in the early 1980s, Shultz replied, "Well, I think that's right." Shultz also stressed that, while various advisors may have helped to further develop the idea of the Accord, the original concept began with Ronald Reagan himself. "The North America idea was something he [Reagan] had in his mind for a long time."

A third commentary on the Accord is offered by Richard Allen. Like the others, Allen worked on Reagan's presidential campaign, and he was also evidently an original contributor to the idea of the Accord. Following the election, he served as Reagan's national security advisor until 1982. In light of his national security focus, Allen was in a position to appreciate whether the Accord concept pertained to issues other than trade. As he explained to the author, the initial idea of the Accord was that it would serve as a diplomatic device to address the threat of communism in the region. From Allen's perspective, however, the utility of using enhanced North American economic relations as a complement to US military – rather than strictly diplomatic – policy in the region is perhaps better understood as an idea that was arrived at as events in the Arctic subsequently developed. To illustrate the original diplomatic goals of the initiative, Allen compared the Accord to Reagan's other regional efforts at the time, such as the Caribbean Basin Initiative, which, for instance, was intended to promote closer bonds between the United States and certain Caribbean nations in response to the Soviet threat in the Caribbean area in the early 1980s.[106]

Thus we find Reagan and three of his top foreign and economic policy advisors all stating that the North American Accord pertained in important ways to security issues. Along with these statements, the significance of security concerns in helping to prompt the North American Accord agenda – as well as the free trade-promoting effort that followed it – is further reinforced by the manner in which that effort was subsequently carried forward.

As noted, Canadian prime minister Trudeau resisted, as much as possible, the idea of closer relations of a wide-ranging nature with the United States in the early 1980s, with the result that the Accord idea was temporarily dropped. The United States then made an attempt in 1983 at persuading the Canadian regime to begin a free trade process. In this instance, the Canadians responded by promoting the idea of sector-based trade, which would focus on specific sectors of the participating states' economies rather than on free trade between the economies in their entirety. Given its narrower focus as compared to the agenda initially associated with the North American Accord, sector-based trade was less threatening to the Canadian regime and presumably to the Canadian public. The US administration, for its part, recognized the political rationale for this diplomatic repackaging and thus agreed to go along with this narrower approach. Furthermore, it was the Canadians who now publicly took the lead in calling for new trade talks. As William Brock, the US trade representative at the time, pointed out in an interview with the author, the Reagan administration encouraged the Canadian regime to take the public initiative in formally launching the process of new trade negotiations.[107] If the Canadian regime appeared to be taking the lead, and if this new initiative was focused on relatively narrow trade issues, then it would be less likely to generate the backlash that had accompanied the airing of the Accord idea. And, in fact, this strategy worked as expected, with relatively little protest from the Canadian public transpiring in response to the announcement of these new trade negotiations.

Yet, notwithstanding this narrowed trade agenda, George Shultz points out that the free trade effort that began in 1983 built upon the North American Accord attempt and was prompted by some of the same sorts of policy concerns.[108] Indeed, it is reflective of the continuing, larger agenda on the part of the United States at the time that, despite the lack of public protests, the US and Canadian regimes were unable to reach agreement in this new round of talks, for much the same reason as before. Shortly after the negotiation process began, the United States took the position that the sector-based approach was an insufficient method for addressing the trade issues between the two states and that full free trade should be pursued.[109] The Trudeau administration balked at this suggestion, and thus by 1984 the trade negotiations had once again come to a standstill. They would likely have remained there had Trudeau not suddenly declared his decision to retire in 1984, thereby precipitating a new election for prime minister, which was won by Brian Mulroney. Soon thereafter the free trade discussions were back in motion.

During his campaign to become prime minister in 1984, Mulroney had displayed less resistance to the idea of US-Canadian free trade than had his opponents. Not surprisingly, therefore, the Reagan administration was fairly enthusiastic about Mulroney's candidacy, and it was in the midst of that campaign – in June 1984 – that Mulroney paid his first visit to Reagan in Washington and apparently made a "good impression."[110] Just eight days after Mulroney assumed office he paid another visit to Reagan in Washington. This meeting, which was held in September 1984, focused primarily on security issues; among other things, Reagan requested that Canada send aid to the anticommunist regime in El Salvador, and that Canada double the number of its troops under NATO command.[111] This meeting between the two leaders also set the stage for their next and most important conference, which was held in Quebec City in March 1985.

It is noteworthy that, between these meetings of September 1984 and March 1985, the United States conducted three cruise missile tests in northern Canada.[112] As such things had in the past, these tests generated protests from the Canadian public, but the Mulroney administration showed little sign of backing away from still-closer relations with its southern neighbour. Indeed, when Mulroney met with Reagan in Quebec in March, Mulroney's intention to support Reagan's North American defence policy was made clear. Their meeting in Quebec – known as the "Shamrock Summit," since it was held around St Patrick's Day – turned out to be nothing short of a historic turning point in US-Canadian relations. In the Canadian collective memory, the image that figures most prominently is that of Reagan and Mulroney standing on a stage with their wives and singing "When Irish Eyes Are Smiling." That performance, however, hardly hinted at the much deeper level of agreement that was reached at that time.

At the Shamrock Summit two important decisions were made. First and foremost, Mulroney formally agreed to endorse the United States' amplified effort to address the Soviet military threat, to coordinate Canadian policy with this effort, and to enhance Canadian forces so as to assist with this overall agenda to the highest degree possible. Of particular note, it was at the Shamrock Summit that negotiations regarding the US Air Defense Master Plan were brought to completion and where agreement was reached on the enhancement of NORAD.[113] At the same time, a second key agreement was reached at the summit, pertaining to economic policy. Specifically, Mulroney and Reagan issued a declaration calling for an examination of ways to reduce and eliminate barriers to trade.[114] Or in other words, a process of policy-advocacy that had begun with Reagan's arrival in office and that had twice been rebuffed – first in its form as the North American Accord, and then as a seemingly more limited trade agenda – was now embraced by the Canadian regime.

Following Reagan and Mulroney's declaration of intent in Quebec City, US-Canadian free trade negotiations were subsequently undertaken during the remainder of 1985 and stretched on throughout 1986 and 1987. Detailed analyses of the vicissitudes of that process have already been undertaken by other scholars, and it is unnecessary for the purposes of the present argument to examine them here. What is relevant is that, although the negotiating process was subjected to an array of difficulties, complications, and various points of near collapse, in a final session of talks in October 1987 the two sides arrived at mutually acceptable terms for a Canadian-US FTA, henceforth to be known as CUFTA. Once the negotiating process was complete, Mulroney ran for re-election in November 1988 with a hard-fought campaign focusing largely on the issue of free trade – a campaign that was reminiscent of the campaign run by Wilfrid Laurier in 1911, when Laurier staked his political career on the passage of a reciprocity treaty with the United States. Laurier's efforts had set US-Canadian relations on a new course, even though his attempt to secure freer trade had failed. Seventy-seven years later, Mulroney completed the process that Laurier began by winning his own election and thus returning to office with a referendum in favour of the trade deal. Securing passage of the treaty was less challenging in the United States, and the FTA was subsequently implemented on both sides, resulting in a wide-ranging liberalization of trade regulations between the United States and Canada. This ambitious agenda was further amplified by the fact that the FTA also established a dispute resolution mechanism, through which a binational panel of experts would be empowered to examine major trade disputes between the two sides.[115] Indeed, as one Canadian affairs specialist in the Reagan administration stated in the context of the Shamrock Summit, and in anticipation of the enhancement of the bilateral relationship, it was "a revolution in US-Canadian relations."[116]

The nature of that revolution was not confined strictly to the area of trade. The initiative for dramatically enhanced bilateral relations was pushed by a US administration that was determined to address the security threat posed by an Arctic-based Soviet attack; that recognized the necessity of far closer connectivity between the US and Canadian military establishments to address that threat; and that viewed the free trade effort as part of that larger agenda. Furthermore, the 1985 agreements in Quebec City that set the stage for this FTA were reached in the context of primarily security policy–focused summits, between leaders who shared a similar perspective in terms of the threats that menaced their states. And all of this, in turn, reflects a larger pattern in US-Canadian relations, spanning the last 220 years, whereby the United

States has repeatedly sought to use trade agreements with Canada as a means to bring the two countries diplomatically closer together, so as to ensure that a powerful, third-party state does not take advantage of Canadian territory to threaten the United States.

Although it therefore seems justifiable to claim that security motivations played a significant role in the US-led effort that eventually resulted in the FTA, the question remains as to what exactly Mulroney himself thought about all this. In light of his background, it is plausible that he would be in favour of greater US-Canadian trade. Prior to entering politics, for instance, he was a businessman who spent part of his career working for a US company. He was thus a natural candidate for appreciating the potential benefits of greater US-Canadian business relations. And although before running for prime minister he had sounded some anti–free trade notes, such statements appear to have been primarily tactical, so as to secure the support of a sufficient number of conservative subgroups to ensure his nomination as the Progressive Conservative Party candidate.[117] During his 1984 campaign and subsequently, he then moved more in the direction of endorsing greater US-Canadian trade as a means to improve the Canadian economy.

In addition to favouring stronger US-Canadian trade relations, Mulroney consistently supported the enhancement of US-Canadian defence relations. He had done so before his public endorsement of greater US-Canadian free trade, and throughout his term as prime minister he remained consistently focused on the security concerns that the two states shared, as well as on the need to improve the Canadian military so as to address those concerns. It would be surprising, therefore, given his championing of closer economic and security ties with the United States, if he had not recognized the connection between these two issue areas and how progress in one might facilitate progress in the other. But the question of how much Mulroney viewed the trade issue in terms of the security context remains. Was the latter central to his calculation about pursuing an FTA?

In an interview with the author regarding his decision to pursue free trade with the United States, Mulroney emphasized first and foremost that "you have to remember the context. The context at the time was the height of the Cold War. Nuclear missiles pointed at New York, and Washington, and London, and so everything we did at the time was within the context of the Cold War. In fact, at the meeting in Quebec City on March 17, I had just come from Moscow, where Gorbachev was installed as the new leader of the Soviet Union. In fact, I was able to give Reagan his first effective debrief on Gorbachev and what [Reagan] might expect there."[118]

Mulroney also stressed that, while he and Reagan disagreed on many foreign policy issues, the two were both committed to resisting the communist threat. When asked whether he therefore viewed the free trade issue as part of the larger security issue, Mulroney replied, "Absolutely," and added, "You can't see anything through the prism of small-bore national interest. If you see relations only in terms of soft wood lumber and Rhode Island potatoes ..." That is to say, a limited focus on traditional trade items would miss the larger point of the agreement.

The importance that Mulroney attached to the FTA, and to its relevance beyond the limits of trade policy, is corroborated by Derek Burney, who served as Mulroney's chief of staff from 1987 to 1989, and who had a specialty in trade issues, having previously worked in the Canadian Foreign Service. As Mulroney notes regarding Burney, "In truth he was, at the critical moments, my key agent in the free trade negotiations. He played an absolutely vital role in their successful conclusion."[119] In line with this, Burney explained to the author,

> One of the reasons he [Mulroney] told me that he wanted me to become his chief of staff, which was kind of an unusual appointment, frankly, for a foreign service officer ... in our system, this was a bit different, because I was a career public servant, and the chief of staff to the prime minister is a highly political position, but Mr Mulroney's view was, look, I don't have political strategists, I'm the political strategist, but I want somebody to organize my office, and I want somebody to help me on the major issues of the day, one of which is free trade. And he said, you know that one inside out ... So from 1987 until the time I left that was the dominant issue for him and for our government.[120]

Burney points out that, in the month of September 1987, there were over twenty cabinet meetings on the trade issue, reflecting the fact that "the risk for the Canadian government was huge."[121] Noting Mulroney's singularly important role in establishing the FTA, Burney explained,

> He did things that very few leaders would have had the courage to do ... Free trade will probably be one of his proudest legacies because he took the risk that other people would have shied away from, and let me tell you, there was not unanimity in his cabinet on this initiative. I characterize

some of those cabinet discussions as Lincolnesque. What I mean by that is, they used to say, about Lincoln's cabinet, the vote was nine to one, but the one prevailed. We had those kinds of discussions in the cabinet. Mr Mulroney pulled his government along with this initiative; he wasn't following, he was leading, he saw a broader context.[122]

Of course it is true that the Macdonald Commission – which had been established by the Canadian regime to examine the costs and benefits of an FTA with the United States – already concluded in 1985 that an FTA would have an overall beneficial impact on the Canadian economy. And indeed, scholars such as Greg Inwood have focused specifically on the influential role of that commission in bringing Canadians around to an acceptance of the FTA.[123] Yet, as Burney explained to the author, Mulroney was already in favour of an FTA before the Macdonald Commission made its pronouncement; he did not need the commission to convince him. Likewise, although the commission's conclusions may have helped persuade various people of the benefits of free trade, Mulroney's leadership was essential in bringing certain of his officials into line.

As Burney further emphasized, "Mr Mulroney thought big, in terms of the relationship with the United States." More specifically, "he was a strong believer in NORAD. In North American defence." Furthermore, "he was a strong believer in NATO. He increased our strength in NATO, that was one of the first things he did. He acknowledged quite openly that Canada hadn't been playing what he thought was an appropriate role in partnership with the United States and he was going to change that." At the same time, "he took very substantial risks in large initiatives with the United States that other people would have shied away from because the political benefits were not obvious to anybody."[124]

In short, Mulroney took those risks because he was motivated by a larger vision, a vision that compelled him to overcome the inevitable resistance and political pitfalls that such a policy would engender. Canadian history, after all, is a history of wariness towards its powerful southern neighbour – a sentiment that has persisted long after the two countries ceased to be likely military antagonists – and Mulroney was seeking nothing less than a fundamental sea change in US-Canadian relations. Despite vociferous resistance from many sectors of Canadian society, and despite the risk of losing office, Mulroney managed to effect that change in the latter 1980s when both the FTA and the defence white paper were approved by the Canadian parliament. Ronald

Reagan, for his part, welcomed the FTA's implementation by harkening back to the origins of the initiative, as first articulated during his presidential campaign of 1978–1980: "This Free Trade Agreement," he declared, "is the cornerstone for that North American Accord, that new era of growth, opportunity and friendship on our continent."[125]

Assessing the Data

The foregoing analysis of CUFTA's creation appears to provide evidence that corroborates the assumption that trade agreements can be – and sometimes are in fact – used by states to help them address security concerns. More specifically, this case study offers evidence that corresponds to the particular hypotheses presented in chapter 1. And since the purpose of this study is not simply to recount the factual record but also to test those specific hypotheses against the data, it is both useful and necessary to consider now the precise ways in which the five functions related to the two hypotheses play out within the case. As noted in chapter 1, an FTA can serve to 1) enhance trade, and thereby increase economic strength, 2) provide voice opportunities, 3) help resolve disputes, 4) provide insurance of a lasting relationship, and 5) lay the groundwork for still greater integration.

We can begin by considering those functions as they pertain to the trading-to-oppose hypothesis. For function 1 of that hypothesis, the observable implications are 1) statesmen in the relevant states identifying a specific threat to their state, 2) those statesmen indicating that the establishment of an FTA will help them to address a specific threat, by facilitating a power-aggregating effort against the threatening state – specifically, that an FTA will increase trade between the FTA member states, thereby increasing their overall economic strength, and hence allowing them to act more effectively against the threatening state, and 3) those statesmen attempting to establish an FTA. Similar sorts of observable implications should likewise be looked for with regard to functions 2 through 5 of the trading-to-oppose hypothesis, although observable implication number 2 – regarding the manner in which an FTA is expected to assist a trading-to-oppose effort – should differ for each function.

Clearly, the observable implications regarding statesmen identifying a threat – observable implication number 1 – and regarding the attempt to enact an FTA – observable implication number 3 – are found within the factual record. Reagan, Mulroney, and others who worked most closely on the FTA initiative were explicit about the threat they thought was posed by the Soviet Union, and they were successful in their efforts to enact an FTA.

With regard to these statesmen seeking to use the FTA to assist their anti-Soviet effort – observable implication number 2 – we also find facts and statements that correspond with each of the five functions that an FTA can serve in this regard. With regard to function 1 – increasing trade, so as to increase military strength – we find both Reagan and Mulroney explicitly stating that increased trade would serve the purpose of more effectively opposing Soviet power. When Regan announced his North American Accord idea, he specifically noted, "A developing closeness among Canada, Mexico and the United States – a North American accord – would permit achievement of the potential in each country beyond that which I believe any of them – strong as they are – could accomplish in the absence of such cooperation."[126] And Mulroney likewise clearly sought to enhance Canadian strength both economically and militarily and demonstrated his recognition of the interconnectedness of those issues.

With regard to function 2 of the trading-to-oppose hypothesis – an FTA can provide member states with voice opportunities through which they can influence each other's policies – the evidence clearly shows a desire by both sides to gain a more determinative say in one another's policy processes, and to use trade agreements to obtain such. This point was made with particular clarity by Prime Minister Mackenzie King when, during the early years of the Cold War, he noted how the Americans "would want to get Canada under their aegis. If I was an American, I would have the same view, especially considering Russia's position." With regard to the 1988 FTA in particular, the data shows a desire by US statesmen to gain diplomatic leverage that they could then bring to bear in persuading the Canadians to work more closely with the United States against the perceived Soviet menace, while we also see Mulroney's administration seeking to enhance its relations with the United States, in part to be able to have more of an influence on US policies that were vital to both Canadian security and trade.

With regard to function 3 of the trading-to-oppose hypothesis – an FTA can be used to resolve disputes between states engaged in a strength-aggregating effort – we observe statesmen clearly seeking not simply to amplify but to improve the US-Canadian relationship, and viewing the FTA as part of that effort. The significance of the dispute-mitigating role of the US-Canadian FTA is highlighted, furthermore, by both the historical context in which the FTA was established and the structure of the FTA itself. The FTA-creating effort was launched at a time when US-Canadian relations had reached a particularly low point, in the wake of Prime Minister Trudeau's efforts to distance Canada – economically and diplomatically – from the United States. Differing perspectives on trade issues had the potential to flare into larger disputes, as they often had in the past. Thus the United States and Canada sought to avoid an aggravation of trade disputes and of more general relational difficulties by establishing an FTA that contained within it a detailed dispute-settlement mechanism.

Function 4 of the trading-to-oppose hypothesis – an FTA can provide insurance that the power-aggregating relationship will last – also appears to have been operative in this case, although perhaps not of central importance. Clearly, both the United States and Canada viewed closer relations with the other as vital in light of the Soviet threat, and any reinforcement of that relationship was desirable. That said, the likelihood that one of the states would fully "defect" from the anti-Soviet effort was fairly low. Trudeau's policy of distancing Canada from the United States, after all, had produced undeniably adverse effects for Canada and hence was unlikely to be repeated in substantial form. Furthermore, the general orientation of Canada towards ever-closer relations with the United States had been underway since the early 1900s. As such, while the FTA offered further solidity to the trading-to-oppose effort, providing such added insurance of a long-standing partnership was arguably not the core function of the FTA.

As for function 5 of the trading-to-oppose hypothesis – an FTA can lay the groundwork for still greater integration – this is clearly demonstrated in the factual record. All of those most closely involved in the FTA creation process – Reagan, Anderson, Shultz, Allen, Mulroney, Burney – viewed the FTA as a first step in a much larger process, which would lead to a wide-ranging "accord" between the two states. Whether that accord was envisioned as leading to thoroughgoing "integration" is debatable, but clearly a far greater degree of interstate interconnectedness was envisioned than merely an FTA. And yet the FTA was simultaneously viewed as integral to that larger process.

It appears, in other words, that each of the five functions that an FTA can perform, in terms of reinforcing states' power-aggregating efforts against a threatening, third-party state, was relevant in varying degrees to the creation of the US-Canadian FTA. Statesmen acknowledged the Soviet threat, they claimed that an FTA would assist in aggregating power against that threat, and they then proceeded to enact an FTA. The legitimacy of this claim is then reinforced, as noted, by the timing of the negotiations and the manner in which they were carried out, and in light of the larger historical pattern.

As for the trading-to-control hypothesis, the observable implications pertaining to the five security-facilitating functions of an FTA are less manifest in the case of the 1988 FTA than are the observable implications for the trading-to-oppose hypothesis. Nonetheless, there are hints of trading-to-control behaviour to be found. From the American perspective, for instance, Canada in the 1980s was not a serious "threat" per se, as it had been in the past via its tendency to align with Britain. However, as the behaviour of the Trudeau administration during the 1970s demonstrated, Canada still had a tendency to seek non-US options for its alliance partners, and thus it is plausible that there was an element of trading-to-control that was operative in US policy. So too, the Canadian regime under Mulroney's leadership clearly did not view the United States as a serious threat, but Mulroney certainly did want to work closely with the United States to ensure that Canada at least had some say – some voice opportunities – in the development of a North American defence policy that could involve Canada in a risky military competition with the Soviets. Furthermore, if we consider the trading-to-control hypothesis in light of US-Canadian relations before the 1980s – and in particular, during the period of the 1770s to the 1890s – then we clearly see the use of trade agreements for the sake of exerting control. During that earlier period we consistently find the United States seeking to control Canadian behaviour, and Canada seeking to exert some sort of influence over US policy, in response to their reciprocally inspired senses of threat.

Overall, therefore, it appears valid to claim that the trading-to-oppose and – to a lesser extent – the trading-to-control hypotheses are corroborated by the CUFTA process, and that any effective counterargument made against this claim would need to demonstrate 1) that the threat facing the United States and Canada in the 1980s was not particularly serious, 2) that the statements made by statesmen with regard to the need to respond to that threat via trade techniques were misleading, 3) that the timing of the security and trade initiatives, which were launched in-tandem, was purely coincidental, and 4) that the many instances of trading-for-security that have occurred throughout the history of US-Canadian relations are irrelevant to an analysis of the events leading up to the creation of CUFTA.

Future Integration

If CUFTA was indeed created in response to not only economic incentives but also security concerns, then the factual implications for the
post-1988 US-Canadian relationship are potentially different than
would be the case if only economic motives played a role. Simply put, a
far more complex and involved relationship may lie ahead for the two
states than would be the case were they merely interacting over issues
of trade. Two questions immediately suggest themselves, however, in
light of this observation. First, why would relations need to become
more involved? And second, how would they do so?

The answer to the first question is perhaps not immediately obvious,
given that the threatening state most relevant to CUFTA's creation was
the Soviet Union, which has since ceased to exist. Likewise, any military
posturing in the Arctic region is currently of less intensity than was the
case during the 1980s. An answer to the question of why closer security
relations will occur, therefore, depends in large part on one's analysis
of the nature of state relations within an environment of global anarchy. For instance, if we accept the idea that states fear one another, that
such fear is generated by a states' power, combined with the elements
of geography, military capacity, and perceived intent, and hence that
states are constantly seeking ways to consolidate and/or amass power
in response to the threats posed by other states, then we should expect
to find states continually experiencing threats in relation to other states,
even if the intensity of one particular threat happens to temporarily
recede. Indeed, the history of US-Canadian relations itself attests to the
insecurity-laden nature of state relations, insofar as security concerns
have repeatedly arisen for these two states even though the specific
sources of greatest threat – Britain, Germany, the Soviet Union – shifted.
Thus although the Soviet Union has disappeared, Russia continues to
exist, as do China and other powerful states, as well as groupings of
states. These states possess their own military arsenals, strategies, and
intentions, and it is not only possible but also likely that the United
States and Canada will continue to view certain of these states warily.
Such wariness, in turn, will likely lend the United States and Canada
renewed reason to cooperate/integrate, and if we assume that the
benefits of such behaviour are greater in proportion to the degree of
cooperation/integration that is achieved, then greater and greater co-
operation/integration may well proceed.

If the rationale for close security relations does in fact persist, then the
other question to address pertains to the manner in which US-Canadian

relations are likely to become more institutionally complex and involved than they already are. After all, the United States and Canada are not only participants in a free trade regime but also the two constituent members of NORAD. The level of interconnectedness between them is therefore already both extensive and of some depth. Thus how might they move forward from here? One obvious thing to do would be to continue expanding the scope of their economic integration/cooperation. In general terms, further economic integration would entail transitioning from the existing free trade area into more involved projects such as a customs union, then eventually the creation of a common market, a common currency, and so forth. At the same time, there are a variety of specific, institution-strengthening actions that can be taken in order to move the trilateral NAFTA process along, and such actions will then enhance any integration involving Canada and the United States. CUFTA, after all, was folded into NAFTA with the latter's enactment in 1994, which means that the furthering of Canadian-US integration will have to take place within the context – or at least against the backdrop – of NAFTA's evolution. This point applies not simply to further economic policy intermeshing but also to security policy integration since, as the foregoing has demonstrated, policies of trade and security have become tightly intertwined in the US-Canadian case. Any understanding of where NAFTA is ultimately headed, in turn, requires an accurate analysis of why NAFTA was created in the first place. And that sort of analysis necessitates an appreciation of the US and Mexican motives for establishing the bilateral FTA that subsequently evolved into the trilateral, continent-encompassing trading arrangement that now characterizes North America.

3 NAFTA

The establishment of NAFTA in 1994 was a watershed moment in North American history. Never before had the continent's three states signed on to such an extensive trilateral trading agreement. Yet, notwithstanding the singular importance of NAFTA, its significance is typically only partially appreciated – a partialness that reflects a general lack of recognition of the security motivations that helped prompt its creation. Those motivations, in turn, were part of a longstanding pattern of trade-and-security seeking behaviour involving the United States and Mexico, just as the creation of CUFTA was but one step in a larger pattern of trade-and-security seeking activity involving the United States and Canada. To fully appreciate the nature of US-Mexican relations in the late 1980s and early 1990s, therefore, and hence how those relations ultimately culminated in NAFTA's enactment, it is essential to first understand the way in which policies of trade and security played themselves out between the two states in the eras before NAFTA began.

US-Mexican Relations, 1820s–1980s

Prior to NAFTA's enactment, US-Mexican relations – as in the case of US-Canadian relations – went through three phases. The character of those phases was different, however, in the two cases. Whereas the US-Canadian relationship grew progressively closer over time, the US and Mexico continued to regard each other as imminent or potential threats during all three of the pre-NAFTA phases, while what changed were the third-party states that became intertwined in the US-Mexican relational dynamic.

1820s–1860s: Engaging the British and the French

The first phase of US-Mexican relations spanned the period from the 1820s to the 1860s. During this phase, the United States feared Mexico's intentions to ally with powerful European states – particularly Britain and France – which in turn might capitalize upon Mexico's geographic position and hence threaten the United States, while Mexico feared the proximity, intentions, and military capacity of the United States.

Initially, relations between the United States and its southern neighbours were relatively amicable. This was due to the fact that, at the time when the United States came into being, the regions to its south were dominated by Spain, which sided with the Americans against the British during the Revolutionary War. The United States and Spain might nonetheless have been fated for eventual large-scale conflict were it not for Spain's rapidly receding hold upon its American colonies. In contrast to British power, which in the late 1700s was waxing towards its colonial apex, Spanish power was on the wane, thanks in part to the rise of British power. Thus when the United States began pressing its claims to Florida in the second decade of the nineteenth century, Spain was obliged to grudgingly relinquish its territorial possession without putting up too much of a fight.

Following the US acquisition of Florida in 1819, the only Spanish territory that still bordered the United States was New Spain, which included present-day Mexico and extended up to the northern border of Texas and west to the coast of California. In 1821, however, Mexico successfully completed its own revolt and thus Spain lost much of this territory as well. The leader of the Mexican revolt – a general in the Spanish army – then had himself proclaimed emperor of Mexico, which inspired a counter-revolution of sorts, with the end result that in 1824 a federal republic was established in Mexico that resembled in many ways the political structure of the United States.[1]

It was thus at this time, as a southward-expanding United States encountered a newly independent Mexico, that relations between the two states truly got underway. It was also during this period that the US regime was formulating its Monroe Doctrine. As noted in chapter 2, the core concept of this doctrine was that the United States would seek to prevent European powers from establishing strategic footholds in the newly independent states of the western hemisphere, since such footholds would allow European powers to threaten the United States. This policy was applied not only to Canada but also to Latin America; indeed the primary focus of the doctrine was on countries located south of the United States. As such, when the new republican regime in Mexico proceeded to establish close relations with Britain – and began negotiating with the British for a commercial treaty – the US regime was alarmed by the prospect that its primary enemy might establish strategic footholds to its south. It thus responded by attempting to establish a commercial treaty of its own with Mexico. US agents in Mexico also simultaneously engaged in efforts to ensure that a more pro-US party came to power in Mexico City. These latter machinations, however, generated consternation in the Mexican senate, which therefore temporarily refused to ratify the trade agreement with the United States.

The temporary nature of this refusal was due to the fact that the United States did indeed manage to get the pro-British, Conservative Party in Mexico removed from power; a feat that was accomplished by supporting a Mexican general, Antonio Lopez de Santa Anna, in his leadership of a pro-Liberal Party revolution. After Santa Anna succeeded in overthrowing the sitting president and putting a Liberal in his place, however, the Conservative vice president overthrew this Liberal president, only to himself be overthrown by Santa Anna, who in turn sought to enhance his legitimacy by having himself elected president in 1833.[2] Twenty-plus years of political instability ensued, with thirty-six presidential transitions taking place during that time period, many of which were effected through armed revolt. Santa Anna himself held the office eleven different times, and when not in power he still managed to control much of Mexican political life.

In the meantime, ratification of the trade deal between the United States and Mexico did eventually occur in the 1830s, during President Andrew Jackson's administration. Jackson had long believed that the United States was vulnerable along its southern border – insofar as Britain might establish military bases in Mexico as it had in Canada – and that for the sake of its security the United States needed to acquire the Mexican state of Texas. Jackson thus pushed to ratify the commercial treaty with Mexico as part of his overall plan to establish closer US-Mexican relations, which he hoped would serve as a prelude to persuading Mexico to cede Texas to the United States.[3] Yet even though Jackson did manage to get this trade treaty ratified, its relevance quickly receded as US-Mexican relations entered a particularly strained period, due precisely to the issue of Texas.

In the mid-1830s Texas was populated by both immigrants from the United States and native Mexicans, and various disputes between these two groups – and between the US immigrants and the federal regime in Mexico City – eventually culminated in an immigrant-led Texan revolt in 1835.[4] In response, the Mexican forces – under the command of Santa Anna – launched a series of attacks against the Texans, with some .success, although ultimately Santa Anna was defeated at the Battle of San Jacinto and was compelled to agree to Texan independence in 1836. This newly independent Texan state, however, was hardly secure, faced as it was with the prospect of still further attacks by a hostile Mexico. The Mexicans, for their part, had reason to attack Texas as soon as conditions allowed, because an independent Texas run by settlers from the United States might seek to integrate with the United States, thereby bringing the US border even further south and thus amplifying the potential US threat to Mexican territory.

In light of this situation, the Texan regime did the rational thing and promptly sought to integrate its state into the United States. Yet the timing was problematic, given that the United States was in the midst of its slavery debate, with anti-slave politicians opposed to annexing Texas because Texas would enter the United States as a slave state and pro-slavery politicians afraid of championing Texan annexation for fear of losing too many northern votes in upcoming national elections.[5] The Texans, however, were not inclined to wait for long. In 1841, with Santa Anna readying for a new invasion, the Texan regime initiated a foreign policy calculated to disturb the United States – namely, it threatened to establish close relations with European powers, and in particular with Britain, in order to protect itself against the Mexican threat.[6] This policy produced the desired result, and in 1845 the United States, fearing a Texan-British alliance, agreed to integrate with Texas.[7]

Although the United States thereby effectively addressed the threat that Texas might come under British control, the annexation of Texas paved the way for military conflict along the Texas-Mexico border, as relations between a southward-expanding United States and a wary and territorially aggrieved Mexico steadily deteriorated. Eventually full-scale fighting erupted between the two states in April 1846. In marked contrast to its various invasions of Canada, however, this southern US offensive was strikingly successful, with US forces securing a string of victories in northern Mexico and also managing to seize Mexico City. Mexican authorities then sued for peace and in February 1848 the war officially ended, leaving the United States in control of what is presently much of its western territory.

As might be expected, tensions persisted between the two states in the aftermath of the war. Various armed incidents occurred along both sides of the US-Mexico border, and American citizens periodically undertook independent campaigns to seize portions of northern Mexico.[8] This continuing sense of threat from the United States prompted Mexico to look once again to European states for power-aggregating assistance, and this time its partner of choice was France. The French during this period were expanding their presence in the Caribbean region and thus a strategic alliance with the Mexican regime made sense.[9] One result of this alliance was that when civil war subsequently erupted in Mexico in the late 1850s, France threw its support behind the ruling Mexican regime. Predictably, this growing French influence in Mexico disturbed US president James Buchanan, fearing as he did that France would use its alliance with Mexico as a means to extend French power into the Caribbean region and – as part of that same strategy – to threaten the United States. In response to this threat, therefore, Buchanan sent various sorts of aid to the Mexican forces fighting the pro-French, Mexican regime.[10] When the anti-regime elements in Mexico appeared unlikely to win the fight quickly, however, Buchanan went to Congress – first in 1859, then in 1860 – to ask for authority to assemble a military force with which to invade Mexico and thereby prevent French consolidation.[11] Congress, for its part, was still wholly taken up with the slavery debate and refused to give him permission. In conjunction with his military-related efforts, Buchanan also sought a commercial treaty with the Mexican anti-regime forces during the period of 1859–1860, as a further means of preventing foreign interference in Mexico. This treaty, however, failed to secure ratification by the US Senate.[12] Thus when the United States slid into its own civil war in 1861, Mexico was left vulnerable to not only France but also Britain and Spain, all three of whom claimed that Mexico owed them the payment of various debts.

These three European states, not surprisingly, invaded Mexico later that year, although disputes soon arose among the invaders, with the result that the British and Spanish troops returned home, leaving French forces to conquer Mexico for themselves, which they proceeded to do, completing their conquest in 1863. Yet by 1866 events had already turned against them. With its own civil war over, the United States began applying pressure on the Franco-Mexican regime, sending large arms shipments and other supplies into Mexico to aid the anti-French resistance. Simultaneously, France began pulling its troops in Mexico back to France in response to the growing threat posed by a territorially expanding Germany. The result was predictable: in 1867 the French forces in Mexico were overrun and the French-installed Mexican emperor, Maximilian, was executed via firing squad. A new republican regime was then established in Mexico City, but it too was overthrown in 1876 by Porfirio Díaz, who subsequently managed to hold on to power until 1911.

1870s–1940s: German Influence

The United States and Mexico clearly experienced a sense of mutual threat during the first phase of their relationship, and, as the record demonstrates, they periodically sought to use trade agreements to help them address their security issues. As in the case of US-Canadian relations, however, the characteristics of the US-Mexican strategic environment shifted over time. In the US-Canadian case, the shift occurred as Britain became less of a threat to the United States and more of a threat to Canada. Thus in the early 1900s Canadian prime minister Laurier took steps to align Canada somewhat more with the United States and somewhat less with Britain. Subsequently, as Canada and the United States were both faced with threats from the Germans and then from the Soviets, US-Canadian relations grew closer still, albeit slowly. In the case of the United States and Mexico, however, the shifting threat dynamic evolved rather differently after the initial relational phase. For the United States, Mexico continued to constitute a threat based upon Mexico's geographic proximity and its intentions to ally with other states, while for Mexico the United States continued to be a serious threat due to its geographic proximity, perceived hostile intent, and military capabilities. What changed, beginning in the 1870s, was the third party involved in the threat scenario. Rather than Britain or France, it was now Germany – which, following its territorial consolidation in central Europe in 1871, became active in the Caribbean – that represented Mexico's most attractive partner in terms of power-aggregating purposes, while, from the US perspective, Germany was viewed as the most dangerous European threat in the Caribbean. Mexico therefore sought to use techniques of trade to enhance its relations with Germany, while the United States sought to prevent such by establishing its own trade deals with Mexico.

These countervailing strategies displayed themselves with particular clarity during the early years of the Díaz presidency in Mexico and the presidency of Chester A. Arthur in the United States. It was in this period that a major push for trade reciprocity treaties with Latin American states was made by the United States. In terms of economic policy, it was logical for the Arthur administration to seek to secure markets in this part of the world at a time when American trade was expanding westward and southward.[13] Important security imperatives were also at play. Secretary of State Frederick Frelinghuysen, for instance, who was the guiding force behind the policy, was a firm promoter of the Monroe Doctrine and hence of the security imperative of preventing European influence in the Americas. Yet Frelinghuysen was also convinced that, for a variety of reasons – including the potential for igniting war with European states, as well as his assumption that the political cultures of Latin America would not mesh with that of the United States – outright annexation of Latin American states was impractical.[14] As such, he viewed the establishment of American influence over these states via trade treaties as a logical middle approach, with economic relations serving as a means of establishing tighter political ties.[15]

This perspective was applied in particular to the Caribbean region, where the United States was actively seeking to prevent foreign powers from establishing strategic footholds.[16] Mexico, naturally, figured prominently in this Monroe Doctrine–promoting economic policy, given its position as the United States' most immediate neighbour, its size as the largest state in the region, and the fact that European powers were indeed seeking to attain influence with it.[17] When Frelinghuysen set out to establish reciprocal trade treaties with several of the states in the Caribbean region, therefore, the first such treaty was sought with Mexico.

The Mexican regime, for its part, initially resisted the idea, fearing that a reciprocity treaty with the United States would damage Mexican trade with Europe and likewise serve as a prelude to further US attempts to acquire Mexican territory.[18] Nonetheless, Mexico did eventually agree to the treaty, although not to all that the United States wanted. Most notably, one month before signing the treaty, Mexico signed another commercial treaty with Germany in which it agreed to give Germany most-favoured-nation status, such that, if Mexico then signed a reciprocity treaty with the United States, Mexico would be obliged to grant Germany the same reciprocal trade privileges as well. From a strategic point of view, this allowed the Mexican regime a means of resisting American influence within Mexico by providing equal German access. More specifically, it offered a legally binding means of resistance should the United States press Mexico for exclusive reciprocity privileges. Not surprisingly, Frelinghuysen was displeased by the Mexican-German agreement and pressured the Mexicans to renounce it, but the Mexican regime refused, claiming that the provisions of the agreement with Germany were of "transcendental importance to Mexico."[19] Thus Frelinghuysen was ultimately obliged to agree to Mexican terms, although this was without effect since the US-Mexican trade treaty, like all of the reciprocal trade treaties pursued by Frelinghuysen, was not enacted by the US Congress.

Another wide-scale US attempt to establish reciprocity agreements in Latin America subsequently occurred in the late 1880s and early 1890s. Motivated by the desire to extend US influence into the region, so as to preclude European domination, US secretary of state James Blaine – who served under President Benjamin Harrison, and who, as noted in chapter 2, employed economic policies to achieve broader security goals – set about seeking to establish a series of free trade agreements with Latin American states.[20] This effort was rendered irrelevant, however, by a US tariff in 1894 that abrogated the reciprocity treaties through the restrictions it placed on the sugar trade.[21] As a result, for the remainder of the 1800s no other ambitious efforts at free trade with Latin America were made by the United States.

US concerns about the Caribbean region nonetheless continued to grow. In 1904 President Theodore Roosevelt crafted his Corollary to the Monroe Doctrine, which stated that the United States not only refused to tolerate foreign – particularly German – influence in the Americas but also would pre-emptively intervene in those Latin American states whose financial weakness offered a likely target for a foreign takeover. Roosevelt's policy was then further refined by his successor, William Howard Taft, who sought via financial means to ensure stability and solvency in Latin American states so as to prevent European powers from gaining a strategic foothold in the region. Taft referred to this policy as "dollar diplomacy." By "substituting dollars for bullets," the idea was that the US regime would encourage private American bankers to invest in Latin American debtor states, thereby providing funds to buy up the foreign debt. The result would be the dominance of US financial interests in the receiving state, which itself would then be more stable, less prone to European interference, and hence pulled more firmly into the US political orbit.[22]

Although dollar diplomacy was aimed primarily at Central America, US relations with Mexico were strongly influenced by the policy as well. Indeed, with the encouragement of the US regime, American business investment in Mexico doubled between 1900 and 1910, and by the end of that decade it was estimated that 43 per cent of Mexican property was owned by Americans.[23] Ironically, however, it was precisely this US policy of promoting investment in Mexico for the sake of stability that was a major cause of the instability that eventually erupted in that country. In 1910 an anti-Díaz revolution broke out, rallying around the banner of "land for the landless and Mexico for the Mexicans," and by 1911 the revolution had gained sufficient strength that Díaz was forced to flee Mexico. His departure was followed by a series of intrarevolutionary coups, with the end result being that one of the revolutionaries, Venustiano Carranza, eventually consolidated power in 1914.

Relations between Carranza and the US regime – now headed by Woodrow Wilson – quickly became strained.[24] This strain was partly due to the fact that Wilson was sceptical about Carranza's ability to bring real stability to Mexico in the wake of so much revolutionary violence.[25] This perceived inability to pacify Mexico, in turn, had important security implications for the United States, given that instability in Mexico might serve foreign – particularly German – strategic interests. The primary concern was that Germany could capitalize upon Mexico's instability to gain influence over the Mexican regime.[26] And indeed, precisely as the United States feared, Germany at this time was seeking to establish close relations with Mexico in order to use Mexican territory as a launching pad for challenging US supremacy in the Caribbean region. Simultaneously, Germany was also actively seeking to instigate a conflict between Mexico and the United States so as to compel the United States to engage militarily in Mexico, thus making it that much more difficult for the United States to challenge Germany militarily in Europe.[27]

This US-Mexican-German strategic triangle took on yet another dimension in March 1916 when the US military entered Mexico in an attempt to capture the Mexican national Pancho Villa, who had been staging raids into US territory. As US forces pushed deep into Mexican territory, they predictably clashed with Mexican troops, and in response to these developments Carranza began preparing for war. Both sides wished to avoid this eventuality, however, and ultimately agreed to resolve the issue peacefully.[28] As a result of their negotiations, all US troops were out of Mexico by early February 1917.[29] A key part of Wilson's willingness to accept this withdrawal of US troops was his abiding concern about Germany's growing strength both in Europe and the Caribbean, and hence his fear that the United States might get drawn into a war against Mexico at the same time as the German threat was mounting.[30] And his worries, as it turned out, were completely justified. In late October and early November 1916, before US-Mexican negotiations regarding US troop withdrawal had been completed, and in the ongoing context of Mexican fears regarding US aggression, Carranza informed the German regime that Mexico was strongly pro-German in sympathy and that Mexico wished to establish close relations with Germany. To demonstrate this point, Carranza offered to supply Germany with submarine bases in Mexican ports. The German foreign secretary responded with a telegram – the famous Zimmerman telegram – which indicated that if the United States entered into a war against Germany, Germany would propose an alliance with Mexico upon the following terms: joint conduct of the war, joint conclusion of the peace, German financial support for Mexico, and an agreement that Mexico would gain back territory lost to the United States at a prior period.[31]

While these messages were being exchanged, US-Mexican troop-withdrawal negotiations continued, and indeed these latter talks were still underway when the Zimmerman telegram was publicized. The United States thus gained explicit confirmation of potential Mexican-German collusion should war break out between the United States and either of the two states. It was, as such, against the backdrop of this potentiality that Wilson agreed to resolve US-Mexican differences peacefully and pulled US forces out of Mexico. To put it another way, via its relations with Germany, Mexico had once again managed to balance against the US threat and also managed to prevent an escalation in US-Mexican tensions. When the United States then declared war against Germany in 1917, Mexico stayed neutral and remained so for the duration of World War I.

US-Mexican relations took another turn for the worse after the war ended – this time regarding a dispute in Nicaragua – but the relationship improved considerably in the 1930s.[32] This improvement was due to the fact that the United States now began implementing a new policy when dealing with Latin America.[33] This new approach, which reached its apogee in the form of the Good Neighbor Policy, which was put in place during the presidency of Franklin Roosevelt, amounted to a full US renunciation of the principle of intervention in Latin American states.[34] Such a dramatic departure from previous US policy reflected two aspects of the global security situation of the 1930s: 1) during this period, the major powers in Europe as well as in Asia were preoccupied with building up their military strength in their own regions and as such had temporarily ceased to engage in overt power competition in the Americas, and 2) the power competitions in these other regions were widely feared to presage the outbreak of another major war, and it was assumed that such a war would inevitably draw in the American states. Thus, the absence of great power encroachment in Latin America temporarily allowed the United States to take a nonaggressive approach to the region, while the fear of an eventual war and of its potential to spread to the Americas simultaneously drove the United States to seek cooperative relations with its Latin American neighbours.[35]

Between 1933 and 1945, therefore, FDR's administration spearheaded a series of conferences, attended by the majority of Latin American states, which were intended to enhance inter-American relations in the face of the growing threats from Europe and Asia. Along with promoting diplomatic and military cooperation between the American states, a parallel effort was undertaken to enhance the economic relations between these states as well. This economic project's chief architect was Roosevelt's secretary of state, Cordell Hull, and as Hull repeatedly notes in his memoirs, his focus on free trade was based primarily upon his appreciation of its use as a mechanism for binding the United States and Latin American states together diplomatically and thus serving as a security-providing measure in light of the looming German threat.[36]

As a result of Hull's efforts, a new free trade agreement between the United States and Mexico was eventually negotiated. Yet before this negotiation process could reach a conclusion, complications arose. In 1938, while Hull was in the midst of his free trade–promoting efforts, Mexico nationalized its oil industry, thereby assuming control of property previously belonging to US, British, and Dutch oil companies. This oil nationalization was the culmination of the "Mexicanization" of Mexican resources that had begun during the Mexican Revolution in 1910, and it had the potential, from the Mexican point of view, of eliciting another US invasion. The Mexican regime calculated, however, that, due to the fear of an impending new war with Germany, and hence out of a desire to avoid other military entanglements, the United States and Britain would not take retaliatory military action in response to the nationalization.[37] As it had previously, in other words, Mexico sought to use German power as a means to resist US power, although in this instance Mexico refrained from direct cooperation with Germany to achieve this goal.

The Mexicans' strategic calculation proved correct.[38] Mexico was indeed able to nationalize its oil industry without major incident, although relations with the United States were certainly put under strain. And when WWII erupted the following year, the sources of strain became even more complex. The complexity stemmed from the fact that, as a result of the war, Mexico was impeded from selling oil to certain European markets and it therefore needed to sell much more of its oil to the United States. Under Hull's leadership, however, the United States refused to reach a new oil deal unless Mexico agreed to participate in Hull's free trade agenda, which required the signing of a general reciprocity agreement with the United States. Mexico thus had good economic reasons for agreeing to Hull's program. It also had good security reasons. One such reason – which serves to demonstrate the complexity of the US-Mexican relationship at the time – was the widespread rumour of an impending pro-fascist coup in Mexico. The primary threat in this regard, from the Mexican point of view, was that US fears of a Mexican coup might prompt the United States to engage in hostile actions against Mexico so as to preclude a pro-German regime from taking power in Mexico City. To quell US concerns, therefore, it was necessary for the Mexican regime to increase its military strength so as to crush the domestic, pro-fascist forces. This strengthening could be most effectively achieved, in turn, by buying military equipment from the United States. Yet in order to buy such equipment, the Mexican regime needed to raise revenue by selling the United States its oil. And to sell its oil, Mexico needed to sign Hull's trade agreement, which it eventually did.[39] With the trade agreement issue settled, Hull was then able to announce in November 1941 that the two states had also agreed upon means of settling the oil dispute.[40] The following month Japan attacked the United States, and in June 1942 Mexico declared war against the Axis.

1945–1989: The Cold War

As in the case of US-Canadian relations, the third phase of US-Mexican relations began with the onset of the Cold War. Yet whereas the Cold War provided a context for pushing the United States and Canada closer together via their anti-Soviet power aggregation, such was not the case for the United States and Mexico. During the Cold War the threat scenario that characterized US-Mexican relations remained essentially the same as it had been. The United States continued to view Mexico's geographic proximity and its intentions to ally with states hostile to the United States as sources of threat, while Mexico continued to see a threat from the United States based upon US proximity, intent, and military capabilities. What changed during the Cold War was the third party involved in this relational situation. Instead of aligning with the Germans as it had since the 1870s, Mexico now partially aligned itself with the Soviet bloc.

This new phase in the relationship got underway shortly after the end of World War II. A first step in this reorientation was taken when Mexico repudiated its reciprocity treaty with the United States. A second step transpired when the United States discarded its policy of non-intervention in Latin America in the 1950s. This change in US policy orientation – essentially a reversion to its previous, long-standing policy towards the region – followed in the wake of the 1951 assumption of power in Guatemala by a regime suspected of communist sympathies, which was followed by anti-American riots throughout South America in 1958 and then by Fidel Castro's arrival in power in Cuba in 1959.[41] Taken together, these events suggested to the US regime that Latin America was highly susceptible to communist infiltration, and hence that the USSR, which championed the communist cause, might become well positioned to threaten the United States via a beachhead to the south. As it had since the early years of the nineteenth century, therefore, the United States reacted vigorously and at times violently in response to this potential European interference in the western hemisphere.

In light of this more aggressive, post–Good Neighbor US approach towards Latin America, it was predictable that Mexico would look once again to some European state as a power-aggregating partner against the United States. Yet in this new geostrategic environment, Mexico could no longer turn to its previous European allies to play the part-nering role, since all of Europe was locked into the new superpower stand-off, with the major states of Western Europe now members of the US-dominated NATO alliance. Indeed, in the case of Germany, the state was not only dominated by the superpowers but also had been divided in two. Mexico's only option for effective anti-US power aggregation was thus to forge some sort of relationship with the communist countries. However, as the US-backed overthrow of the left-leaning Guatemalan regime in 1954 demonstrated, too close an affiliation with the USSR might prompt US military action against Mexico.

A solution to this puzzle soon presented itself, as US fears grew of a Latin American backlash against US military activity in the region. Between the overthrow of the Guatemalan regime in 1954 and the Cuban revolution of 1959, the United States became both more concerned about the spread of communism in Latin America and more wary in its approach to dealing with that threat. For instance, when, following Castro's ascent, US legislators argued for full-scale invasion of Cuba, President Dwight Eisenhower responded by suggesting a more restrained approach, out of fear that the United States might alienate Latin America if it moved too overtly against the Castro regime. In particular, Eisenhower worried that, if the Mexicans became "disgruntled" with US tactics in Cuba, "and if we were to see the Communists come to power there [in Mexico], in all likelihood we would have to go to war about this."[42] That is to say, he would feel compelled to order a major military offensive against Mexico.

Thanks to this wary US disposition, therefore, Mexico was able to stake out a middle-road approach on various issues pertaining to the Cold War stand-off. This approach was affected most notably with regard to the Castro regime in Cuba, which Mexico neither overly criticized nor outright endorsed. Rather, the Cuban revolution provided a tangible policy issue to which Mexico could respond with concrete actions and hence via which it could demonstrate its independence from US domination. In the wake of Castro's seizure of power, for instance, Mexico championed a position of total non-intervention in Cuba's internal affairs, it refused US pressure to condemn the Castro regime, it voted against Cuba's expulsion from the Organization of American States, it did not endorse economic sanctions against Cuba, and it was the only country in the western hemisphere to retain air service and diplomatic relations with Cuba. At the same time, however, Mexico distanced itself from certain Soviet policies regarding Cuba, most notably by condemning the placement of Soviet nuclear missiles in Cuba in 1962. The United States, in turn, concerned as it was not to push Mexico further into the communist camp, responded by taking a relatively tolerant approach towards Mexico and tacitly accepted Mexico's partial distance from US positions so long as Mexico did not side too closely with the communist cause.[43]

This Mexican strategy of maintaining a diplomatic distance from the United States via a moderately pro-Castro policy persisted throughout the following decades and was amplified in the latter 1970s when large oil discoveries were made in Mexican territory.[44] These finds turned Mexico into the world's fourth largest oil producer and, via the strengthening of its economic position, provided a new means for Mexico to assert its political independence. Thus, for instance, when the US administration sought in the 1970s to substantially improve relations with Mexico, the Mexican regime responded by criticizing US policy in general.[45] Likewise, when President Reagan arrived in office championing the idea of the North American Accord, Mexican president José López Portillo responded with a cold shoulder. Similarly, it was under Portillo in the 1980s that Mexico demonstrated its independence from the United States by recognizing the leftist guerrillas in El Salvador while likewise lending diplomatic support to leftist rebels in Nicaragua.[46] Such policies were strikingly at odds with American strategy in the region, and, indeed, they represented a high-water mark of Mexican independence from US domination. This particular era, however, was about to come to a sudden and dramatic end due to events that would ultimately result, via the creation of NAFTA in 1994, in an unprecedentedly close US-Mexican relationship.

The Security Context of the 1980s and Early 1990s

To understand why the decision was made to create NAFTA, it is essential to appreciate the larger context in which that decision occurred – that is to say, the relational context that existed between the United States and Mexico in the late 1980s and early 1990s. More specifically, it is necessary to consider that relationship as it pertained to issues of security policy, since, as the foregoing indicates, policies of trade and security have often overlapped within the context of US-Mexican affairs. Yet, as noted in chapter 1, relatively little has been written about the security motivations that lay behind the creation of either of the two North American FTAs. With regard to the US-Canadian FTA, this neglect on the part of IR scholars is understandable, given that the creators of that FTA did not – except on rare occasions – go out of their way to publicly enunciate their security-based motives. In the case of NAFTA, however, certain crafters of that policy – particularly Mexican president Carlos Salinas de Gortari, who played the primary role in NAFTA's creation – have been quite explicit about their security-based motivations. Indeed, after leaving office Salinas wrote a 1371-page book in which he detailed, among other things, the security issues that were relevant to his NAFTA-promoting policy. In light of the scholarly neglect of these issues, therefore, I asked Salinas if he wished to elaborate upon them, to which he replied, "I believe that what I wrote in my book explains by itself the reasons that compelled us to promote the NAFTA negotiation."[47] But in an effort to explain the lack of scholarly appreciation of the subject, he continued, saying, "Nevertheless, I try to understand the reasons behind the scholarship that disregards the context in which decisions are taken." His conclusion was that

it reflects a total incapacity of understanding of any political process, or for that matter how decisions are taken when you have a political responsibility. These decisions are not the product neither of an enlightened ruler or a selfish politician. In the everyday life of a decision-maker, it is contexts that matter, and above all the national, local and international contexts (politics is not always merely local politics).

He went on to suggest that

observers with the benefit of time (hindsight they tend to call it) start out of certitudes. And politics is most of the time having to face uncertainties. As it has been clearly pointed out, when there is certain knowledge, true science or absolute right, there is no conflict that cannot be resolved and thus there is no necessity for politics. But reality works differently.[48]

In the case of the Mexican decision to negotiate NAFTA, in other words, analysts cannot simply assume that set "laws" of economics or anything else were the sole determinant of political behaviour. Rather, that behaviour was a response to a specific geopolitical context that, as it turned out, caught practically everyone by surprise. "In the real world," Salinas explained, "you have to attend to circumstance, time, place, and actors. And in the case of the NAFTA negotiation the circumstances had changed dramatically in a few weeks: the end of the Cold War, which had dominated international and domestic politics since before I was born!"[49]

The correlation in timing between the end of the Cold War and the decision to create NAFTA is indeed a key point. As indicated, the US-Mexican relationship during the Cold War was part of the long-term pattern of relations between the two states, with the United States afraid that Mexico might ally with a foreign power, and with Mexico periodically doing precisely that, out of fear of the United States. Yet the Cold War also partially altered the traditional patterns because the United States was somewhat limited in what it could do in the western hemisphere, given its fear of creating a pro-Soviet Latin American backlash, while Mexico's most preferred European power-aggregating partner – Germany – was unavailable to perform such a role. When the Cold War ended in 1989, however, the more traditional behaviour patterns rapidly reasserted themselves. The United States no longer needed to fear the prospect of close Mexican-Soviet relations and thus could behave more proactively towards the Mexican regime, as well as towards the other states of the Caribbean region. Mexico, conversely, was deprived of the global, bipolar power structure that had allowed it to maintain some diplomatic distance from the United States, and thus it needed a new power-aggregating partner. Germany, for its part, not only was now more liberated to pursue the foreign policy of its choosing but also, thanks to the unification of West Germany with East Germany, had re-emerged as Europe's dominant power. It is therefore logical to expect that Mexico might turn once again towards Germany to help it resist a more assertive United States. Which is precisely what occurred. This course of action then resulted, counter-intuitively, in negotiations between the United States and Mexico for a new trade agreement, and that agreement became trilateral when Canada subsequently joined, thereby leading to the creation of NAFTA.

To fully appreciate how this all came about, it is necessary to return to the early days of the Reagan presidency. As noted, the United States began exploring the possibility of closer ties with both Mexico and Canada during the early 1980s. And, as noted, Reagan said in his first campaign speech in September 1979 that "the world has become a place where, in order to survive, our country needs more than just allies – it needs real friends." Reagan therefore suggested that "a developing closeness among Canada, Mexico and the United States – a North American accord – would permit achievement of the potential in each country beyond that which I believe any of them – strong as they are – could accomplish in the absence of such cooperation." The nature of the Accord was somewhat unclear in the public discourse – it was variously described as something akin to the integration project of western Europe, as a trade-oriented effort, as a "state of mind" – although in interviews with the author certain key officials from the Reagan administration clarified the purpose of the proposal. They stressed, as noted in the previous chapter, that the concept of the Accord went "way beyond economics" and that a central motivation for the Accord was to counter communist inroads close to US borders. With regard to Canada, a primary security concern pertained to the advent of Soviet cruise missiles and to the manner in which Canadian military weakness might provide an entrée for a Soviet attack on the US mainland. Canada, however, was not the only state that the United States had in mind for the Accord; Mexico was to be another partner, and indeed, it was to Mexico that President Reagan first travelled, following his assumption of the presidency, in order to promote the Accord idea.

Mexico was a natural target for Reagan's cooperation/integration strategy, given the very real security concerns that Mexico raised for the United States. As mentioned, Mexican president López Portillo had begun in the late 1970s and early 1980s to actively support the leftist rebel groups that the United States and its allies were fighting in Central America. Not only was this support for leftist insurgencies in the 1980s a step beyond the sort of behaviour that Mexico had previously exhibited during the Cold War, but it also occurred at a time when the United States was experiencing a heightened sense of Cold War threats, which were emanating from the north in the form of the Arctic arms build-up and from the south via the appearance of communist regimes in Central America and the Caribbean. In response to the northern cruise missile threat, the United States sought closer military and trade relations with Canada. So too, it responded to the general threat in the Caribbean and Central America by directly attacking certain communist-leaning regimes – in Grenada, for example – or funnelling arms to local groups that were fighting communist-leaning regimes, such as in Nicaragua. It also sought to ensure that Caribbean states did not engage in cooperative, trade-based efforts against the United States. Most notably in this regard, the United States sought to stifle the CARICOM project, which was an integration scheme spearheaded by the communist-leaning regime in Jamaica. In that case, the United States not only managed to have that regime in Jamaica toppled from power and replaced with a pro-US administration, but also, in concert with that new Jamaican regime, it established the Caribbean Basin Initiative, which was a trade-based project whose explicit goal was to prevent communist inroads into the region.[50] At the same time, Reagan likewise pushed to directly incorporate Puerto Rico into the United States, so as to preclude left-leaning Puerto Rican separatists from dislodging Puerto Rico from US control.

Paralleling all of these initiatives, meanwhile, Reagan repeatedly expressed the fear that a communist-controlled Central America would offer an entrée for communist efforts in Mexico, and that were Mexico to go communist, this would prove a grave threat to US security. As he put it, "The conflagration in Central America appears too close to ignore. Like a fire in one's neighborhood, this threat should be of concern to every nation in the hemisphere."[51] This sense of threat for the United

States was present not only during the López Portillo presidency but also persisted after López Portillo was succeeded by Miguel de la Madrid in 1982. As was reported at the time,

> President Reagan, in an obvious criticism of Mexico's policy towards central America ... told Mexican President Miguel de la Madrid that "responsible governments of this hemisphere cannot afford to close their eyes" to the threat of a communist takeover in the region. In welcoming de la Madrid to the White House, Reagan noted that the United States and Mexico disagree "not on goals ... but on the means by which to achieve those goals." But his words also implied stern disapproval of Mexico's friendship with Cuba and Nicaragua and its advocacy of negotiations with El Salvador's leftist guerrillas.[52]

On another occasion, Reagan attributed conflict in Central America to communist aggression originating in the Soviet Union, Cuba, and Nicaragua, and warned that "this Communist subversion poses the threat that 100 million people from Panama to the open border on our south could come under the control of pro-Soviet regimes."[53] It was Reagan's ambassador to the United Nations, Jeane Kirkpatrick, however, who made the most memorable statement along these lines, when, at the Republican Party's national convention in 1984, she declared,

> Today, foreign policy is central to the security, to the freedom, to the prosperity, even to the survival of the United States. And our strength, for which we make many sacrifices, is essential to the independence and freedom of our allies and our friends. Ask yourself: What would become of Europe if the United States withdrew? What would become of Africa if Europe fell under Soviet domination? What would become of Europe if the Middle East came under communist control? What would become of Israel, if surrounded by Soviet client states? What would become of Asia if the Philippines or Japan came under Soviet domination? What would become of Mexico if Central America became a Soviet satellite? What then could the United States do?[54]

These concerns, therefore, prompted the Reagan administration to seek from its earliest days to establish closer relations with Mexico. Yet when Reagan visited López Portillo in 1980 and presented his North American Accord idea, as noted, the latter resisted the initiative, as did Canada's Trudeau when Reagan met with him. And, as noted, there was fear in both of these states that the Accord might be a clandestine grab for Canadian and Mexican natural resources. As such, the United States was obliged to temporarily put its integrative attempt with Canada and Mexico on hold. In 1982 the United States focused instead on its Caribbean initiative. Then in 1983 it began revisiting its attempt to enhance relations with Canada, and by 1984 a new Canadian prime minister was in power who was willing to work extensively with the United States in addressing the relevant threats. This period of the mid-1980s did not, however, witness a similar scenario with regard to US-Mexican relations, despite the security rationale for closer bilateral ties. An obvious contributing factor to this delay was a continuing determination on the part of Mexican leaders to resist US domination. Whereas Canada had, since the early 1900s, made a slow transition towards closer and closer relations with the United States, Mexico's sense of wariness towards its powerful neighbour had not undergone a similar evolution. Indeed, since the early 1900s the United States had invaded or contemplated invading Mexico on multiple occasions. Thus when Reagan visited López Portillo and promoted his North American Accord, the Mexicans predictably resisted Reagan's overture and continued to resist it throughout the remainder of the 1980s.

Another key contributing factor to the delay in establishing closer US-Mexican relations was the state of the Mexican economy, which during the 1980s experienced a period of intense troubles. As one scholar summarizes the situation, "In 1982 Mexico was in a deep economic crisis. The international environment was adverse to a Mexico saddled with foreign debt. World interest rates were high, the price of oil, Mexico's main export, was falling, and commercial banks had stopped lending. This unfavorable international environment exacerbated the consequences of domestic imbalances and contributed to rampant inflation, capital flight, and chaos in the financial and foreign exchange markets."[55]

For the next several years the conditions remained dire. By 1984 the peso began to slip against the dollar and then began to plunge on the free market. The foreign debt simultaneously grew exponentially, as did inflation.[56] Thus although President de la Madrid – like Mulroney in Canada – was pro–free market and had lived for a time in the United States, and would therefore have seemed a likely candidate for agreeing to work with the United States on a trade deal, the state of crisis in the Mexican economy and the vulnerability this brought to the Mexican state provided an unpropitious environment for either the United States or Mexico to seek a major new trade deal with the other.

Nevertheless, Mexico did take certain policy measures during this period that began moving it in a direction more in line with US trade objectives. These included, most notably, the decision to join the General Agreement on Tariffs and Trade (GATT) in 1986, which marked a fundamental shift away from the closed-door economic policy that Mexico had adopted in the wake of the Mexican revolution. The GATT, with its promotion of open trade relations among its member states, was long viewed by many Mexican officials as dominated by particular – namely, US – interests and thus as a threat to Mexican economic sovereignty.[57] Under the leadership of the de la Madrid administration, however, greater openness to trade was viewed as crucial to Mexico's economic recovery, and hence Mexico joined the GATT after engaging in numerous meetings with GATT and US officials in order to agree to the terms of Mexico's accession.[58] That same year, the United States and Mexico also agreed to institute what came to be known as the Baker Plan, named after US treasury secretary James Baker. Via the Baker Plan, a deal was reached between the Mexican regime and various commercial banks to begin rescheduling some of Mexico's foreign debt obligations. Following this, the two countries signed a US-Mexican Framework of Principles and Procedures for Consultation Regarding Trade and Investment Relations, and in 1989 they subsequently signed another agreement, known as the Understanding Regarding Trade and Investment Facilitation Talks.[59] All of these efforts thus pointed in the direction of a closer relationship between the United States and its southern neighbour, yet, notwithstanding these positive measures, US-Mexican relations still fell far short of the extensive sorts of agreements pertaining to trade and security that the United States was concurrently engaging in with Canada.

Towards the end of the 1980s, however, two developments occurred that substantially altered the prospects for closer engagement between the United States and Mexico. The first development was a partial improvement of Mexico's economic situation. By the time de la Madrid left office in 1988, some of the most serious economic haemorrhaging had begun to be effectively addressed, thanks in large part to the modernizing and liberalizing policies of de la Madrid's secretary of budget and planning, Carlos Salinas, who went on to become Mexico's next president. Due to these improved conditions in Mexico, the US rationale for closer economic relations with its southern neighbour was at least partially enhanced. The second key development allowing for closer US-Mexican relations was, as noted, the end of the Cold War. As Salinas explains in his book, and as he reiterated to the author, "At the end of 1989, four international events occurred that had enormous repercussions in Mexico."[60] The first of these events was the fall of the Berlin Wall on 9 November 1989, and hence the end of the division of Germany. The second event was a meeting in Malta on 2 December 1989 between US president George H.W. Bush and Mikhail Gorbachev, the general secretary of the Soviet Union. This meeting "confirmed the end of the Cold War."[61] The third event was the arrival in power in Chile of a democratic regime, thereby symbolizing a more general democratic turn in the Latin American region. The fourth event was the US invasion of Panama. Taken together, these events appeared to indicate that the United States would no longer be held in check in Latin America by the threat of the Soviet bloc, that a democratic tide was complementing this American triumph, and that the United States was acting, as per its historical pattern, in an aggressive manner to address perceived threats in the western hemisphere. The fact that the invasion of Panama occurred on 20 December 1989 – only eighteen days after the Cold War officially "ended" – added dramatic emphasis to this return of traditional power plays. Indeed, the invasion of Panama was, as Salinas explained to the author, "a reminder of the enormous difficulty of the everyday relationship with our inevitable neighbour to the North."[62]

Essentially, Salinas viewed the situation in the following manner: "These important events formed part of a new world transformation. All of this made us see that new paths were opening up, but that, at the same time, enormous risks lay ahead." As for the types of risks this posed to Mexico, Salinas was clear: "The speed of the transformation precipitated the disappearance of some nations and the reconstruction of others. These were times of challenge for political leadership, and of risks to sovereignty."[63] In light of these concerns, therefore, Salinas refused to condone the US invasion of Panama when he and Bush discussed the possibility of such an action in October 1989.[64] When the Panamanian invasion subsequently occurred, Salinas reiterated his opposition to it in a conversation with Bush, and, following the installation of a US-friendly regime in Panama City, Salinas notes in his book, "I recalled the Mexican ambassador to Panama, and for over two years, we had no diplomatic representation in that sister nation. The new world order still had interventionist elements. The risks were evident."[65]

In explaining the sense of threat that Mexico was experiencing at this time, Salinas's reference to a "new world order" is particularly telling, as that phrase received its most famous utterance from President Bush.

Having served as Reagan's vice president for eight years, and assuming the presidency himself in 1989, Bush presided over the transformative period of the late 1980s and early 1990s. It was thus Bush who, in the context of the end of the Cold War, the fall of the Berlin Wall, and the subsequent invasion of Kuwait by Iraq, famously declared that, in the post–Cold War era, a "new world order" was at hand, wherein closer relations between the United States and the USSR would allow for more effective efforts, under US leadership, to resist tyrannical – that is to say, nondemocratic, anti-US – regimes. As Bush put it, "Clearly, no longer can a dictator count on East-West confrontation to stymie concerted United Nations action against aggression."[66] Nor could Latin American states – and Mexico in particular – hope that East-West confrontation might prevent assertive US initiatives in the western hemisphere.

With regard to Latin America more specifically, the Bush administration moved quickly following the collapse of the Berlin Wall to consolidate its influence in the region. For instance, it actively advocated the ideas of democracy, free markets, and close relations between the United States and its southern neighbours via its Enterprise for the Americas Initiative (EAI). The EAI was a concept that the Bush administration began discussing with Latin American leaders in late 1989 and early 1990. The program was then launched in September 1990.[67] As Bush explained at the time,

> The last fourteen months have been a remarkable time for the world. Yet the rapid changes at which we have marveled in Eastern Europe are not unique. Freedom has made great gains in our hemisphere, as a resurgence of democratic rule has swept through the Americas. Parallel to this political shift has come a realignment of policies in the economic sphere. As the people of Latin America and the Caribbean search for prosperity following a difficult decade of painful economic adjustment, their governments are focusing on economic growth and the free market policies needed to nourish it. For the benefit of all the people of this hemisphere, the United States needs to reach out to support the efforts of these countries as each undertakes its own approach to economic reform.[68]

And, as Bush observed one year later,

> As a nation, we are re-engaging with our friends and partners as never before. For this generation of leaders in the Americas, north and south,

share a common vision. Together we are building something the world has never seen before: the first completely democratic hemisphere ... But our common vision is broader still. For we are also building a new relationship among the developed and developing nations throughout the Americas, an authentic partnership in which trade is free from Alaska to Tierra del Fuego.[69]

The EAI thus constituted a portion of Bush's larger vision of a world in which democracy and free markets were on the march via the leadership of the United States. It also built naturally on the trading-for-security policy concepts that were formulated by the Reagan administration with regard to the Latin American region. From a longer-term historical perspective, the creation of the EAI indicated that the United States would be actively engaging in relations with its southern neighbours in a manner reminiscent of numerous previous US initiatives, whereby the United States sought to consolidate its influence over the region via the promotion of free trade and democratization. The carrot for inducing such transformation in the target states was the prospect of enhanced economic growth within those states, aided by the world's sole remaining superpower. The stick, on the other hand, would be the prospect of invasion by that superpower's army, as occurred in the case of the democratically questionable and insufficiently pro-US Panama.

Thus, in sum, at the end of the 1980s and in the early 1990s we find the United States in a position to suddenly consolidate its influence in Latin America, and we concomitantly find Mexico experiencing a sense of threat to its sovereignty that appeared to be as intense as any it had ever confronted. Not coincidentally, it was at this time that the two states agreed to negotiate a new FTA.

The Decision to Establish an FTA

In light of a historical record that indicates that the United States and Mexico have often sought to use trade agreements to address security issues involving one another, it would be unsurprising if security and trade policy overlapped in the context of the initial NAFTA negotiations. One obvious means, in turn, of determining why that FTA was established, and thus whether such a policy overlap occurred, is to examine the statements of the individuals who were most influential in the FTA policymaking processes in each state. And since President Salinas clearly played the key role in bringing NAFTA into being, his statements are crucial. Nonetheless, as in the case of the US-Canadian FTA, so too in this instance it was the United States that took the first steps.

In the wake of the Reagan administration's early, unsuccessful efforts to establish a close relationship with Mexico, the idea of a comprehensive US-Mexican trade agreement was not broached again by the United States until 1988. It was in November of that year that George H.W. Bush and Carlos Salinas – who had both been recently elected as presidents of their respective states, though neither had yet been sworn into office – held their first formal meeting in Houston. Salinas arrived at the meeting expecting to discuss Mexico's debt issues. From his point of view, his first task as president was to restart economic growth in Mexico now that a certain degree of economic stability had been achieved.[70] And his first priority in this regard was to reduce Mexico's foreign debt so that less of Mexico's GDP would be spent servicing that debt and hence draining capital out of Mexico.[71] As Salinas recounts, however, Bush had other topics that he wished to discuss.

> Right from the start, President Bush proposed the establishment of a free trade zone between Mexico and the United States. The free exchange zone between the United States and Canada had just been created. Bush's proposal, however, came unexpectedly. I preferred that two subjects as broad and complex as free trade and the reduction of the debt should not be mixed in a single negotiation. I was concerned that the Americans would attempt to gain trade concessions in exchange for the negotiation of the debt ... And so I answered that while we were agreeing on reduction of the debt, it would not be time to begin negotiating a free trade agreement.[72]

Bush's push for a US-Mexican FTA fit in naturally with his larger EAI project and with the general effort of US-promoted North American integration. Clearly, now that the US-Canadian trade agreement had been agreed to, and with the Mexican economy appearing more stabilized, the United States was seeking to complete its continental project of closer, broad-based relations with its neighbours – relations pertaining to issues of economics, security, and more. Indeed, as Bush explained in a correspondence with the author, "I did view NAFTA as serving goals beyond economics. I think it did a lot to bring our countries closer together." When asked whether he viewed such non-economic goals in terms of foreign policy, security policy, or cultural policy, Bush answered that it was not a question of NAFTA serving one particular, isolated policy, such as security. Rather, "it was a question of the overall bilateral relationship."[73]

Bush's point regarding the broad motivations for the proposed FTA was corroborated by James Baker, who, as President Bush's secretary of state, was a close collaborator on the trade initiative. Baker, as noted, had previously served as treasury secretary during Reagan's second term in office. In that capacity he had played a vital role in the negotiations to draft the Canadian-US FTA. As likewise noted, he had also helped negotiate certain limited economic agreements between the United States and Mexico in the 1980s. He was thus well prepared to work on behalf of a US-Mexican FTA agenda. In an interview with the author, Baker emphasized that, along with the economic rationale for an FTA with Mexico, the chance to establish closer diplomatic relations was paramount.

> It [the FTA] has increased economic growth in both Mexico and the United States, and I know one thing for sure – it has brought Mexico and the United States closer together ... There were political issues here too. You can understand why a secretary of state would be for it – the one who negotiated the Canadian free trade agreement, with all the economic benefits of that. So, the economic benefits were not something that was up in the air, as far as I was concerned, and there were clear diplomatic benefits ... Improved relationships with our southern neighbor. I mean, it really brought the two countries a lot closer together. We still have the same old irritants, you got immigration, you got drugs, but we're a heck of a lot closer to Mexico today post-NAFTA than we were pre-NAFTA.[74]

Other members of the Bush administration viewed the potential FTA in a similar light. John Negroponte, for instance, who was US ambassador to Mexico during the Bush administration and who had previously served as US ambassador to Honduras during the 1980s, observed that "a Free Trade Agreement would institutionalize acceptance of a North American orientation to Mexico's foreign relations," thereby precluding Mexico from establishing close relations with countries that the United States found threatening.[75] Similarly, Carla Hills, the US trade representative during the Bush administration and the person who subsequently took the lead on negotiating NAFTA on behalf of the United States, argued that a Mexican foreign policy more friendly towards the United States would be a "necessary consequence" of the trade pact.[76]

Of course, statements such as these by Bush administration officials are suggestive, yet restrained. None of them directly states that the Mexican potential for aligning with another major power posed an imminent threat to US security. And it is important not to attempt to stretch an interpretation of their statements beyond their intended significance. At the same time, however, it is worth noting two points. First, regardless of the relational dynamic between the United States and Mexico – that is to say, a dynamic of repeated US attempts to dominate its southern neighbour – it would simply be impolitic, to say the least, for US officials to state too directly that the purpose of a trade agreement with Mexico was to fundamentally constrain Mexican foreign policy so as to achieve US security goals. Thus when President Bush, for instance, responded to the question of whether security issues were relevant to his FTA-promoting agenda, he did in effect answer in the affirmative – "It was a question of the overall bilateral relationship" – yet he did so in a way that was indirect, and hence – to use a term that he was inclined to use himself – prudent.

Second, this couching of the responses takes place against the backdrop of a particular geostrategic context – namely, the context of the United States explicitly seeking to ensure a pro-US orientation in Mexican foreign policy, at the same time that it was also attempting to more generally lock in its advantage in Latin America in the immediate post–Cold War era, following a decades-long struggle with the Soviet Union for influence in the region. The somewhat larger context, furthermore, is that of the policy process set in motion by Reagan with the North American Accord, which ultimately led up to this 1988 US-Mexican FTA discussion and whose original impetus was explicitly security-based. The still larger context is the US pattern of repeatedly seeking to gain influence over Mexican foreign policy – often via trade agreements – to ensure that Mexico does not ally itself with another powerful state. And this is a strategy that itself ties into a more general pattern of US policy that stretches all the way back to the early 1800s and the formulation of the Monroe Doctrine.

In light of these various points, therefore, it seems fair to suggest that security issues were of relevance to the US decision-making process when it came to the topic of establishing the FTA with Mexico. To say anything more would be to force the evidence. What is quite clear, on the other hand, is that security concerns were of direct relevance to the Mexican decision to pursue the FTA. And since it was the Mexican decision that represents the key turning point – because Bush was carrying forward an agenda that was set in motion by Reagan, whereas Salinas was putting Mexico onto a dramatically different path in terms of its approach to its northern neighbour – it is the Salinas decision to pursue the FTA that requires the closest analysis.[77]

When the idea of an FTA was first presented to Salinas by Bush in 1988, Salinas, as noted, resisted, given that he wished to resolve the debt reduction issue before discussing a full FTA. In his Houston conversation with Bush, therefore, he explained that he wanted to take a sector-by-sector approach to trade agreements, at least until the debt reduction issue had been effectively addressed.[78] By July 1989, however, the debt reduction negotiations had been successfully concluded, yet Salinas continued to adhere to the notion of sector-based trade agreements as opposed to a comprehensive FTA.

In October 1989 Salinas again visited Bush, this time in Washington, and an "action plan" for more cooperative US-Mexican economic relations was agreed upon, although Salinas apparently did not at this time indicate a greater willingness to explore a full FTA.[79] Similarly, the following month, when US commerce secretary Robert Mosbacher visited Salinas in Mexico City, Salinas was evidently no more willing than before to explore the full FTA idea. Upon his arrival in Mexico City, Mosbacher expressed optimism about the chances of a US-Mexican FTA; by the final day of his trip, however, Mosbacher's statements displayed notably less confidence. He had concluded that "it was premature to talk about an overall comprehensive agreement," and that instead the two sides should concentrate on what could be accomplished in terms of sector-based trade agreements.[80] In an interview with the author, Mosbacher suggested that Salinas appeared at that time to be particularly concerned about the prospect of US access to Mexican natural resources, and that such fear was evidently playing into Salinas's reluctance regarding the trade deal.[81]

This negotiation scenario has obvious parallels with the US-Canadian free trade effort, which the United States began in 1983 by proposing a trade deal to the Canadians, in response to which Canada agreed to consider the possibility of sector-based trade. In the US-Canadian case, the United States subsequently sought to expand the agenda to encompass a full FTA between the two states, although these full-FTA efforts eventually collapsed in the face of Canadian resistance. It was only when a new Canadian prime minister arrived in office – a prime minister who shared the Reagan administration's sense of threat from the Soviets, and who embraced the strategic logic of using a trade deal to bring the two states closer together – that full FTA negotiations commenced. In the case of Mexico, however, it was not a change of administration but rather a change in its strategic situation that convinced the Mexican regime to move beyond a sector-based approach and to agree instead to a full FTA with the United States. As Salinas points out,

> The reduction of the debt seemed enough to create conditions that would allow the country to start growing again and generate opportunities for employment, which Mexicans demanded. We were on the road to growth, but this itself would bring new challenges. Just by continuing on the same path we could have recovered economic growth and price stability ... In other times, it might have been like that. But in 1989, world reality changed drastically and altered our expectations. We found ourselves faced with a global transformation and, in consequence, new political and economic circumstances.[82]

These circumstances, as noted, included the end of the Cold War, the emergence of the United States as the sole superpower, the invasion of Panama, Bush's call for a new world order, and so forth. Yet, while these events provided fresh cause for Mexico to fear for its sovereign independence vis-à-vis the United States, and hence to fear for its security, Salinas's strategic calculations were complicated by the fact that, although he had thus far resisted a full FTA with the United States, he recognized that improving trade relations with the United States was an obvious approach to growing the Mexican economy. More generally, Salinas calculated that he had a better chance of securing Mexican interests by engaging with the United States than by resisting it outright. Indeed, his rationale represented the essence of a trading-to-control strategy. Despite a history "marred by American violations, unilateral acts of force, arrogance, and misunderstanding ... geopolitical reality and new historical, economic and cultural circumstances required that Mexico – rather than emphasizing differences – propose a constructive approach to complex bilateral issues."[83] As he further explained,

> Consciously taking the initiative to negotiate the terms to regulate the close economic relationship with our powerful neighbor in the north was a step that represented a big risk, contrary to the traditional Mexican position of resistance and isolation in the face of United States proposals ... Our new strategy had to establish clear rules for economic relations. It was necessary to establish trade rules that would be based on norms and

verifiable by independent bodies. We had to ensure that certain issues, fundamental to Mexico's growth, should not depend on the power games of the United States. This had been historically a basic aspiration in our relations with our neighbor to the north. We had to make it come true and build an additional means of strengthening Mexico's sovereignty.[84]

Even if Salinas was not yet ready to contemplate a full FTA with the United States, in other words, he realized that some sort of constructive partnership needed to be maintained. Mexico simply could not rely upon outright power-resisting as it had in the past. As Salinas noted, "The United States was emerging as the world's sole superpower. Its hegemonic character meant that, in the international arena, we could no longer keep the colossus of the north in check by means of counterbalances, as Mexico had done at the beginnings of the twentieth century with Europe and later, with the Socialist bloc."[85] Yet this does not mean that Salinas rejected the strategy of resistance altogether. Rather, he combined his strategy of trading-to-control with a simultaneous trading-to-oppose initiative. Indeed, the fact that the United States was now the world's sole superpower only further necessitated the effort of resisting the United States, since enhanced US-Mexican relations would lead to increased US dominance. The obvious option therefore, in light of Mexico's historical pattern, was to turn to some European power – most likely Germany – for a strategic partnership – both economic and diplomatic – which would allow Mexico to resist, as much as possible, US influences, yet to do so in such a way that would simultaneously help to improve US-Mexican relations.

A convenient opportunity to explore the possibility of a new strategic partnership with Germany and other European states arose little more than a month after US troops arrived in Panama City, when Salinas flew to Europe to attend the annual meeting of the World Economic Forum in Davos, Switzerland. Salinas had already planned – before the fall of the Berlin Wall or the US invasion of Panama – to attend the Davos conference, but in the wake of those events his motivation for making a European trip was considerably increased.

En route to Davos in January 1990, Salinas made a few stops in certain European capitals. He first visited Lisbon, Portugal, where he met with Prime Minister Mario Soares, and then he flew to London for a meeting with Prime Minister Margaret Thatcher. In his meeting with Thatcher, Salinas expressed his concern that "the industrialized world was totally absorbed in the changes taking place in Europe, and that this was negatively impacting the level of foreign investment being sent to developing states like Mexico." Thatcher told him that he was right to be worried. Salinas then flew to the West German capital of Bonn for a meeting with Chancellor Helmut Kohl. In his book, Salinas recounts in detail how he and Kohl "had a long, private conversation," in which Kohl emphasized the importance of Mexico joining a North American integration project. Kohl predicted that "in the year 2000, there will be three great zones in the world." One would be in Asia, another in Europe, and the third in North America. "The prospects for Mexico are clear," Kohl told him, "either it becomes part of the North American zone, or it can be left behind as a country outside any bloc. You are introducing big economic changes into your country. If you join one of these blocs, I forecast a great future for your nation in the twenty-first century." By joining the North American bloc, furthermore, Mexico would become more attractive to Germany. "We will give priority to the countries with a future, and Mexico is one of them," Kohl said. And, as Salinas notes, "Then he added a comment that showed how much things had changed in comparison with the early years of the twentieth century: 'Now, the Americans don't seem to be worried about our interest in Mexico.'"[86]

Yet, while things may have changed somewhat in terms of European relations with the United States, things had not changed all that much regarding relations between the United States and Mexico, as demonstrated by Salinas's larger motivation for coming to Europe and for meeting with Kohl in particular. His comments on this point, overlooked by many NAFTA scholars, are worth quoting at length.

> When he [Kohl] finished, I spoke to him emphatically about how important it was for Mexico to balance the growing economic link with the United States with a strong relationship with Europe, especially with Germany. He answered that three years earlier, the Chinese Prime Minister, Deng Xiao Peng, had shown his interest precisely in promoting a greater German presence in China, to balance the relationship with Japan. When we returned to the initial topic, he stated: "The changes in the East are irreversible." Kohl's tone said it all. The fact was that the merely instrumental motivation of having recourse to other strong countries and using them as an instrument to obtain temporary balances was not sufficiently attractive to Europe. It was not even so in the case of markets as big as that of China, or as important from the point of view of their strategic location as Mexico. He concluded with a comment of great importance: "I am especially interested

in cultural exchange. The French have had more presence than us in Latin America because they are more skillful in projecting their culture."

I understood the double meaning of his message: on the one hand, he was letting me know that Mexico would be more attractive for investment as a part of one of the three great international trade blocs. Only in this way would we ensure our economic viability under the new conditions imposed by globalization. At the same time, he seemed to imply that definitely the European region, and perhaps the Asian region, would keep us in mind for serious, long-term, and not merely opportunistic, trade negotiations – but only if we joined the North American bloc.

The situation was paradoxical: in order to diversify our trade relations with parts of the world other than just the United States, we first had to concentrate on joining the enormous and powerful market of our neighbor in the north. Willy Brandt, the respected leader of the International Socialist Movement and ex-Chancellor of Germany, with whom I met later, confirmed this. Forging closer economic ties with the United States and sharing its market would attract European interest in Mexico. By making it permanent, the balance we sought would operate more efficiently. Time confirmed this. Years later, once NAFTA was ratified, Europe agreed to negotiate a free trade agreement with Mexico.[87]

Salinas was thus worried about the power of the United States, and was seeking –"emphatically" – some means of opposing it. Kohl, however, wanted something more than a temporary power-aggregating partner. He wanted a permanent relationship with an integrating North America. Mexico could potentially help Germany to obtain this goal if Mexico were to establish a closer relationship with the German regime. Yet for Mexico to be sufficiently attractive to Germany in this regard, Mexico first needed to engage in a free trade scheme with the United States. Or in other words, to more effectively oppose the United States, Mexico first needed to begin integrating with the United States, so as to be able to establish closer relations with Germany, and with Europe more generally.

After his conversation with Kohl, Salinas flew on to Davos, where he found little European enthusiasm for investing in Mexico, thereby reinforcing Kohl's point.[88] It was at Davos, therefore, that Salinas apparently made his fateful decision to begin negotiations with the United States for an FTA. Against the backdrop of the snowy Swiss Alps, he held a meeting with his top economic advisors and informed them of his decision. As he relates in his memoirs, it was "in the early hours of Friday February the 1st 1990," that he finally decided to pursue an FTA.[89] Yet, while the decision was made at Davos, the critical point in Salinas's thinking was evidently reached during the earlier meetings of his trip. Salinas had gone to Europe seeking to obtain greater means of resisting US influence in Mexico – and hence to secure Mexican sovereignty – and had come to realize that this could be achieved only by interacting more closely with the United States.

This is by no means to claim that economic rationales were absent from Salinas's FTA calculations. Indeed, an FTA with the United States made abundant good sense in terms of Mexican economic growth. Not only would it significantly increase US-Mexican trade, but it would also send a message to the international community that Mexico was a responsible player in the global economy and could be trusted as a reliable destination for foreign investment. And yet the very obvious economic arguments in favour of an FTA only serve to further emphasize the relevance of security issues to Salinas's decision when consideration is given to the manner in which that decision was made.

In light of the clear economic rationale for pursuing the US-Mexican FTA, it would have made most sense for Salinas to begin negotiating with the United States about the prospects for such beginning in July 1989. As he told Bush at their first meeting in November 1988, he wished to wait until the debt reduction negotiations had been completed before beginning negotiations on an FTA. The debt reduction talks, however, were successfully completed – from Salinas's perspective – in July 1989. Nonetheless, following their completion, Salinas did not move on to full FTA discussions but continued to stick to the position originally iterated in his meeting with Bush – namely, adherence to the principle of far more limited, sector-based trade. The economic benefits of more limited trade deals, however, would by their nature be more limited than those gleaned from a full FTA. On the other hand, sector-based agreements would mean greater political independence for the Mexican regime vis-à-vis the United States. Thus a noneconomic incentive would appear to have been relevant to Salinas's bargaining position at that time.

More significant still, as 1989 wore on it became clear to Salinas and his economic team that the limited agreements that they were pursuing with the United States were unsatisfactory from a strictly economic point of view. As Jaime Serra Puche – who served as Salinas's commerce secretary – explained to the author, "Indeed, at the beginning of the Salinas administration conventional wisdom was that sectoral agreements were preferable. However, as time went by, it was obvious that those agreements were creating uncertainty for Mexican exporters."[90] The limited agreements meant that current trade preferences might not last, and it was unclear whether they would allow for trade growth over time. "All this inhibited major investment projects to increase the export platform of the country," Serra Puche added. Yet, despite these economic problems, which were recognized before the Davos trip, it was not until the Salinas team made that trip in January–February 1990 that the critical decision was taken to begin serious negotiations with the United States about an FTA. This point about the timing of the decision not only is made clear in Salinas's writings on the subject but also was reiterated to the author by Serra Puche and by Pedro Aspe, who served as Salinas's finance secretary.[91] The decision to pursue a free trade agreement with the United States was therefore made in the context of a trip through Europe during which Salinas expressed his "emphatic" interest in resisting the United States via a close European partnership, and during which he realized that such a goal could be attained only after first agreeing to a US-Mexican FTA. It is logical to assume, therefore, that, in light of the timing of his decision to accept the FTA option, the trading-to-oppose rationale entered into Salinas's decision-making process in a significant way.

The logic of this assumption becomes all the more manifest when consideration is given to the fact that, economically speaking, the Europeans had only modest prospects to offer Mexico. Historically, European investment has been, while notable, nonetheless much less than US investment in Mexico, at least since the end of the nineteenth century.[92] This is not to say that European investment in Mexico in the late 1980s and early 1990s was negligible. Although each of the largest European investors in Mexico before 1990 constituted a small percentage of the total foreign investment into Mexico – for instance, in 1989 the cumulative investment from Britain accounted for 6.7 per cent, that from West Germany for 6.4, that from Switzerland for 4.5, that from France for 3, and that from Spain for 2.6 – nonetheless when taken as a whole they did add up to a fairly notable 23.2 per cent. In that same year, however, US cumulative investment in Mexico accounted for 63 per cent.[93] Thus not only was the US percentage substantially larger than that of all the Europeans taken together, but in order to significantly increase Europe's investment percentage it would have required that all of the extant European investor states, and presumably other European states as well, dramatically increase their percentages at the same time. This sort of outcome was improbable, however, given – to name simply the most obvious factor – differing fluctuations within individual states' economies from one year to the next.

Yet even if we assume that a collective surge in European capital might have been possible for Mexico to attract in a "good year," 1989–1990 was by no means a good year, for the simple reason that Europe's attention was directed eastward. By the summer of 1989 – when eastern Europeans were allowed free transit into western Europe – it was obvious that the half of Europe that had been cordoned off behind the Iron Curtain was now opening up to the outside world. The logical result of this was that western Europe was bound to devote much of its focus – diplomatic and financial – to this newly liberated part of the world. It could hardly be expected, therefore, that now, of all possible historical moments, the Europeans would be interested in significantly enhancing their investment commitments in Mexico. Although this point was reinforced for Salinas during his European travels, still surely he – with a Harvard PhD in economics, an acute sense of the economic issues facing Mexico, and a demonstrably strong grasp of geopolitical history and present reality – was alive to this dynamic before his departure for Europe.

All the more revealing is that one of the primary states with which Salinas was seeking an agreement was West Germany. Although Germany had, at various times, been a major figure in Mexican power-aggregating calculations against the United States – in the early 1880s, in 1914, in 1939 – this was due primarily to German military clout, not to its economic engagement in Mexico. And, as noted, in 1989 the accumulated foreign investment in Mexico from West Germany was only 6.4 per cent of the total such foreign investment. Nor was West Germany's percentage the largest among the Europeans in the two years before Salinas's European trip; Britain's was slightly larger.[94]

Salinas's interest in reaching an agreement with the Germans is made even more noteworthy by the fact that, of all the European states, West Germany was the most distracted by events in the east and the most impacted by them, since the fall of the Berlin Wall meant not only the liberation of eastern Europe but also the liberation of East Germany. That liberation, in turn, set the stage for the subsequent integration of East Germany into West Germany, the planning for which Kohl had already begun by the time Salinas visited him. Of course, this recombining of the two Germanys would amplify German political influence, but it would also – as was anticipated by many West Germans – likely have a negative impact on the overall German economy for some years to come, given East Germany's economic stagnation at the time. Since vast West German resources would need to be devoted to enhancing the economic status of the former East German region, it simply was not plausible to assume that any major increase in German foreign investment would be available to Mexico in the early months of 1990 or even in the next few years thereafter. Yet, as Salinas told Kohl during their January 1990 meeting, it was important "for Mexico to balance the growing economic link with the United States with a strong relationship with Europe, especially with Germany."

In light of all these points, therefore, the economic rationale for Salinas's decision to accept the FTA option appears to be only part of the calculus. He resisted the FTA idea when it was first broached by Bush in late 1988; he continued to resist it even after the debt-payment issue was settled; he still continued to resist it when sector-based trade agreements proved unlikely to deliver the kind of economic benefits that Mexico was seeking; he then travelled to Europe seeking a much closer and more comprehensive economic arrangement with various European states, even though the United States was a far larger economic actor in Mexico than all of the European states taken together; he did this at a time when he, better than most people, would have known in advance that geopolitical and economic considerations would be directing European attention to the east; and one of his primary target audiences was West Germany, even though West Germany had not been Mexico's largest European investor in the years just prior to the Davos trip, and even though West Germany, more than any other western European state, was likely to be politically and financially focused on eastern Europe. Yet when the Germans indicated that they would explore a closer economic relationship with Mexico only after Mexico had established such a relationship with the United States, Mexico decided to pursue an FTA with its northern neighbour.

Assessing the Data

The foregoing analysis appears to provide evidence that corroborates the assumption that trade agreements can be – and sometimes are – used by states to help them address important security concerns. In particular, this case study offers evidence that supports the hypotheses that an FTA can reinforce states' efforts to aggregate power against other third-party states, and that an FTA can reinforce states' efforts to

control other states that pose a threat. Since, as noted, a central task of
this study is to test these specific hypotheses, it is appropriate at this
point to consider the precise ways in which the assumptions of those
hypotheses play out in this case. As previously stated, there are five
functions that an FTA can perform in order to reinforce a security strategy. An FTA can 1) enhance trade, and thereby increase economic and
hence military strength, 2) provide voice opportunities, 3) help resolve
disputes, 4) provide insurance of a lasting relationship, and 5) lay the
groundwork for still greater integration.

We can begin by reviewing these functions insofar as they relate to
the trading-to-oppose hypothesis. The observable implications of the
five functions with regard to that hypothesis are as follows: for function
1, we should observe 1) regime leaders in the relevant states identifying a specific threat to their state; 2) those statesmen indicating that the
establishment of an FTA will help them to address a specific threat, by
facilitating a power-aggregating effort against the threatening state –
specifically, that an FTA will increase trade between the FTA member countries, thereby increasing their overall economic strength, and
hence allowing them to oppose the threatening state more effectively;
and 3) those statesmen attempting to establish an FTA. Similar sorts of
observable implications should likewise be looked for with regard to
functions 2 through 5 of the trading-to-oppose hypothesis, although
observable implication number 2 – regarding the manner in which an
FTA is expected to assist a power-aggregating effort – should differ for
each function. As such, what do we find?

It does appear that the observable implications of the trading-
to-oppose hypothesis are found within the factual record of the US-
Mexican case, particularly with regard to Mexican foreign policy.
Salinas made it clear that he viewed US behaviour following the collapse of the Berlin Wall as highly threatening to the sovereign integrity
of his state. He likewise made it clear that he sought to more closely
associate Mexico with European powers – notably Germany – so as to
more effectively resist the threat of US power, and that the decision to
pursue an FTA with the United States reflected, at least in part, his desire to ultimately establish an FTA with the Europeans.

With regard to the specific trading-to-oppose functions that an FTA
can serve, some appear to have been operable in this case while others
appear less relevant. Function 1, for instance – that an FTA can enhance
trade, and thereby increase economic and hence military strength –
does not appear particularly relevant to Mexico's behaviour towards

Germany and towards Europe in general. Not only was the prospect of greatly increased economic strength for Mexico – as a result of its trade relations with Europe – unlikely, but also the utility of building up the Mexican military in response to a potential US military threat is highly questionable, simply because the US military is so disproportionately stronger than the Mexican military. Similarly, function 2 – that an FTA can provide voice opportunities to influence member states' policies – and function 3 – that an FTA can help resolve disputes among the trading partners – appear to be only marginally relevant, because the Mexican-German relationship – and the Mexican-European relationship, more generally – was very limited at this point, and thus was not characterized by either abundant voice opportunities or trade-related problems. Yet clearly function 4 – an FTA serving as insurance of a longer relationship – was operable, because Salinas explicitly stated that he was looking for concrete guarantees of stronger ties with the European states. So too, function 5 – an FTA serving as the starting point for greater integration – appears relevant to Salinas's strategic calculus, since he not only claimed to want a trading relationship with Germany and the other European states but also "emphatically" wanted it to grow into a close partnership of some sort, to offset the complex and close relationship that was developing with Mexico's northern neighbour. The credibility of Salinas's statements in this regard is reinforced, furthermore, by the timing of his decision, of which there are two elements: 1) his decision took place immediately after the end of the Cold War, when the threat to his state was heightened, and at the same time that Germany was suddenly available again to play its historical role of assisting Mexican efforts to resist US power, and 2) it would have made more sense – from a strictly economic standpoint – to begin pursuing an FTA with the United States before Salinas's trip to Europe, when the key FTA-creating decision was made. Still further credibility is then lent by the historical precedent, wherein Mexico has repeatedly sought throughout its history to resist US assertions of influence by seeking to ally itself with a European power. At the same time, the question remains open as to whether Germany was seeking an FTA with Mexico to somehow oppose US power. The evidence presented here does not lend strong support to that idea. Thus, although trading-to-oppose behaviour was being engaged in, only one of the states in the Mexican-German relationship appears to have been using that relationship as a mechanism for pushing back against US pressure.

As for the United States in its relations with Mexico during this period, it does not display a great deal of trading-to-oppose behaviour. With its Cold War victory apparent, and with its economic and military strength unrivalled in the world, the US concern was evidently less that of pairing its power with another state – such as Mexico – and more that of consolidating its control over the region to its south so as to preclude the establishment of anti-US power-aggregating arrangements involving Latin American states.

As for trading-to-control behaviour in this case, we see the observable implications of the five functions playing out very clearly. With regard to US behaviour towards Mexico, for instance, evidence indicates that the United States sought to use the FTA as a means of influencing Mexico's behaviour, so as to make Mexico more disposed to align itself with the United States rather than with another foreign power. Although function 1 – using an FTA for the sake of increasing economic strength, so as to increase military strength and thus the potential capacity for influence – does not appear highly relevant, because US military strength was already so much greater than that of Mexico, the other four functions do appear to have been pertinent to the US strategic calculus. For example, with regard to function 2, George H.W. Bush was fairly clear about the fact that he was seeking a means to more directly influence the policies of Latin American states – and Mexico in particular – in the post–Cold War era, so as to ensure that US-friendly policies were put in place, which in turn would help consolidate the security gains brought by the Cold War's demise. As per function 3, US policymakers were also quite clear that they viewed the FTA as providing a platform for resolving long-standing tensions between the two states. As per function 4, various US officials stated that the FTA would reorient Mexico's foreign policy towards the United States, thereby placing limits on Mexico's range of options, and hence making Mexico less likely to ally itself with other states. And as per function 5, US statesmen indicated that this FTA would serve the longer-term US goal of building a close partnership with Mexico, at a time when the United States was pursuing similar such relationships with the Latin American states in general. Indeed, when asked whether he anticipated that NAFTA would continue bringing the two states together on a variety of policy fronts, former secretary of state James Baker replied, "I mean, that's pretty darn obvious. You don't need a crystal ball to see that."[95]

Statements by the relevant US policymakers regarding the manner in which the FTA would serve a trading-to-control strategy are further reinforced by the historical pattern whereby the United States has repeatedly sought to influence Mexican behaviour via trade agreements, so as to impede Mexico's ability to associate itself with another foreign power. The United States engaged in such behaviour in the 1820s, the 1830s, the 1870s, the 1890s, the 1910s, and again in the 1930s and early 1940s. Then in the 1980s, as Cold War tensions escalated, the United States sought once more to establish some such relationship, though to no avail. As soon as a new opportunity presented itself in the late 1980s and early 1990s, however, another attempt was made and that effort ultimately proved successful.

The evidence also suggests that a sophisticated trading-to-control strategy was in play in Mexican policy. Salinas clearly felt compelled to engage the United States more directly than had previous, post-Revolution Mexican presidents. The economic rationale for this behaviour is obvious, but it also seems fair to conclude from his statements that he recognized the necessity of engaging with the United States in order to protect Mexican sovereignty. Following the US invasion of Panama, in particular, there could be little doubt that a safer course of action for Mexico was to be "friends" with the United States rather than appear to be hostile. European encouragement then caused that approach to evolve into an FTA. As to the specific trading-to-control functions that an FTA can provide, although the relevance of function 1 – using an FTA to increase trade so as to be able to enhance the member states' military strength and hence the capacity for exerting influence – is debatable, given the vast discrepancy between the relevant militaries, the other four functions do appear to have been in play. For instance, with regard to function 2 – using an FTA to provide voice opportunities – Salinas clearly viewed closer trade relations with the United States as a means to exert some influence over US policy in general. As per function 3, he also saw increased formalization of the bilateral trade relationship as a means to resolve dangerous disputes between the two states. Similarly, as per function 4, the desire to constrain US behaviour, and thereby gain greater insurance of a US commitment to amicable relations, was evidently uppermost in his mind when he sought a more engaged bilateral relationship. And as per function 5, although it is debatable as to how far Salinas would have wanted integration between the United States and Mexico to proceed, the evidence does indicate that he was willing to go quite some ways to establish a less threatening bilateral relationship.

One can also think of Salinas's strategy in the following manner: Salinas was compelled to engage in a trading-to-control strategy with the United States in order to get what he most wanted, which was a closer relationship with the Europeans. In this mildly complex scenario, therefore, all the benefits of a trading-to-control policy vis-à-vis the United States were accentuated, insofar as pursuing such a policy with the United States allowed for enhanced trading-to-oppose activities – directed against the United States – with the Europeans, and that trading-to-oppose policy with the Europeans then allowed Mexico to be a stronger trade partner vis-à-vis the United States, and hence to more effectively make use of the benefits of its US-targeted trading-to-control agenda.

In sum, therefore, it appears valid to claim that the core assumptions of both the trading-to-oppose and the trading-to-control hypotheses find strong support in the evidence pertaining to the creation of NAFTA. Any effective counterargument made against this claim would need to demonstrate 1) that the threat scenarios facing the United States and Mexico at the time of the decision to establish the FTA were not particularly serious, 2) that the statements made by statesman with regard to the need to respond to those threats via trade techniques were misleading, 3) that the timing of the security and trade initiatives, which were launched during the same period, was purely coincidental, and 4) that the many instances of trading-for-security that have occurred throughout the history of US-Mexican relations are irrelevant to an analysis of the events leading up the creation of NAFTA.

Future Integration

In the wake of the decision made by the United States and Mexico to establish an FTA, Canada – whose economic interests were linked to those of the United States, due in part to the 1988 FTA – joined the negotiations as well, and this resulted, ultimately, in the creation of the trilateral NAFTA. The NAFTA-creating treaty that eventually came into effect in 1994 is, as Cameron and Tomlin point out, "a very big deal. The document itself is 1 1/2 inches thick, consisting of more than one thousand pages of text organized into twenty-two chapters, with numerous annexes, plus supplemental agreements on the environment and labor."[96] The chapters of the treaty, more specifically, are devoted to topics such as customs procedures, energy, agriculture, investment, telecommunications, competition policy, and so forth. More broadly, via the manner in which these topics are addressed, the NAFTA treaty seeks to establish a moderately institutionalized, integrative arrangement – essentially a version of a free trade area with a light supranational framework. With regard to that framework, the trading system is to be presided over by a North American Free Trade Commission (NAFTC), which consists of cabinet-level officials or their designated representatives and which is to be headquartered in Mexico City. As Gruber explains,

> Acting on the basis of consensus (unless otherwise agreed), the commissioners are charged with the formulation of policies affecting trade in manufactured goods, agricultural products, textiles and financial services. The supranational body is also responsible for developing common rules of origin, customs procedures, transportation regulations, sanitary measures, and labeling standards. To assist the commissioners in performing these tasks, the NAFTA accord explicitly provided for numerous standing committees and subcommittees, as well as over a dozen working groups and advisory panels.[97]

In addition to this, "NAFTA's three signatories also established an overarching system for the settlement of intraregional trade and investment disputes. When invoked, this system calls for 'panels of experts' to exercise what are, in essence, powers of judicial review."[98] Indeed, an array of institutional mechanisms – executive, judicial, bureaucratic – were called for by the NAFTA treaty, and, if allowed to function fully, would have established a network of overlapping governing functions among the three member states, which would, in turn, have allowed the trade relations made possible via NAFTA to be that much more effectively managed. Yet many of these institutional tools – including the NAFTC – have to date either been underutilized or simply not used at all, which is not particularly surprising. The mere enactment of NAFTA, after all, represented a sea change in North American affairs. It was the most wide-ranging trade agreement ever established between any of the signatories, and it was also the only such agreement to ever include all three regimes. It was, as such, inherently controversial; not only did George H.W. Bush's strong advocacy of the treaty go a long way towards costing him the 1992 presidential election, but simply enacting NAFTA helped prompt a guerrilla uprising in southern Mexico, which was led by individuals who feared that NAFTA might constitute yet one more attempted land-grab by foreign-dominated – particularly US – business entities. Thus, to then expect the far-reaching, institutional ambitions of the treaty to be fully realized from the get-go seems a bit more hopeful than reality would allow. The only exception that proves the rule in this regard is the one robustly realized institutional tool of the treaty – that which pertains to trilateral adjudication of trade issues; in particular, those provisions pertaining to chapter 11, which itself managed to cause substantial controversy when initially acted upon.[99]

Yet, even though a degree of institutional stasis has ensued, it is important to note that continental-scale integration has progressed. In various sectors of the three economies, for instance, markets have been established that are comprehensive of all three states, and this combining of economic sectors requires regular interactions not only between economic actors but also between these actors and political agencies. In industries such as energy, agriculture, and steel, for example, the markets have become truly North American, and this phenomenon has required the combining of authority purviews among the three member states.[100]

Furthermore, in addition to such generally-progressing integrative trends, sudden geopolitical jolts have also pushed the integration process forward, although in certain cases some results have also been counterproductive. Most notably, the Al Qaeda attacks of 11 September 2001 prompted a robust implementation of NORAD's continental defence capabilities in the days immediately thereafter, and, in line with NORAD's suddenly invigorated role, a new US military command – the Northern Command – was paired with the joint US-Canadian authority structure that exists within the NORAD framework. This heightening of emphasis on NORAD's role set the stage, in turn, for further US-Canadian coordination on the issue of strategic missile defence. The Al Qaeda attacks, however, also drove the United States to clamp down on border security both to its north and to its south, thereby raising a variety of impediments to many of the cross-border trade flows that NAFTA was meant to facilitate.[101]

It was against this backdrop of some increased integration, therefore, as well as some stalled integration, along with some real strains in the trilateral project, that the three states' regimes decided to re-evaluate the NAFTA arrangement and determine ways to improve it. In each of the three states, influential organizations devoted to analysing foreign policy were tasked with providing recommendations along these lines, and various of these recommendations were then packaged together by the three regimes. The ultimate result was the Security and Prosperity Partnership (SPP) of 2005.[102] The founding declaration of the SPP reads,

We, the elected leaders of Canada, Mexico and the United States, gather in Texas to announce the establishment of the Security and Prosperity Partnership of North America ... Over the past decade, our three nations have taken important steps to expand economic opportunity for our people and to create the most vibrant and dynamic trade relationship in the world. Since September 11, 2001, we have also taken significant new steps to address the threat of terrorism and to enhance the security of our people ... But more needs to be done. In a rapidly changing world, we must develop new avenues of cooperation that will make our open societies safer and more secure, our businesses more competitive, and our economies more resilient.[103]

Specifically with regard to security,

We will establish a common approach to security to protect North America from external threats, prevent and respond to threats within North America, and further streamline the secure and efficient movement of legitimate, low-risk traffic across our shared borders. As part of our efforts, we will: implement common border security and bioprotection strategies ... enhance critical infrastructure protection ... implement improvements in aviation and maritime security, combat transnational threats, and enhance intelligence partnerships.[104]

Enhancement of economic relations would likewise include steps to "improve productivity through regulatory cooperation to generate growth ... promote sectoral collaboration in energy, transportation, financial services, technology ... reduce the cost of trade through the efficient movement of goods and people ... enhance the stewardship of our environment." The founding declaration also called for the establishment of "Ministerial-led working groups that will consult with stakeholders in our respective countries." For instance, "Security working groups chaired by ... the Department of Homeland Security will address: external threats to North America ... streamlined and secured shared borders ... etc."[105]

As noted in chapter 1, although the SPP did cause a few changes to occur – most notably, annual trilateral summits became more common – its ambitions largely went unrealized and since 2009 the SPP has been shelved.[106] Explanations vary as to why the SPP failed to be more successful. Derek Burney – Mulroney's chief of staff during the US-Canadian FTA negotiations – pointed out in his interview with the author that advancement during the first years of the SPP was hindered in part by the domestic political realities of the three heads of state: a weakened US president, a minority government in Canada, and a controversially elected president in Mexico. Once the three states' leaders were in stronger positions, however, Burney thought that greater cooperative and/or integrative action might be more likely.[107] Conversely, various analysts view the SPP approach as inherently flawed, based as it was on limited, step-by-step expansion of the NAFTA agenda into new issue areas as opposed to taking a more comprehensive approach.[108] Still others suggest that a key problem was simply that the process of putting together the SPP proposals was too rushed to allow for coherence, regardless of whether the general philosophy of integrative progression was the right one.[109] Whatever the case may be, the larger question is whether further attempts are likely to be made to enhance the North American integrative endeavour. The answer to that question would seem to be in the affirmative.

Along with a variety of economic rationales for further integration, there are reasons both general and specific to suspect further security-driven advancements as well. The general security-related reason is that, as the history of US-Mexican and US-Canadian relations demonstrates, there is an abundance of factual evidence that lends credence to the claim that the world is indeed a dangerous place; that states find each other threatening; and that a logical response to those threats is for states to establish more regimented – and potentially institutionalized – relations with one another.

As for the specific types of threats that might prompt greater integration in the near future, these can be found in both the northern and southern portions of the continent. To the north, a rapidly thawing Arctic Ocean is opening an array of possibilities for both cooperation and competition among states. In the first decade of the new century, for instance, a series of tense interactions transpired between states in the region as they vied for control of newly accessible territory, sea lanes, and natural resources, with the tension reaching its crescendo around 2007–2008.[110] Although effective diplomacy prevented that trend from escalating into outright military action, and although certain issues have been temporarily addressed, the scene is still set for new rounds of power competition, especially now that China is moving proactively to establish a strong presence in the region.[111] It is not at all difficult to imagine, in turn, that further cooperation or integration may well occur among the North American states in response to these evolving threat dynamics.

With regard to threats emanating from North America's southern region, these are also likely to continue. While it is true that US-Mexican relations have been greatly improved via NAFTA, still NAFTA itself resulted in part from Mexico's desire to ally itself closely with another foreign power in response to the threat posed by the United States. Thus, as the cooperation/integration process between the United States and Mexico continues, it is likely that Mexico will seek closer and closer relations with other foreign powers, thereby prompting the United States to seek still closer relations with Mexico. At the same time, the Mexican regime's ongoing domestic battle with drug cartels might weaken the regime to the point where Mexico again becomes vulnerable to interference by extraregional states, and just as such interference has in the past, so too such interference in the future might prompt still greater integration efforts with Mexico by the United States. Meanwhile, threats within the Caribbean region likewise continue to be of concern to US policymakers. One example is the recent effort undertaken by Cuba and Venezuela to establish a regional, anti-US grouping of some sort. Indeed, the establishment of CAFTA-DR – the Dominican Republic–Central American Free Trade Agreement – in 2005, which includes the United States, Guatemala, Honduras, El Salvador, Nicaragua, and the Dominican Republic, and which in certain respects extends the NAFTA project south of the Yucatan Peninsula, is viewed by the United States partly as a means to address the threat of Venezuela seeking to export its leftist ideology to the rest of the region. As President George W. Bush stated when he signed the FTA-creating legislation, "CAFTA is more than a trade bill. It is a commitment among freedom-loving nations to advance peace and prosperity throughout the region. The United States has a moral obligation and a vital national security interest in helping democracies in our neighborhood succeed."[112] In words widely interpreted as being directed against the Venezuelan regime, Bush also said that this new FTA would help still-fragile Central American democracies to better defend "against forces that oppose democracy, seek to limit economic freedom and want to drive a wedge between the United States and the rest of the Americas."[113] More generally, Venezuela's penchant for allying not only with Cuba but also with states from outside the western hemisphere – especially with states whose relations with the United States are strained, such as Russia and Iran – falls in line with the sort of behaviour that has always caused the United States to be concerned about the activities of its southern neighbours. Such behaviour patterns will no doubt continue to cause the United States disquiet well into the future.

If, therefore, security issues continue to face the North American states and if closer economic and security cooperation/integration help to address those issues, then the North American cooperative/integrative effort is likely over the long term to continue moving forward, even as countervailing tendencies – such as protectionist trade sentiments in the United States, or cross-border tensions between the United States and Mexico relating to illegal immigration – continue to persist. In general terms, such forward progress with regard to economic integration would mean moving from the level of a free trade area to something more advanced, such as a customs union or eventually a common market. Speaking more specifically, it could also mean bringing into being any number of institutional mechanisms that were called for by the NAFTA treaty but that were never in fact established or only weakly so.

As for next steps in terms of continental security-policy integration, the picture is somewhat unclear due to three factors. First, the North American project is relatively new and undeveloped, and since serious security policy integration typically makes most sense – politically speaking – after economic integration has been achieved, we are presumably some ways off from the time when comprehensive, trilateral security policy integration will be most likely to occur. Second, the North American picture is skewed somewhat by the existence of NORAD, which allows for tight cooperation/integration on security issues between Canada and the United States but not Mexico. NORAD is a highly unusual institution – the result of US military strength and a Canadian territory too big to be defended by Canada's proportionately small population – and indeed, the very existence of NORAD nearly provides an exception that proves the rule of factor one. Third, extant Mexican laws place exceptionally strong constraints on the degree to which Mexican armed forces can be deployed outside of Mexican territory, as well as on the degree to which foreign militaries can be stationed in Mexican territory, and this raises extra barriers to Mexico's ability to militarily integrate with its North American neighbours. At the same time, however, various forms of military-style cooperation are already underway between the United States and Mexico in response to the security threats posed by Mexico's drug cartels. Most notably, a comprehensive cooperative agreement – the Merida Initiative – came into effect in 2008 that allows for the provision of extensive US military training, equipment, intelligence support, and funding for the Mexican

military. In 2011 this effort was further amplified by even closer cooperation, such as the permanent stationing of CIA operatives at Mexican
military bases – their job being to work in tandem with Mexican authorities to collect information and plan operations against drug cartels.[114] Thus, it remains to be seen exactly whether and how Mexico's
domestic fight against the cartels – and the US assistance with such –
will transform Mexico's legal structure insofar as it pertains to military
relations with other regimes.

In addition to these specific factors that problematize any detailed
predictions about the future of NAFTA, there is the more general fact
that North America is currently awash in various cooperative endeavours that may or may not link up with or overtake NAFTA-based integration. For instance, renewed efforts pertaining to the US-Canadian
Permanent Joint Board of Defense (PJBD) are underway. Meanwhile,
proactive meetings between the three states' foreign ministers suggest
that further cooperation/integration may be handled in the context of
those interactions and not necessarily within the set framework established by NAFTA. At the same time, bilateral agreements on securing
the states' shared borders have recently been announced, thereby providing yet another venue for addressing security issues in a nontrilat-
eral fashion. In the case of US-Canadian relations, the latest formulation
of this approach has been an initiative known as "Beyond the Border";
in the case of the United States and Mexico, the most recent program
was articulated in the "Declaration of the 21st Century Border."

Due to all of these factors, therefore, it is difficult to determine in a
detailed fashion how North American security policy integration will
be likely to progress on a step-by-step basis. Based on the foregoing evidence, such progress is nonetheless plausible in the long run. If we wish
to be any more precise than that in our long-term predictions, then we
need to turn to another method of analysis, one that does not rely solely
on examining North American history. More specifically, we need to
pair the foregoing analysis of the historical integrative patterns within
North America – an analysis of "depth" – with an analysis of the extent –
the "breadth" – of contemporary integrative activity in other regions.
That approach can lend insights by allowing for direct comparisons between separate integration projects, especially with regard to the role
of security concerns in prompting those projects. It can also shed useful
light by placing the North American case within the context of a global
trend. Once the nature of that global trend is understood, then NAFTA
itself can be appreciated for what it is.

4 The Broader Context

There are currently several regional integration efforts underway in various parts of the world. Of all of these, that which is transpiring in North America seems perhaps the least likely – at first glance – to have been motivated by security concerns. Yet, as the foregoing chapters demonstrate, security motivations have played a central role in the North American integration process and will likely continue to do so. Recognition of this fact allows, in turn, for a further recognition – namely, of the similarities between the North American project and those other integration projects in other regions that have likewise been rooted in security-seeking behaviour and that have also used economic policies to achieve their security goals.[1]

The key comparative case is of course that of the EU, given its duration and scope of development. And indeed, if we examine the three most important historical moments in that process – the founding of the European Coal and Steel Community (ECSC) in 1951, the establishment of the European Economic Community (EEC) in 1957, and the rejuvenation of the integration process in the mid-1980s and early 1990s – we find in each instance that those statesmen most responsible for promoting integration cited security concerns as a primary rationale for integrative action. We likewise find that their security concerns correlated with objective security threats that their states were facing at the time.

For example, the European integration process officially began in 1950 when the French foreign minister, Robert Schuman, sent a letter to the West German chancellor, Konrad Adenauer, suggesting the creation of the European Coal and Steel Community. Schuman sent this letter at a time when the bilateral structures established after World War II for regulating the border region between France and Germany – which is also the area where the two states' major coal reserves, and hence their steel industries, were located – were faltering, and thus at a time when tensions between France and Germany were beginning to re-escalate.[2] To ensure, therefore, that war did not re-erupt in Europe and, by extension, throughout the world, it was logical for France and Germany to integrate with each other in order to control one another, and the logical place to begin an integration-directed trading-to-control policy was in the coal and steel industries, since those industries provided the basis for the two states' armaments industries, and since control over the coal-rich borderlands had sparked so many disagreements between France and Germany in the past.

As Schuman noted to Adenauer, "The peace of the world will not be able to be secured without a creative effort on the same scale as the dangers that menace it."[3] He continued:

The contribution that a Europe organized and vibrant can bring to civilization is indispensable to the maintenance of peaceful relations. In acting for more than twenty years as the champion of a united Europe, France always had as its essential object to serve peace. Europe was not made, thus we had war.

Europe will not be made all at once, nor out of an assemblage of different efforts: she will be made through the concrete steps which flow first from solid fact. The organization of European nations requires that the historical opposition of France and Germany be eliminated: the current integration effort must therefore touch first upon France and Germany.

In this goal, the French government proposes to bring action on a point that is limited but decisive:

The French government proposes to place together the Franco-German production of coal and steel, under a High Common Authority, in an organization open to the participation of the other states of Europe.

The placing together of the coal and steel productions will assure immediately the establishment of common bases of development, which is the first step towards a European federation, and it will change the destiny of these regions which have long been menaced by the fabrication of the arms of war of which they are the most constant victims.[4]

Schuman's security motivations for establishing the ECSC could hardly have been clearer, and indeed, if there were any doubt regarding the security-based incentives he was acting upon, further details of his motivations and objectives are provided in his other writings on the topic.[5] So too Adenauer himself was utterly explicit about his integrative perspective:

> The purpose of his [Schuman's] proposal was not economic, but eminently political. In France there was a fear that once Germany had recovered, she would attack France. He could imagine that the corresponding fears might be present in Germany. Rearmament always showed first in an increased production of coal, iron and steel. If any organization such as he was proposing were to be set up it would enable each country to detect the first signs of rearmament, and would have an extraordinarily calming effect in France.
>
> Schuman's plan corresponded entirely with the ideas I had been advocating for a long time concerning the integration of the key industries of Europe. I informed Robert Schuman at once that I accepted his proposal wholeheartedly.[6]

For the sake of their respective states' security, therefore, the two statesmen decided to launch a long-term integration project that, like the North American project, would begin by integrating the respective states' economic policies.[7]

The central actors in initiating the next key step in the integration process – the creation of the EEC in 1957 – likewise provide explicit indications of the security-driven nature of that project.[8] Most notable in this regard is Johann Beyen, the Dutch foreign minister, who was primarily responsible for developing and promoting the concept of a West European customs union, which became the core element of the EEC. Beyen began advocating for such an approach in 1952, as a means to reinforce efforts then underway by the six ECSC states to establish an integrated western European military capacity, known as the European Defence Community (EDC). The EDC effort was explicitly undertaken to aggregate strength, as much as possible, against the threat posed by the Soviet Union, as well as to address the threat of a restrengthening West Germany by seeking greater control over the regime in Bonn.[9] Beyen wanted to reinforce that EDC effort by coupling it with an advance in economic integration. As he argued, "The primary goal of European integration must be, it seems, the elevation of the general standard of living of the European peoples, alongside the reinforcement of the defense by a closer cooperation in the military domain, such as is previewed in the Treaty creating the European Defence Community."[10] He continued:

From the Perspective of the Government of the Queen [of the Netherlands], economic integration, as well as the monetary and social coordination that it necessitates, is for this reason essential to the development of the interests of the European countries, seeing that it is the indispensable condition to maintaining and ameliorating the standard of living, with all the social aspects that this question entails, and that it can serve equally at the same time to reinforce the defence.[11]

Beyen noted that this approach would follow in the integration method established by Robert Schuman – namely, a step-by-step process that would bring concrete results, leading to the creation of a supportive, pro-integration political environment upon which further integration could eventually be built. Beyen subsequently elaborated upon these ideas in 1953, when he wrote,

The Government of the Queen seeks to reiterate its conviction that the *raison d'etre* of a Political Community, which is necessary, derives from the undeniable need and real solidarity which is felt by the people of Western Europe. Although this need manifests itself first in the political domain in the narrow sense of the term, it is evident that this need can hardly be satisfied solely in this restricted domain; in effect, the measure in which the political solidarity is realizable depends, if not exclusively then at least in large part, on the measure to which this new political arrangement contributes truly to the solidarity of the economies of which it is the expression.[12]

Beyen recognized that the fundamental motivation for integration derived from western Europe's post-war political – that is to say, security – imperatives, but that whatever goals might be sought via political integration required an accompanying integration of economic spheres. Without this economic integration, he repeatedly emphasized, political integration would ultimately fall apart. These considerations led Beyen to list the following points:

a. The realization of a Political Community must constitute at the same time a real contribution to a fusion of the essential interests of the member states.
b. The elaboration of this fusion must fall to the Political Community, because it will decide the measure of political solidarity between the member states.

   c. The contribution to the fusion of essential interests must be at the outset
     of a limited character and be applied to all the sectors of the national
     economies.
   d. It is equally in the interest of Europe that the adjustments in the econo-
     mies that result from the envisioned fusion of essential interests not
     lead to serious social and economic perturbations.[13]

In other words, political integration required a simultaneous push towards economic integration, and the best way to ensure the success of that economic policy was to start at a relatively low level of policy and to apply that integrative policy across all sectors of the member states' economies. Given these conclusions, therefore, Beyen logically proposed the establishment of a customs union between the integrating states, which would be relatively limited in its effects on separate economies, could be applied to them equally, and would provide a solid first step towards greater integration.[14] Throughout 1953 and into 1954 Beyen championed this conception of a customs union as the best means of advancing the integrative cause, to be pursued in tandem with the creation of the political structures of military integration. In August 1954, however, the French National Assembly refused to endorse the EDC treaty and thus the prospect of integrating the militaries of the six ECSC states collapsed. The EDC's failed realization, however, did not deter Beyen. Instead, he continued to push for the idea of a customs union that would eventually lead to a common market, and he continued to frame his objectives in terms of the larger goal of European security. In September 1954, for instance, one month after the EDC's rejection by the French National Assembly, Beyen gave a speech in which he reiterated the necessity of European integration.

> The European idea was born of the consciousness that the European spiritual heritage, this civilization, based upon respect of human dignity, is found to be menaced in its very existence, from the exterior and from the interior, by enemy forces, forces spiritual as well as material; the European idea received its momentum from the conviction that any efficacious defense against these dangers was not possible without putting to an end divisions which have been quarrelsome to the point of being fratricidal, which are the principle cause of the weakness of Europe and which, already two times, led it up to the brink of total ruin. Europe has ceased to be the entire world, or even the center of the entire world. So that it does not perish as an eternal source of civilization, of liberty and of progress, it

is necessary that Europe become aware of its solidarity, that the European family be constituted as a cultural, economic and political unity.[15]

Beyen's security motivations for promoting the customs union could hardly have been clearer. This point is reinforced, furthermore, by Beyen's former assistant at the Dutch Foreign Ministry, Edmund Wellenstein, who was at Beyen's side when Beyen first announced his proposal for an ECSC-wide customs union in 1952. When asked by the author whether he thought that security concerns were relevant to Beyen's integration-related efforts, Wellenstein responded as if this was the most unnecessary of questions. "My dear friend," he exclaimed, "we had just come out of a war!"[16]

Beyen's persistence eventually paid off and the customs union approach to integration was followed when the EEC was established in 1957. Shortly thereafter, however, the European integrative project was dealt a series of setbacks by French president Charles De Gaulle, who was disinclined to allow French sovereign independence to be constrained by EEC strictures. His anti-integrative efforts served to diminish the integrative momentum thus far established, and even after he left office in 1969 the integration project remained rather stagnant. The most immediate factor reinforcing this lingering stagnation was a seemingly intractable debate about how much Britain – which joined the integration process in 1973 – should be obliged to pay in membership dues to the Community. In fact it was not until the mid-1980s that this issue was finally resolved and hence integration was at last rejuvenated. More specifically, it was in 1984 that French president François Mitterrand assumed the rotating six-month presidency of the European Council and used that position to promote a resolution to the British budget issue.

At least two points are worth mentioning with regard to Mitterrand's actions, and hence with regard to the rejuvenation of European integration in general. First, Mitterrand's efforts occurred at a time of exceptionally heightened tensions in Europe, when, after a period of MAD-based security stasis in Europe, the region's security situation again became very precarious due the advent of cruise missile technology, and, more specifically, due to the placement of intermediate-range cruise missiles by the United States and the USSR in locations close to the Iron Curtain, this being the European corollary to the North American Arctic arms race.[17] Second, Mitterrand not only repeatedly expressed his concern about this security situation but also explicitly stated his intent to further enhance the trade-based relations of western European states, so as to enable them to increase their military integration efforts so that they, in turn, could act as a third force on the geopolitical scene and not remain beholden to the strategic whims of the two superpowers.[18] As he told the European Parliament in Strasbourg in May 1984,

> I am speaking to you as the President of the European Council for the first half of 1984. ... But I am also speaking to you as a French European whose personal commitment has been in evidence at every stage of the emergence of Europe. When, in May 1948, just three years after the war, the European idea took shape at the congress of The Hague, I was there and I believed in it. When, in 1950, Robert Schuman launched the plan for the European Coal and Steel Community, I supported it and I believed in it. When, in 1956, the vast task of building the common market began, with the very active participation of the French government of that time, I was there and I believed in it. And today, when we have to rid Europe of the Ten of its differences and lead it resolutely along the path to the future, I can still say that I am there and I believe in it.[19]

Mitterrand then tied the founding security rationale of integration to the present security issues facing Europe.

> Today, the Community has achieved the initial objectives it inherited from the war. In the beginning, it had to reconcile and bring together peoples whom force and bloodshed had divided and get them harnessed to a common task. That has been done. Now the choice is between letting other people on our continent and outside our continent decide on everyone's destiny, ours included, and combining all the talent and ability, the creative ability and the material, spiritual and cultural resources that have combined to make Europe a civilization, so, as Walt Whitman puts it in a line I like very much, it can at last become what it is.[20]

The fear of war between France and Germany had been largely addressed – at least for the moment – and now it was necessary to deal with the insecurity that arose between western Europe and the major powers on either side of it. The fate of Europe, simply put, was not yet in European hands; to attain European security, it was necessary to revitalize the integration project so that the region might become what it was always meant to be – a politically integrated structure capable of exerting influence both within Europe and without. After making these points, Mitterrand briefly reviewed the various issues that had been stalling integration, noting how each had been resolved, save for one. "That leaves the dispute modestly referred to as the correction of budgetary imbalance – which in fact means the current discussion about the British contribution."[21]

To deal with this British contribution problem, Mitterrand directed his foreign minister, Roland Dumas, to conduct a series of confidential meetings with the British foreign secretary.[22] Dumas, who had worked with Mitterrand for years, appreciated the larger significance of his task. As he explained to the author,

> The principal motivation of François Mitterrand and myself was double. On the one hand, to un-jam the process of European integration that was blocked by the fact of the refusal of [British Prime Minister] Madame Thatcher, who opposed all solicitous measures so long as her financial problem had not been resolved. We were thus motivated by a sort of "checkbook blackmail." At the same time, clearly, we were of the spirit at that moment that the construction of Europe could only progress in the domains of foreign policy and European security if the countries concerned were in accord.[23]

After Dumas's initial meetings with the British foreign secretary, the budget negotiations were assigned to civil servants in the respective foreign ministries, with Guy Legras serving as lead negotiator on the French side. The subsequent negotiations proved quite productive, and as Legras explained to the author, the success of these negotiations was due in no small part to the fact that the ministers in the French cabinet with economics-focused portfolios – and hence those who might object most strongly to the new budgeting terms given to the British – were largely cut out of the negotiations by Mitterrand. Legras found it understandable that Mitterrand would act in this manner, however, since he viewed Mitterrand's motivations as being primarily noneconomics-focused in nature.[24] As such, thanks to the efforts of Mitterrand, Dumas, and Legras, who were willing to give the British much of what they wanted, the budget issue was resolved and European integration was allowed to proceed, resulting not long thereafter in the creation of the Single European Act (SEA) in 1987 – essentially a commitment to complete the European common market by the early 1990s – and in the relatively robust integration that has transpired ever since.[25]

That integrative momentum was given an additional impetus shortly after the SEA's enactment, thanks to the fact that in the latter part of the 1980s the Soviet Union's grip on eastern Europe began to weaken and, most significantly, in 1989 the Berlin Wall fell. These developments not only helped precipitate the creation of NAFTA but also spurred the European integration process forward as well. The prospect of a united Germany unconstrained by the Cold War, and hence the potential for a new round of power politics in the region, deeply disturbed European leaders, particularly those in France and Britain, as well as in Germany itself.[26] It was thus Mitterrand and Helmut Kohl who now called for still greater European integration to proceed; specifically, they decided to push forward with enhanced integration on foreign and security policy, as a parallel effort to the SEA-based effort to complete the common market – the idea being that the only way to ensure the security of Europe in the new geostrategic context was to bind France and Germany still more tightly together.[27] The result was therefore two intergovernmental conferences – one pertaining to economics, the other pertaining to foreign and security policy – that culminated in the creation of the Treaty on European Union (TEU) in 1992. The TEU, in turn, brought into being the Common Foreign and Security Policy (CFSP), through which the EU member states were provided with a far greater range of goals and capabilities for acting in concert regarding security concerns.

In the years since the CFSP's creation, the relevance of security issues to the integration process has become still more obvious. For instance, although the EU was ill-prepared to address the wars that broke out in the Balkans in the 1990s, those wars helped spur further integration, · with another intergovernmental conference held in Amsterdam in the mid-1990s, and further meetings taking place at the end of the decade, all of which refined the role and capabilities of CFSP. Thanks to these enhancements, by the early 2000s the EU was able to field military-based monitoring and peacekeeping missions in the Balkans and in Africa. In 2009 the EU states then signed the Lisbon Treaty, which gave a still more prominent place to security policy integration within the EU structure, including the creation of a strong role for a foreign minister–like position, as well as the establishment of a permanent position of European Council president, thereby lending the EU as a whole the capacity to act more concertedly on security policy initiatives.

In short, just as in the case of North American integration, so too in the case of European integration the process appears to have been strongly and consistently driven forward by security motivations, while techniques of trade have often been the means for facilitating that integration. Of course, the EU process is highly complex – it currently involves twenty-eight states, numerous institutions, and countless polices – and the study of its history is an involved undertaking. The sampling of facts presented here is simply meant to suggest some ways of thinking about how future North American security policy integration could proceed, and more generally, to indicate that the trading-for-security hypotheses presented in chapter 1 have relevance beyond the limits of the North American case. Indeed, with regard to this latter point, we find that in addition to Europe and North America, other regions of the world – such as South America and Southeast Asia – are also currently engaged in trading-for-security projects.

In the South American region, for example, various attempts have been made at interstate integration, with the initial efforts transpiring soon after these states broke free of colonial control in the 1820s. The earliest attempts were led by the foremost figure in the decolonization of South America, Simón Bolívar, who sought to secure the newly liberated territories against the threat of a return of the colonial powers. These initial integration projects came to little, however, as did subsequent tries, including comparatively recent efforts such as those spearheaded by Argentina in the 1940s and 1950s, the Latin American Free Trade Agreement (LAFTA) of the late 1950s and 1960s, or the Andean Group of the mid-to-late 1960s. It was not until a free trade-based process began in the mid-1980s – led by Argentina and Brazil – that any real progress was made. These two states, fearing domestic threats posed to their newly established democratic regimes, as well as threats posed by other states in the region, including threats posed by each other, began establishing closer trade and security relations with one another. They then actively sought to encourage the establishment of democratic regimes in other neighbouring states, while likewise promoting closer integration with those states to reinforce their mutual security.[28] In 1991 this trade-and-security process was given the name Mercosur (Mercosul in Portuguese), with the founding members being Argentina, Brazil, Uruguay, and Paraguay.[29]

As for Southeast Asia, the project of note is the Association of Southeast Asian Nations (ASEAN), which was established in 1967 by Malaysia, Indonesia, Singapore, the Philippines, and Thailand. ASEAN was initially conceived of as strictly a limited, nonintegrative "security community," and was prompted by the member states' fear of each other, combined with their fear of China and its communist allies in the region.

More specifically, following the liberation of Malaya (subsequently Malaysia) from British colonial control, Malaya began responding to the threats around it – in particular, the presence of Chinese-backed communists in Singapore – by seeking to augment its power via the acquisition of more territory, a course of behaviour that, in turn, appeared threatening to its neighbours, most notably to Indonesia. Thus as war began to appear imminent, Malaysia and Indonesia, as well as some of their neighbours, sought a consultative alternative to violent conflict and ultimately created ASEAN. Since then, ASEAN has evolved in terms of its membership, its level of integration, and its policy range, such that while it continues to exist primarily as a security-focused organization, it also functions more and more as a means of coordinating/integrating its member states' trade policies.[30]

As for other regions of the world, such as Africa and the Middle East, there we find repeated but less successful attempts to establish integrative institutions for the sake of gaining greater security. In the wake of African decolonization, for instance, a series of efforts – initially led by the Simón Bolívar of Africa, Kwame Nkrumah of Ghana – were undertaken to secure the continent's newly liberated territories against the return of colonial powers, via a fully integrated United States of Africa. When that continental-scale state failed to take shape, however, efforts were made – some of which continue to this day – to create large-scale states made up of the subregions of the continent, although these macrostates have likewise failed to materialize. The most notable of these African subregional endeavours is the East African project that currently includes Kenya, Tanzania, Uganda, Rwanda, and Burundi. Although neither free trade nor in-depth security integration has resulted from this project, it was launched in the 1960s specifically to achieve those goals, with the relevant regime leaders stating that the objective was to strengthen the member states via trade and security policy integration, so that those states could then better defend themselves against threats to their sovereignty posed by their former colonizers.[31] Since the 1960s the project's purpose has continued to expand to address other threats, but the project itself remains very much in the conceptual stage. Indeed, to date the only "successful" integration of African states occurred in the early 1960s when Tanganyika and the island of Zanzibar integrated – at the forceful behest of the former – to create the state of Tanzania. The Tanganyikan leadership at the time was seeking control over Zanzibar due to fears that Zanzibar was about to become a superpower pawn in the Cold War power struggle, and that, should such struggles arrive at Tanganyika's doorstep, it could prove perilous for the Tanganyikan regime.[32]

Similarly in the Middle East, we find a pattern of repeated yet thus far largely unsuccessful security-motivated integrative efforts. Following the post-WWII European withdrawal from the region, numerous efforts at interstate integration were attempted, primarily for the purpose of protecting the newly independent states against former colonial powers, as well as against each other, although ultimately to no avail. The most notable of these attempts was the United Arab Republic (UAR), which was founded in 1958 and technically lasted, on paper, until 1961. Comprising Egypt – which was led at the time by Gamal Nasser, the Bolívar of the postcolonial Middle East – and Syria, the UAR was formed as a defensive measure against various Middle Eastern as well as extraregional states that Egypt and Syria viewed as threatening. Real integration never took place within the UAR, however, since the Syrians were disinclined to submit to Egyptian leadership.[33] Indeed, the only unquestionably "successful" instance of integration in the region has been the formation of the contemporary state of Yemen, created out of two previous Yemens, with the motivation for integration stemming from a combination of economic incentives – involving oil – and security concerns – involving each other and Saudi Arabia. This integration effort succeeded, however, only after a postunification civil war gave full executive authority to one of the previous Yemeni leaders.[34] Another seemingly successful – and peaceful – integration scheme in the region is that of the United Arab Emirates (UAE), which was formed by a group of microstates in the 1970s. It was set up essentially as a military alliance between the emirates of Abu Dhabi and Dubai – and then foisted upon the other member emirates – and was meant to function as a defensive, power-aggregating measure directed against Iran. This arrangement initially displayed more cooperation than integration, however, and to this day the degree of real integration between the member principalities remains rather ambiguous.[35]

Overall, therefore, just as with the North American states, so too we find other states across the globe engaging or attempting to engage in integrative efforts – often via free trade means – in order to promote their security-seeking agendas. And this behaviour seems altogether logical, given the threats with which states are constantly beset in an environment of global anarchy. Indeed, it could be argued that almost any technique utilized by states in order to combine with other states so as to reinforce their security is technically rational in that sort of environment, with the most obvious such technique being, of course, territorial conquest. It is hardly surprising, in other words, that, beginning with the first appearance of states roughly five thousand years ago, history has repeatedly exhibited a pattern of states engaging in precisely such behaviour, the most notable conquerors including first Akkad, then Babylonia, Assyria, Persia, Macedonia, and Rome, followed in turn by all the would-be-Rome imitators of Western history, not to mention all the countless states exhibiting similar behavioural patterns during the long histories of East Asia, the Indian subcontinent, and so forth. In light of the logic of security-driven integration, therefore, the next question to consider is why certain states appear able to integrate peacefully with each other, often with the assistance of trade techniques, while other states appear unable to do so and thus are obliged to resort to a more violent power-aggregating approach.

Aside from the economic criteria required for the development of successful, trade-based, peaceful integrative endeavours, the role of democratic governance is perhaps the most obvious variable to consider when examining states' capacity for negotiated integration. A cursory review of the data, for instance, indicates that those contemporary integration projects that are complex – in terms of the level of cooperation/integration between states – and successful – in terms of progressively becoming more complex – are those which also happen to be made up of democratic states. The European project, for instance, has always consisted of only democracies, while in North America the integration process began to really progress only after Canada's democratic regime became fully sovereign and at a time when Mexico's regime was in the process of entering its current democratic phase. Mercosur, for its part, came into being shortly after its member states transitioned to democracy, while ASEAN has become progressively more complex in its scope as its member states have become more democratic. Conversely, those regions of the world that have witnessed the least success in terms of peacefully pursuing genuinely integrative trade-and-security programs – the Middle East and Africa – are also the regions with the least amount of experience with durable democratic regimes.

This correlation between democracy and peaceful integration likewise finds an intriguing degree of corroboration in previous historical periods. For instance, in the late 1700s the thirteen rebellious, democratized colonies of North America engaged in a successful integrative enterprise that was, first and foremost, a defensive reaction against the threat of the British, as well as against the potential threats posed by one another.[36] Going further back to the late Middle Ages, we see the Swiss cantons, which were the most democratized states of their time, engaged in a peaceful, long-term, negotiated integration process that was undertaken to augment their strength against the threat of the Hapsburg Empire.[37] As for the classical period, in that case we find the most notable democratic state – Athens – leading an integration-related enterprise known as the Delian League, which evolved into the Athenian Empire and through which Athens led roughly two hundred other city states in an effort to first consolidate control of the Aegean Sea region and then attempt to extend that control further west into the Mediterranean. Although there was much coercion involved in the Athenians' effort to sustain this project, there are also various indications that a key reason why so many of the member states were willing to remain peacefully within the Athenian structure was the fact that they endorsed Athens's commitment to democracy as a regime type.[38]

This general correlation between democracy and integration does seem logical. Democracies, after all, share compatible notions of political justice, insofar as every citizen in a democracy has the right to participate in political life and to do so – or attempt to do so, via election – at the highest level. Thus democratic regimes can combine their authority structures – entirely, if they so choose – without compromising their fundamental justice notions. Two democracies can integrate, in other words, without either state changing their essential rules regarding who is allowed to rule. Nondemocracies, on the other hand, often embody idiosyncratic notions of political justice, insofar as they allow only a person-specific subsection of the population – that is, one specific person, or a specific family, or a group of specific families or of specific nonrelated individuals – to rule. For instance, the theory of justice in Napoleon's France was that Napoleon, and no one else, should hold the position of supreme command.[39] Likewise in Tudor England, the theory of justice was that members of the House of Tudor, and no one else, should hold ultimate authority in the regime. As for examples of oligarchies – such as have characterized much of El Salvador's history, for instance – there too we typically find only certain specific people allowed to take part in the highest echelons of power wielding.[40]

This fundamental difference between democracies and nondemocracies calls to mind Leo Tolstoy's observation at the beginning of *Anna Karenina* that "happy families are all alike; every unhappy family is unhappy in its own way." The same might be said of states, if we assume that democracies are the most truly just and therefore the happiest of possible states, while nondemocracies are each flawed in their own way, insofar as they grant political authority to a unique, person-specific group. As a result of their idiosyncrasies, in turn, nondemocracies have far more difficulty than democracies when it comes to peacefully integrating with other states, since to blend the regime of a monarchy, or a dynasty, or an oligarchy with another regime would be to impinge upon the current rulers' exclusive rights of authority. And this is an outcome that the monarchic, dynastic, or oligarchic rulers are likely to resist, since the leaders of a regime tend to believe that the theory of political justice that informs their regime structure is in fact just.[41] Indeed, there are essentially two things that any regime must do in order to function as a regime: 1) it must wield coercive force – or at least make a partially effective attempt at such – so as to maintain order within the state, and 2) it must claim to represent true justice via its determination of who is allowed to partake of political authority. As Aristotle puts it in his *Politics*, the state is first brought into being for the sake of establishing an order that allows its inhabitants to secure the basic needs of life, but it continues in existence to secure the "good life," and central to the concept of the good life is the concept of justice.[42] Since democracies share the same fundamental notion of what constitutes justice and hence of what accords with the good life, they can combine their regimes without any of their regimes – and hence, fundamentally, any of their states – ceasing to survive. Nondemocracies, on the other hand, have differing notions of what the good life entails, and thus any integrative behaviour involving such states would typically need to remain limited to relatively low levels.

That said, there are certain circumstances that do facilitate peaceful integration between idiosyncratic nondemocracies, the most obvious being that of dynastic intermarriage, whereby two distinct ruling families become part of one extended family, thus allowing for authority over their respective states to become shared. For instance, one of history's great empire-building exercises was carried out by the Hapsburg dynasty, whose members were also the all-time masters of marrying well. Nonetheless, dynastic intermarriage is typically fraught with all sorts of complications, leading as often to state fragmentation and war – as occurred even with the Hapsburgs – as to consolidation. In addition to this, in the modern era the options for dynastic intermarriage among nondemocracies are greatly reduced due to a variety of factors. Not only are there relatively few such regimes remaining, but also some of these regimes are separated from each other by vast distances. Furthermore, some of their family cultures are so different as to seriously impinge upon any integrative attempts. For example, it is difficult to imagine a peaceful intermarriage involving the Kim dynasty in North Korea and the House of Saud in Saudi Arabia, although such an attempt would be fascinating to observe.[43]

The implication of all of this, therefore, is that over time North America and other highly democratized regions of the world may become more and more integrated while less democratized regions will be unable to follow suit. In such a scenario, democratized regions would experience increasing consolidation in terms of their economic and hence military power, they would be less preoccupied with interstate squabbles within their regions, and they would be better able to both defend themselves against and project military power towards states in other regions. In fact we need not wait for some far-off future for certain of these benefits to be reaped. Security pay-offs can already be observed, for instance, insofar as interstate wars between democracies in the modern era are exceptionally rare, and it is probably not a coincidence that democracies are also much better at peacefully integrating with each other in response to security threats – including threats that are posed by one another – than are nondemocracies when faced with threats posed by either democracies or other nondemocracies.[44]

If this assessment is accurate, furthermore, then certain cases of integration are also interesting to consider in light of the mixture of regime types within specific regions. The ASEAN case is of particular note in this regard, not only because of the growing importance of Asia in world affairs but also because of the mélange of regime types in that region and because of the relations that exist between the ASEAN states and important third parties, such as China. As mentioned, ASEAN was formed in the 1960s partially in response to the threat posed by China and its communist allies. In the 1970s, however, ASEAN took on the added role of serving as a coordinating mechanism for the member states in their efforts to resist Vietnamese power, at a time when North Vietnam was proceeding to assert control over South Vietnam while also establishing dominance over Laos and Cambodia.[45] These Vietnamese efforts at controlling neighbouring states, in turn, were driven in no small part by a desire to increase power vis-à-vis China. Ultimately, however, Vietnam evidently determined that it could best seek to compete against the Chinese by joining the ASEAN grouping.[46] The ASEAN states, in turn, recognized the benefits of adding not only Vietnam but also other Southeast Asian states to their organization, so as to better aggregate power vis-à-vis China, and thus expanded ASEAN's membership in the 1990s.[47] More recently, China's efforts to extend its power out into the Pacific Ocean and the South China Sea have seriously unsettled many of ASEAN's members, which therefore look primed for still further ASEAN-based integration in response. Yet it is also noteworthy that since the late 1990s China has sought to move closer and closer to the ASEAN bloc in terms of economic relations, to the point where it now has extensive trading arrangements with many of the ASEAN states; indeed, in 2010 a region-wide ASEAN-China FTA came into effect. Thus the question arises as to whether China's relations with the ASEAN states will serve to impede or intensify integration within the regional grouping. China's regime, after all, retains significant nondemocratic elements – as do certain ASEAN members – and this will presumably constitute a limiting factor for potential integration should China itself become a full participant in the group. On the other hand, India, Japan, and South Korea have also sought closer ties with ASEAN, and these relationships may potentially reinforce the democratic nature of the organization. It will therefore be interesting to see whether China ultimately is able to dominate ASEAN internally and hence prevent the project from becoming highly integrative, or whether the democratic trend within ASEAN will win out, thereby allowing for further integration among the member states and hence limiting the Chinese role within the grouping and perhaps within Asia more generally.

The possible future of the Asian region and of other incompletely democratized regions can also be considered from another angle, however, if we pair the hypothesis about a democracy/integration correlation with the observation that democracy as a regime type not only has spread across the globe but also is continuing to make inroads into underdemocratized areas. Indeed, as these words are being written, various nondemocratic regimes in the Arab world are being challenged by massive popular uprisings, at the same time as certain nondemocratic rulers in sub-Saharan Africa are likewise succumbing to the democratic tide, while in China the odds appear better than even that eventually that state's population will likewise demand a more democratized environment in which to fully realize its tremendous potential. This democratizing trend thus points to the possibility that security-driven, trade technique–using, peaceful interstate integration may someday occur in a thoroughgoing fashion in all of the world's regions. That, in turn, would mean that the current global arrangement – whereby many independent states interact within the context of global anarchy – might eventually be replaced by a world comprising only a handful of regional political groupings. Of course the dynamics of anarchy would continue to persist in such an environment, as the few regional-scale, state-like structures responded to their reciprocal senses of threat by engaging in still further security-driven integration among themselves. Initially they would do so to both oppose and control one another, but eventually they would seek solely to control each other once every region was highly integrated with every other. And thus all of this activity would ultimately point towards the creation of some sort of a global state structure; towards a type of universal political community; towards the cosmopolis.[48]

That is, admittedly, an outcome that any number of people might find unattractive, because such a fate might be assumed to be associated with the loss of unique cultural identities or with the end of other cherished aspects of the contemporary political order.[49] Yet the claim that specific cultural identities or anything else – aside from global anarchy – would inevitably end with the establishment of a global political structure is open to debate. Indeed, it is just as likely that, to paraphrase Winston Churchill, the establishment of such a structure would not be the end; it would not even be the beginning of the end; but it would be the end of the beginning. For example, the European integration process has been accompanied by a parallel phenomenon whereby various member states of the EU have begun to disaggregate into smaller, more culturally specific political units. We thus see Scotland asserting greater autonomy vis-à-vis the British parliament in London, and Catalonia asserting more autonomy vis-à-vis the Spanish regime in Madrid, while in Belgium the culturally Dutch north and the culturally French south appear to be disaggregating from each other. Such disaggregation is logical against the background of simultaneous European integration, because many of the European states were formed out of culturally heterogeneous parts, often as a means to enhance their strength vis-à-vis other states in the region. Yet now, thanks to European integration, the EU states pose far less of a threat to one another, and thus there is a less pressing security-based rationale for keeping these heterogeneous parts bundled together within the same states; hence a more permissive environment exists for subregions within states to press their claims for greater political autonomy. Nor is it contradictory for these more localized political units to seek greater autonomy from existing EU states' regimes while simultaneously remaining within the larger EU superstructure, since the necessarily thin cultural identity of the EU as a whole – which must be fashioned out of generalities that can be applied to all of the EU's culturally diverse parts – would seem to facilitate the assertion of these more localized political identities. In other words, Europe's political unification is allowing for the region's rich cultural diversity to become more politically reinforced. And this is a dynamic that might likewise apply to other integrating regions as well. For instance, if we carry this logic across the Atlantic, and if we anticipate that North American integration will continue moving forward, then the potential implications for that continent's many distinct subregions are interesting to consider.

Of course it remains to be seen exactly what the future will hold. For the time being, all that can be definitively determined is that in the seemingly least likely of cases – that of North America – security issues have played an important role in the free trade–creating process. Through that process, the continent's three states have progressed from viewing each other primarily as threats to viewing each other primarily as partners. In the case of the United States and Canada, we see that the bilateral relationship steadily improved over time, with the capstone to that trend put in place by the 1988 FTA – an FTA that resulted, in no small part, from a shared concern about the Soviet nuclear build-up in the Arctic. US-Mexican relations, in contrast, remained often fraught throughout much of these states' mutual history until the early 1990s, when the Mexican regime recognized that more could be gained by seeking to simultaneously control and to oppose the United States than by simply pursuing a policy of resistance. The result was NAFTA, which itself may yet prove to be just one more step in a long-term, complex, integrative endeavour.

To be sure, it is still entirely possible that North American integration may – as occurred in the European case – experience a protracted stasis, remaining essentially where it is for the next few decades. It may even experience integrative reversals. Current relations between the constituent regimes are by no means so cordial as to utterly negate this latter possibility. In addition to which, as previously noted, relations between the general populations of the three states continue to be at times uneasy, and at times quite strained. Canadians remain concerned about the cultural and economic influence of the United States; US citizens continue to be concerned about the cultural and economic impacts of Mexican immigration; and Mexican citizens remain concerned about the United States in general. Any extant US-Mexican wariness is then amplified by the extraordinary levels of drugs-related violence transpiring within Mexico and along the US-Mexico border. Furthermore, reactions to that violence by regimes – state and federal – on either side of the border have the potential to cause substantial damage to the US-Mexican bilateral relationship and thereby to possibly impede North America's overall integrative development.

And yet, even while acknowledging all of these challenges, it is necessary to recognize the following, fundamental point: in the wake of NAFTA's enactment, trilateral relations on the continent – at least between the three regimes – have improved substantially. Newer attempts, meanwhile, are being made to build upon NAFTA's foundation in order to extend the integrative impetus into other policy domains. In light of all of these initiatives, therefore, it currently appears implausible for war-scale violence to erupt between the United States and its two neighbours, despite the dangerous dynamics of these states' relational histories. Indeed, North America, long a theatre of contestation, is now a more peaceful enterprise.

List of Interviews

(Date Format: Year-Month-Day)

Allen, Richard	2006-3-30
Anderson, Martin	2004-10-21
Aspe, Pedro	2007-11-28
Baker, James	2004-12-9
Brock, William	2004-12-2
Burney, Derek	2007-9-28
Bush, George H.W.	2008-5-28
Carlsson, Ingvar	2006-10-12
Chalker, Lynda	2006-2-6
Dietrich-Genscher, Hans	2006-4-4
Dumas, Roland	2005-10-25
Hannay, David	2006-2-1
Legras, Guy	2006-3-3
Mosbacher, Robert	2004-12-13
Mulroney, Brian	2005-2-21
Renwick, Robin	2006-2-14
Rifkind, Malcolm	2006-2-9
Rutten, Charles	2006-3-14
Salinas, Carlos	2008-4-29, 2008-5-3
Serra Puche, Jaime	2005-2-4
Shultz, George	2005-5-12
Teltshik, Horst	2006-4-5
Trumpf, Juergen	2006-3-22
Williamson, David	2006-9-15
Weenink, W.H.	2006-3-15
Wellenstein, Edmund	2006-3-16

Chronologies of Important Events

Canadian-US Relations

1775:   The Thirteen Colonies send an army to invade Canada.

1794:   Tensions between the United States and UK/Canada rise due to a variety of factors, including the maintaining of British forts along the US-Canada border. The Jay Treaty is signed between the two sides to address these issues.

1800–10: Tensions between the United States and Britain nearly prompt the United States to invade Canada in retaliation.

1812–14: The War of 1812, during which the United States again invades Canada.

1814–17: A US-British naval arms race on the Great Lakes.

1817:   The US secretary of state, John Quincy Adams, launches an unsuccessful effort to establish a reciprocal trade agreement between the United States and the Canadians.

1820s: British plans to build a military road near the US-Canadian border increase tensions between the United States and the Canadians.

1823:   The United States puts forth its Monroe Doctrine, declaring the western hemisphere off-limits to further European colonization.

1830–40:   The "Caroline Affair," as well as a border dispute between New Brunswick and Maine and the "McLeod Incident," nearly lead to armed conflict between the United States and the Canadians.

1840s: Tensions rise between the United States and Britain over disputes regarding the northern border of the Oregon Territories, in response to which the British send warships to the Northern Pacific.

1852:   US-Canadian disputes regarding fishing rights prompt the British to send a naval force to the Gulf of St Lawrence, and likewise prompt the United States to send its own naval force to the coast of Nova Scotia.

1854:   A reciprocal trade agreement is established between the United States and Canada.

1860s: US-British tensions during the US Civil War put strain on US relations with Canada. Following the war, the United States expresses its continuing displeasure with Britain by abrogating the reciprocity treaty with Canada in 1866. Meanwhile, Canadian confederation takes place in part as a defensive reaction against the threat posed by the United States.

1869:   There is an unsuccessful attempt to re-establish reciprocal trade between the United States and Canada.

1874:   There is another unsuccessful attempt to re-establish reciprocal trade between the United States and Canada.

1888–91:   Disputes between the United States and Canada over seal hunting in the Bering Strait prompt the United Kingdom to send naval ships to the Bering Sea. At the same time, efforts are renewed to establish a trade deal between the United States and Canada, but without success.

1898:   Another effort is undertaken to establish reciprocal trade between the United States and Canada. The attempt is unsuccessful, but it is nonetheless highly significant, because it is championed by a Canadian regime that is seeking to partner with the United States in order to resist British power, rather than vice versa.

1911:   Another unsuccessful attempt to establish US-Canadian reciprocal trade.

1914–17:   During WWI, the United States and Canada fight as allies.

1920s: A period of worldwide high tariffs impedes any possibilities of reciprocal US-Canadian trade.

1931:   The Statute of Westminster gives Canada official control over its own foreign policy.

1935:   The Canadian-US Reciprocal Trade Agreement is established.

1938:   US president Franklin Roosevelt issues his Kingston Proclamation, in which he states that the United States will not stand idly by if Canada is threatened by another empire. In the same year, Canada agrees to another, preliminary treaty with the United States, in order to demonstrate willingness to explore the possibility of freer trade.

1940:   The United States and Canada sign the Ogdensburg Agreement, which establishes the Permanent Joint Board of Defense (PJBD).

1940–5:   Canada and the United States fight as allies in World War II.

1947–8:   The United States pushes, unsuccessfully, for an FTA with Canada.

1948:   US diplomats are sent to Ottawa to persuade the Canadians to agree to a further development of the defence arrangements under the Ogdensburg Agreement, in response to the threat posed by the Soviet Union.

1949:   The North Atlantic Treaty Organization (NATO) is established, of which both Canada and the United States are members.

1953:   The US secretary of defense promotes the idea of an FTA with Canada, but without success.

1954:   The Pine Tree network of radar stations, built just north of major Canadian population centres and operated jointly by the US and Canadian militaries, is completed.

1957:   Another radar station network, the Mid-Canada Line, is completed. That same year, work begins on the Distant Early Warning (DEW) System, comprising a string of radar stations along
Canada's northern coast.

1958:   Canada and the United States establish the North American Air
Defense Command (NORAD).

1959:   The stationing of US nuclear weapons in Canada causes a public outcry.

1965:   The Canadian-US Auto Pact is established.

1960s: The development of intercontinental ballistic missile (ICBM)
technology renders the strategic utility of US-Canadian military
coordination less relevant. US-Canadian relations simultaneously enter a more general period of strain.

Early 1970s: Key breakthroughs occur in the development of cruise missile
technology.

**Late 1970s
through
mid-1980s:**   The advent of cruise missile technology prompts the United
States and the USSR to begin an Arctic arms race. This leads to
greatly enhanced military relations between the United States
and Canada.

1980:   The United States promotes the idea of the North American
Accord. Canada resists the initiative.

1983:   The United States and Canada return to exploratory talks
regarding an FTA. Eventually the negotiations stall.

1984:   FTA negotiations resume.

1985:   At the Shamrock Summit, the United States and Canada agree
to greatly enhance their military relations and to launch a negotiating process for an FTA.

1987:   The United States and Canada arrive at mutually acceptable terms for the FTA.

1988:   The Canadian-US FTA (CUFTA) officially comes into being.

1994:   The North American Free Trade Agreement (NAFTA) officially comes into being.

US-Mexican Relations

1770s: Spain supports the Thirteen Colonies in their war against Britain.

1803:   The United States acquires the Louisiana Territory.

1819:   The United States acquires Florida.

1821:   Mexico revolts against Spain.

1823:   The United States puts forth its Monroe Doctrine, declaring the western hemisphere off-limits to further European colonization.

1824:   Mexico emerges as an independent state, with a federal republican structure somewhat akin to the US political structure.

Late 1820s and early 1830s: Spain tries unsuccessfully to retake Mexico by force. Mexico allies itself with Britain, via a trade agreement. The United States, concerned about a Mexican-British alliance, employs various means to try to rupture Mexican-British relations, including a failed attempt to establish a trade agreement with Mexico.

1833:   Mexican general Santa Anna assumes control of the Mexican regime.

1830s: The United States and Mexico ratify a trade agreement, but then relations between the two states deteriorate rapidly due to issues pertaining to Texas.

1835–6:   Texas revolts from Mexico and emerges as an independent state. Texas then begins to establish close relations with the British, which alarms the United States.

1845:   The United States agrees to the accession of Texas as a US state, which in turn displeases the Mexicans.

1846–8:   The Mexican-American War takes place. Via its victory in this war, the United States acquires territory stretching to the Pacific Ocean.

Late 1850s: Civil war breaks out in Mexico. France supports the ruling Mexican regime, while the United States supports the Mexican rebel forces.

1859–60:   US president James Buchanan unsuccessfully seeks permission from the US Congress to invade Mexico to prevent French consolidation. Buchanan likewise seeks a commercial treaty with Mexican anti-regime forces, but similarly without success.

1861:   The United States descends into its Civil War. France, Britain, and Spain invade Mexico, although Britain and Spain quickly abandon the effort.

1863:   French forces complete the conquest of Mexico.

1866:   The civil war in the United States draws to a close, allowing the US regime to send further supplies to the Mexican rebel forces. At the same time, France begins pulling some of its forces in Mexico back to France, to prepare for the coming military contest with Germany.

1867:   French forces in Mexico are overrun. A new republican regime is established in Mexico City.

1871:   The state of Germany is consolidated in its modern form.

1876:   Porfirio Díaz overthrows the republican regime in Mexico.

1880s: The United States pushes unsuccessfully for a commercial agreement with Mexico, while Mexico pursues a commercial agreement with Germany.

**Late 1880s
to early 1890s:**   The United States pushes for reciprocity agreements with various Latin American states.

1898:   The Spanish-American War transpires, via which the United States acquires the territory of Puerto Rico and de facto dominance over Cuba.

1904:   US president Theodore Roosevelt issues his Corollary to the Monroe Doctrine, as a warning to European states – and to Germany in particular – not to interfere in the western hemisphere.

**First decade
of the 1900s:**   The United States implements "dollar diplomacy," which promotes the increase of US commercial activity with Latin American states, including Mexico.

1910–14:   The Mexican Revolution transpires, prompted in part by US dominance of the Mexican economy.

1916:   The US military enters Mexico in pursuit of the Mexican national Pancho Villa. Meanwhile, Mexico contacts the German regime, seeking closer Mexican-German relations.

1917:   The Zimmerman telegram comes to light, indicating German interest in an anti-US alliance with Mexico. All US troops are removed from Mexico. The United States declares war against Germany.

1920s: US-Mexican relations enter a period of strain due to competing agendas in Nicaragua.

1930s: US-Mexican relations improve as a result of the United States' Good Neighbor Policy. In conjunction with this Policy, the United States also promotes liberalized trade agreements with Latin American states.

1938:   Mexico nationalizes its oil industry.

1941:   The United States and Mexico agree to the terms of a reciprocal trade agreement. The United States enters World War II against Germany.

1942:   Mexico declares war against the Axis powers.

1941–5:   During WWII, US reciprocity agreements with Latin American states are suspended. Immediately following the war, Mexico repudiates its reciprocity treaty with the United States.

1951:   A regime takes power in Guatemala that is suspected by the United States of having communist sympathies.

1954:   The United States helps facilitate the overthrow of the Guatemalan regime.

1959:   Fidel Castro comes to power in Cuba.

1961:   The US-backed Bay of Pigs invasion in Cuba takes place.

1962:   The Cuban missile crisis occurs.

1960s–80s: Mexico establishes a diplomatic middle ground between the United States and the USSR, as demonstrated most pointedly via its partial support of the Castro regime in Cuba.

Late 1970s: Large oil discoveries are made in Mexico.

1980:   US president Ronald Reagan visits Mexico, promoting his idea of a North American Accord. The Mexicans resist the idea.

Early 1980s: Mexico enters a period of deep economic crisis.

1984:   The Mexican peso goes into free fall.

1986:   Mexico decides to join the General Agreement on Tariffs and Trade (GATT). The United States and Mexico agree to institute the Baker Plan, which pertains to rescheduling Mexico's foreign debt. This is then followed by the US-Mexican Framework of Principles for Consultation Regarding Trade and Investment Relations.

1988:   US president-elect George H.W. Bush proposes to Mexican president-elect Carlos Salinas that their two states pursue an FTA. Salinas replies by saying that he first wants to focus on restricting Mexico's debt.

1989:   The United States and Mexico sign the Understanding Regarding Trade and Investment Facilitation Talks. The Berlin Wall falls in Germany. The United States invades Panama. Debt reduction negotiations between the United States and Mexico are completed. The United States reiterates its idea for a US-Mexican FTA, to which Mexico responds by suggesting the exploration of sector-based trade agreements.

1990:   President George H.W. Bush promotes his Enterprise for the Americas Initiative (EAI). President Salinas travels to Europe and seeks European leaders' endorsement of a strong trading relationship with Mexico, in order to offset Mexico's trade relationship with the United States. European leaders inform Salinas that, if he wants a trade agreement with European states, Mexico will first need to establish a comprehensive FTA with the United States. Salinas starts negotiations with the United States for an FTA.

1994:   NAFTA comes into being.

Notes

1. Core Concepts

1 A sampling of analyses of the US-Canadian FTA includes Doern and Tomlin (1992); Bognanno and Ready (1993); Hart, with Dymond and Robertson (1994); Barry, Dickerson, and Gaisford (1995); Orme (1996); Coffey, Dods, Lazcano, and Riley (1999); Cameron and Tomlin (2000); and Thompson and Randall (2002). Analyses of the decision to create NAFTA can be found in Bognanno and Ready (1993); Garber (1993); Barry, Dickerson, and Gaisford (1995); Grayson (1995); Orme (1996); Mayer (1998); Coffey, Dods, Lazcano, and Riley (1999); Cameron and Tomlin (2000); Robert Pastor (2001); and Clarkson (2008).

2 As Doern and Tomlin argue, "In the second half of 1980, the US economy quietly entered a downward spiral into an economic collapse on a scale not experienced since the Great Depression of the 1930s ... The economic crisis also unleashed forces that would transform Canada's relationship with the United States, leading to a free trade pact between the two countries" (1992, 15).

3 Ibid., (33).

4 Hart, Dymond, and Robertson (1994, 15).

5 Ibid. (14–15).

6 See, for instance, Inwood (2004), as well as Doern and Tomlin (1992).

7 Robert Lawrence, "International Competition and the Evolution of a North American Free Trade Area," in Bognanno and Ready (1993, 151–2).

8 Cameron and Tomlin (2000, 56–7).

9 Ibid. (58–9). Cameron and Tomlin employ a relatively detailed interstate negotiating model, which is similar to models used to analyse free trade in the context of European integration. As they explain, "We argue that the

NAFTA negotiations were critically shaped by three factors: (1) asymmetries of power between the three states [with "power" understood as "market power"]; (2) sharply contrasting domestic political institutions; and (3) differences in the nonagreement alternatives, patience, and risk orientations of the heads of government and their chief negotiators" (2000, 15). Essentially, what this means is that the state with the strongest bargaining position – based upon its market size, decentralization of domestic authority, and range of trading alternatives – will obtain results from a trade negotiation that most closely approximate its negotiating goal.

10 Ibid. (59–63).

11 Mexico under President Carlos Salinas "originally sought a trade pact with Washington because it needed foreign investment, and there were limits to what Mexico could accomplish on its own. Mexico had already given investors the three things they need most: political stability, a growing market, and predictable, intelligently managed macroeconomic policies. But it could not unilaterally guarantee access to the US market, or even the long term survival of Salinas's economic reforms. NAFTA did both" (Orme 1996, xix).

12 Cameron and Tomlin (2000, 5–6).

13 See, for instance, Mayer (1998) and Cameron and Tomlin (2000). More generally, with regard to issue linkage in the context of North American integration, see Clarkson (2002).

14 A partial exception to this general categorization is provided by Clarkson and Mildenberger (2011), who consider ways in which relations with Canada and Mexico serve to extend US security-seeking capacity.

15 Gruber (2000, 7).

16 Ibid. (132).

17 This trend in NAFTA scholarship is one expression of the larger trend in international relations scholarship in which IR realists focus on states' military relations and IR liberals focus on states' economic relations. The realist tendency was set in place by Hans Morgenthau, with his foundational tome *Politics among Nations* ([1948] 1985), and carried forward by subsequent realists such as Waltz (1979) and Mearsheimer (2001). On the liberal side, a predominant focus on economic issues was inaugurated by scholars of European integration such as Haas (1958 and 1964) and Lindberg (1963), and then carried forward by others such as Keohane and Nye (1979) and Moravcsik (1998). The result is that, while various IR scholars have sought to combine the examination of states' security and economic policies into one analytical framework, the "hegemonic" character of the two main IR

theory schools has resulted in a continuing bifurcation of the discipline, with one consequence being that phenomena such as NAFTA end up being analysed primarily by scholars who are focused on issues of economics.

18 Waltz (1979, 192).

19 As Walt notes, "All else being equal, the greater a state's total resources (e.g., population, industrial and military capability, and technological prowess), the greater a potential threat it can pose to others" (1987, 22).

20 Ibid. (5).

21 Waltz, championing the position known as "defensive realism," argues that states will seek a limited amount of power, which will result in a rough balance, whereas Mearsheimer, the most notable proponent of "offensive realism," suggests that states will seek to obtain as much power as they possibly can. Both of these realist positions fall under the rubric of structural – or "neo-" – realism, as opposed to the classical realist position promoted by Morgenthau, in which states are presumed to seek power simply because they are run by human beings, who are understood as innately power-driven.

22 This approach has a certain – though not complete – resemblance to a balance of power strategy. In addition to Waltz, recent treatment of the topic can be found in Vasquez and Elman (2003), and Kaufman, Little, and Wohlforth (2007). Much contemporary IR theorizing regarding state relations within global anarchy, and hence regarding balance of power strategies, rests, in turn, upon the models of anarchy-induced, security-seeking behaviour articulated in the early modern contract theories of Thomas Hobbes, John Locke, Jean-Jacques Rousseau, Emmanuel Kant, and so forth.

23 This approach has a certain though not complete resemblance to a bandwagoning strategy. There are multiple ways to think about the concept of bandwagoning. The most typical way is to think of it in a passive sense – namely, of the weaker state simply allying itself with the strength of the more powerful state. Mearsheimer formulates this strategy – as it applies to wartime – as follows: "With bandwagoning, the threatened state abandons hope of preventing the aggressor from gaining power at its expense and instead joins forces with its dangerous foe to get at least some small portion of the spoils of war" (2001, 139). The other way to conceive of bandwagoning is to think of it in a more active sense – namely, as an attempt to not only ally with a stronger state but also influence the stronger state's behaviour. Mearsheimer refers to all such proactive bandwagoning strategies as "appeasement." He writes, "Appeasement is a more ambitious strategy. The appeaser aims to modify the behavior of the aggressor

by conceding it power, in the hope that this gesture will make the aggressor feel more secure, thus dampening or eliminating its motive for aggression" (ibid). For still further treatment of the topic, see Schweller (1994, 72–107).

24 The typical IR term for a noninstitutionalized arrangement between states is "regime." However, because the term "regime" is also used to refer to the governing structure of a state – which is highly institutionalized – the term "regime" is introduced into the main text of this work only in order to denote the second meaning.

25 In addition to the integration scholars noted earlier, the most prominent examples of scholarship that is focused on how regimes and institutions can facilitate cooperation include Krasner (1983); Keohane (1984); Lipson (1984); Snidal (1985); Oye (1986); Kupchan and Kupchan (1991); Martin (1992); Yarbrough and Yarbrough (1992); and Milner (1997).

26 This idea of voice opportunities is treated, most notably, in Grieco (1995, 1996). It is indicative of the current state of IR scholarship that Grieco's analysis became a prime target of other scholars' efforts to discredit attempts to combine security and economic analyses. In this regard, see Legro and Moravcsik (1999).

27 One reason IR realists tend to downplay the importance of economic relations between states is the assumption that, when faced with serious security threats, states will pay less heed to their economic relationships with each other and hence cannot be counted on to abide by their agreements; indeed, states often have an incentive to defect from trade agreements. This assumption rests on the classic game-theory models of actor interaction, in which the costs for actor A are much higher for maintaining an agreement with actor B if actor B defects from the agreement, than if actor A and B both defect. As such, both actors are motivated to defect and thus the agreement falls through. However, such models are easily rendered void if the costs for actor A of not cooperating with actor B are higher than the costs for actor A of cooperating even if actor B defects, which is the assumption on which this present argument rests. Some of the earliest scholarly work done on tracing out these cooperation-inducing logics is the most useful. Axelrod (1984) is a seminal text in this regard. See also Oye (1986); Snidal (1991); and Powell (1991).

28 A nation may lack a state, while states may have only a very thin sense of nationhood associated with them. Conversely, there may be a very tight connection between a state and a nation.

29 This is another reason why in-depth cooperation/integration is presumed to be possible, despite realists' claims of states' wariness towards

one another – namely, the slow, evolutionary growth of cooperation/ integration, where each step leads to a further solidifying of the relationship.

30 One formulation of how a trading-to-oppose policy might function – and one that shares certain similarities with the ideas developed here – is supplied by Rosato (2006). Whereas Rosato focuses on European integration, however, the primary focus here is on North American integration. Furthermore, whereas Rosato argues that it is only the threat of being conquered, and hence of ceasing to exist as an independent state, that will prompt states to accept a certain degree of economic and military integration, I do not accept that limiting claim.

31 Grieco (1995, 1996).

32 The case study methodology used in this analysis is of a qualitative as opposed to quantitative nature. With regard to the testing of theories and hypotheses via qualitative case studies, this present analysis draws particularly upon George and Bennett (2005).

33 As George and Bennett point out, the observable implications of a theory, once established, constitute its predictive capacity (2005,178). See also King, Keohane, and Verba (1994, 28–9).

34 To conduct this examination I employ a process-tracing methodology. A process trace is an explicit account of how one part of the theory's explanation is connected to the next part of the explanation. As George and Bennett explain, process tracing is a method of detailed explanation that links all the observable implications of the theory to one another (2005, 207). There are various approaches to process tracing, some more specific and some more general. A process trace, for instance, can simply function as a detailed narrative, linking a series of events together without explicit reference to a theory, or even a causal hypothesis. Another type of process trace is what George and Bennett label an "analytic explanation," which "converts a historical narrative into an *analytical* causal explanation couched in explicit theoretical forms" (ibid., 210–11). In this case, the narrative is approached with a specific theory in mind, and the variables to be examined are specified and explained in terms of their place in the causal chain. This approach differs from the pure narrative approach not only by its explicit use of theory but also by its more selective use of facts, focusing as it does on the most relevant details of the case, rather than on telling a fully detailed story. The process-tracing method used in the present argument is of the more theory focused, analytical type, although with less emphasis on variable interplay and more on the underlying logic of key assumptions.

35 The factual material for this analysis is gleaned from multiple sources.
I draw, of course, from extant scholarship of the two North American
cases. This scholarship is both specific to the creation of the two FTAs and
more general insofar as it applies to the history of either the US-Canadian
relationship or the US-Mexican relationship. Although much of this material disregards the interconnections between trade and security policy,
it provides a vast amount of basic factual data – such as when decisions
were made and so forth – that is useful for this project. I likewise utilize
data gleaned from multiple archives, including the National Archives of
Canada, the National Archives of Mexico, the US National Security Archives, the Netherlands Foreign Ministry Archives, and the archives of the
Presidential Libraries of Ronald Reagan and George H.W. Bush. Here too,
much of the material is useful in terms of providing basic facts relevant to
decision-making processes. At the same time, some very valuable docu-
ments exist in these archives that offer statesmen's security rationales
for establishing FTAs. To reinforce this textual research, I also conducted
interviews with individuals who played key roles in the creation of the
FTAs examined in this book. In all, I conducted twenty-six such interviews
between 2004 and 2009. I sought in each instance to interview those individuals who were most closely associated with the key decision-making
processes under analysis. Furthermore, I sought out individuals who
would, presumably, be particularly disposed to offer evidence that would
run counter to my thesis: in particular, individuals with economics-focused
jobs – commerce secretaries, for instance – and/or bureaucratic actors –
civil servants, for instance – who would potentially be most interested in
the nuts-and-bolts details of a trade agreement and thus would be perhaps
less inclined to support a reading of events that focuses on long-term patterns of security-seeking behaviour.

2. CUFTA

1 Orchard (1993, 15–18).
2 For more on this topic, see Carroll and Ashworth (1948, 162–4, 194, 237–9).
3 Malone (1974, 426–8, 482, 576).
4 Thompson and Randall (2002, 19–21).
5 Brant (1941, 18).
6 Bemis (1949, 229–35). It is also interesting to note, along these same lines,
that the original capital of the combined provinces of Canada was Kingston, Ontario, but this location was ultimately considered too vulnerable to
US attack, situated as it was on the shores of Lake Ontario, across

from Sacket's Harbour, where some of the 1812 naval engagements transpired.

7 Setser (1937, 2).

8 Bemis (1949, 299).

9 Ibid. (457–9). Parsons (1998) also notes that Adams wanted to annex Canada as well as Spain's North American territories, but he did not want to acquire them through conquest (137–8).

10 Bemis (1949, 298).

11 For more on the military road issue, see H. Jones (1977, 10–19). Regarding the other three instances, the first was the "Caroline Affair" of 1837 (ibid., 20–32). The second instance involved disputes between New Brunswick and Maine over their shared border, shortly after the Caroline Affair was settled (ibid., 33–43). The third near-war situation grew out of the "McLeod Incident" in 1840 (ibid., 48–68).

12 H. Jones (1990, 203–17).

13 The Oregon region had been jointly occupied by the United States and Britain, as had been agreed upon in the treaty of 1818 (Bergeron 1987, 114). The dispute over the Oregon border helped fuel the well-known "54-40 or Fight" movement in the United States, which in turn prompted the Canadian regime to move more rapidly to include British Columbia in the Canadian federation and also to build the east-west national railway.

14 Ibid. (113–28). Even after the agreement, however, differing interpretations persisted regarding the location of the western US-Canada border, giving rise to various tense episodes, the most notable being the rather comic stand-off between the two sides known as the "Pig War" in 1859.

15 Scarry (2001, 208).

16 Ibid. (208–9).

17 Gara (1991, 140).

18 Ibid. (xii, 131–3).

19 Dowty (1971, 41).

20 Gara (1991, 133).

21 Morton (1983, 44–6).

22 Orchard (1993, 45).

23 Thompson and Randall (2002, 37).

24 Nevins (1957, 412). For Prime Minister Sir John A. Macdonald's fears, see, for instance, his speech in favor of the Washington Treaty, in Thomson (1960, 137).

25 Nevins (1957, 249–50).

26 Ibid. (413). Nonetheless, a general conference dealing with an array of outstanding issues between the United States, Canada, and Britain was

held in Washington in 1871. Given Canada's fears of conflict with the United States, and the United States' fears of conflict with Britain while US efforts against Spanish holdings in the Caribbean were underway, and with Britain concerned about rising tensions in the Black Sea region and thus a potentially renewed war against Russia, and hence wishing to avoid a simultaneous war against the United States, a wide-ranging settlement was able to be achieved, thereby reducing tensions temporarily between the United States and its northern neighbour.

27 Thomson (1960, 188–207).

28 In 1888 tensions between the United States and Canada-Britain flared when American fisherman began plying the waters along the Canadian coast, in response to which British naval vessels began seizing American ships. This occurred following the US abrogation of the Washington Treaty agreements of 1871 (Nevins 1932, 404–5). The situation looked poised to lead to a military confrontation, although British troubles with Russia were still prominent, while in its western territories Canada was facing a rebellion (Creighton 1998, 418–22). As such, Canada and Britain were eager to avoid a military confrontation with the United States at this time. Even if military engagements did not immediately break out, however, it was clear that this issue would lead to perpetual US-Canadian hostility and thus insecurity for both sides so long as it remained unsettled (ibid., 407, 477).

29 Socolofsky and Spetter (1987, 136–9).

30 See Creighton (1998, 547), regarding Canadian fears about reciprocity, and Creighton (1998, 531), regarding Blaine.

31 Crapol (2000). See, for instance, p. 53.

32 Other relevant factors relating to the attempted trade deal include the fact that the late 1880s were a period of economic depression in Canada, and amid the financial strain voices began being heard once again in Canadian business circles calling for free trade with the United States, as an economic palliative. In the United States, the chairman of the Senate Foreign Affairs Committee, John Sherman, sponsored a bill for commercial union with Canada, stating explicitly that the ultimate goal of such a bill would be to bring Canada into the United States in an eventual and complete union (Orchard 1993, 74). In Canada, however, prime minister Sir John A. Macdonald resisted the free trade treaty with the United States for precisely this reason, fearing, as he put it, "the inevitable toboggan slide towards annexation ... which would be created by any system of continental commercial union" (ibid., 75). His point was voiced by other Canadian political leaders as well, and, after calling an election of the issue in 1891, Macdonald won his point and the free trade effort went down in defeat.

33 Schull (1966, 30–5, 203, 217, 237).
34 Ibid. (356–7). For Laurier's resistance to the idea of joining the Boer War, see pp. 378, 392, 407.
35 Despite his resistance, Laurier did eventually agree to dispatch troops to the Boer War: a total of 8,300, with 242 killed in action. See Morton (1999, 113–18).
36 See Schull (1966, 212–13, 347), regarding British prime minister Joseph Chamberlain's desire for an imperial zollverein. Chamberlain saw precisely what a threat Laurier's proposal would be to British-Canadian relations (212). See p. 216 with regard to Laurier's wish to keep the political implications of the treaty quiet and to publicly focus instead on the economic rationale.
37 Ibid. (207, 213).
38 Dobson (1988, 31).
39 Schull (1966, 372). Regarding the Alaskan boundary question, see Orchard (1993, 82). This caused Laurier to remain wary of the United States, even as he subsequently sought closer relations. See Schull (1966, 433, 457).
40 Ibid. (481).
41 Ibid. (481, 489, 494, 496).
42 Ibid. (530).
43 Ibid. (521–3).
44 Ibid. (533). Arguments that suggest that Laurier had electoral motivations for pushing free trade, so as to gain the prairie and maritime states, are problematic since these areas were lightly populated. At the same time, there were some notable economic interests arrayed against reciprocity, because Canada was doing fairly well at this time economically; indeed, it was doing better than the United States. Ultimately, Laurier won only the sparsely populated territories of Alberta, Saskatchewan, and – just barely – the maritime territories.
45 Coletta (1973, 151). When Taft sent his message to the Senate asking for its support of reciprocity, he pointed out that Britain and Canada are "coming to a parting of the ways," and that this bill would help facilitate that dynamic (ibid., 144). In response to such statements, Laurier sent Taft a message warning against "creating any impression that there is a political significance in this treaty. My political opponents are trying to make that an issue" (ibid., 151). Laurier was not helped therefore when Taft's reciprocity-championing partner in the Senate, Champ Clarke, declared that through this bill, he hoped to one day see the American flag flying over all of British North America (ibid., 147).
46 Anderson (1973, 139).

47 Ibid. (136).
48 Ibid. (137).
49 This is not to suggest that concern over the British threat disappeared alto-gether following the first decade of the twentieth century. In the 1920s, for instance, the US War Department drafted a plan for an unlikely yet poten-tial war against Britain, premised on the notion of an outbreak of hostilities that would occur in response to competing trade practices. The plan, like others before it pertaining to the British menace, entailed a US invasion of Canada, so as to pre-empt a British invasion of the United States via Cana-dian territory. See Carlson (2005).
50 Morton (1999, 176).
51 Hull (1948, 528–30). Hull says he had a long talk with Mackenzie King, who understood Hull's reasoning thoroughly (528).
52 Orchard (1993, 94).
53 Ibid.
54 Mahant and Mount (1999, 17).
55 Ibid. (18).
56 Ibid.
57 Ibid.
58 Ibid. (31).
59 Ibid. (20). For more information on related topics, see Sokolsky (1989, 3) and Mahant and Mount (1999, 18). See also Maloney (2007, 4–5).
60 Mahant and Mount (1999, 19).
61 Thompson and Randall (2002, 197–8). See also Maloney (2007, 23–5).
62 Pearson (1973, 46).
63 Thompson and Randall (2002, 199). The level of integration is attested to by the fact that, during the Cuban Missile Crisis, NORAD went to DEF-CON 3, and thus Canadian forces were put on nuclear readiness, without the Canadian PM being consulted first (ibid., 224). For another perspective on this history, see Hayden (1993).
64 In 1949, US-Canadian negotiations were undertaken regarding the US use of the military base at Goose Bay, Labrador, in response to a controversy arising over the stationing of nuclear weapons at the base. Once again, these talks were headed by Nitze. The talks lasted through 1950, thereby giving Nitze a busy year, since it was also in 1950 that NSC-68 – the famous National Security Council document that outlined America's hard-line approach towards the Soviet Union, of which Nitze was the author – was drafted and became official US policy (Mahant and Mount 1999, 20–1).
65 Thompson and Randall (2002, 202).

66 Mahant and Mount (1999, 170). It is interesting to note that, while the Canadians resisted in-depth economic integration with the United States at this time, it had been the United States that put up some resistance to Canada's insistence on including Article II – pertaining to economic relations – in the NATO treaty. The US regime was apparently sceptical about securing Senate approval for a treaty that included further economic support for the Europeans. It is also possible that the United States did not want to promote an arrangement that would facilitate closer Canadian-European trade relations, given the long history of the United States seeking to prevent such. On US resistance to Article II, see Pearson (1973, 55–8).

67 Thompson and Randall (2002, 210).

68 Maloney (2007, 232–94).

69 Instead, attention was now devoted to hardening the silos of the US retaliatory missile force and to the detection of missile launchings by the Soviets, the detection of which did not require the same degree of surveillance equipment as had been put in place to detect Soviet airplanes flying into Canadian airspace (Gellner 1986, 50). This ICBM-based change in the strategic situation was predicted by O.M. Solandt, the chairman of Canada's Defense Research Board, as early as the mid-1950s (Maloney 2007, 62–3).

70 Despite this holding pattern, however, one further attempt at liberalized US-Canadian trade was made between the 1960s and the late 1970s. This was the Agreement Governing Trade in Automotive Products – the "Autopact" – which was signed by President Lyndon Johnson and Prime Minister Lester Pearson in 1964. This agreement is often considered to be an important step towards the establishment of free trade between the two states in the 1980s, although its movement in this direction was fairly modest. Despite this modesty, however, and despite the seemingly innocuous nature of the agreement – insofar as security issues were concerned – the Autopact had its roots in a security rationale. In this case, President Johnson had agreed to the deal in no small part out of a desire to pay his political debts. This debt stemmed from Canadian assistance to the United States during the crisis in Cyprus in 1964. During the height of the crisis – when NATO allies Greece and Turkey nearly went to war against each other over control of the island – Canada was one of the few states to send a significant number of peacekeeping troops to help prevent the outbreak of full-scale violence. Johnson, who recognized that the Autopact was a bad deal from the US angle, gave Prime Minister Pearson a gift in the form of the Autopact in response to Pearson's Cyprus assistance (Thompson and Randall 2002, 232). The Autopact, it should be pointed out, represents a form of managed trade, as opposed to sectoral free trade.

71 Reisman (1984, 43).
72 Ibid. (45).
73 Reisman (1985, 3).
74 Reisman (1984, 51).
75 Reisman (1985, 23–4).
76 Jockel and Sokolsky (1986, 4). To be fair, Trudeau's policies were in part a reaction to President Richard Nixon's decision in 1971 to unilaterally impose a surcharge on all foreign imports (Clarkson 2002, 5).
77 For more on Trudeau's foreign policy, see Granatstein and Bothwel (1991).
78 Werrell (1985, 7–43).
79 Ibid. (225).
80 Ibid.
81 Ibid.
82 Ibid.
83 Ibid. (171).
84 On the history and qualities of the cruise missile, see also Fleeman (2001) and Huisken (1981).
85 Purver (1986, 34).
86 Sokolsky (1989, 8).
87 Young (1985–6, 165).
88 Byers and Slack (1986, 10).
89 Jockel and Sokolsky (1986, 72).
90 Young (1985–6, 167).
91 Sokolsky (1989, 13).
92 Young (1985–6, 167).
93 Sokolsky (1989, 31).
94 Honderich (1985). Another type of interceptor system that was envisioned was one that would impact a Soviet ICBM at a very early phase of the ICBM's trajectory. Known as Excalibur, this involved an x-ray laser that would destroy the missiles soon after their launch. Yet in order to be feasible – if that were even possible – Excalibur would need to be stationed close to the Soviet border, and, given various problems that would arise from using Excalibur from a submarine, the most logical place to put it, once again, was in the Canadian Arctic. Arctic basing, furthermore, would be more defensible against attack than would space-basing, so for this reason as well Canadian territory was critical. As yet another example: the famous and ill-fated MX missile system also played into this Arctic focus, because its basing requirements – involving vast, open tracts of territory, around which the missiles could frequently be moved – were best met in the northern Canadian landscape.

95 Ibid. (30).

96 Further fuel was added to the fire of this debate via statements made around this time by US secretary of defense Caspar Weinberger, as well as by the perennially present Paul Nitze, during their visits to Canada, when they speculated on future linkages between SDI and the Canadian-based anti-Soviet warning systems (Byers and Slack 1986, 12). On the internal debates within the Canadian administration, see Mulroney (2007, 349–54).

97 This defence white paper stood in stark contrast to the defence white paper issued by Trudeau in 1971, in which Trudeau expressed his intent to establish greater independence from US dominance on security issues, although the degree to which Trudeau was then fully able to act upon the points made in the white paper was much less clear-cut. For more on comparing the two white papers, see Bland (1997).

98 Sokolsky (1989, 15).

99 Ibid. (15–16).

100 Ibid. (16).

101 Reagan (1979).

102 C. Jones (1980).

103 Weisman (1981).

104 Martin Anderson (pers. comm.). Furthermore, according to Orme, Sears viewed an economically unified North America as "a colossus" that would be resistant to subversion from the south and to commercial assaults from the east and west (1996, 35).

105 George Shultz (pers. comm.).

106 Richard Allen (pers. comm.). It is also interesting to note a connection between these Reagan advisors – Anderson, Shultz, and Allen – on the one hand, and Paul Nitze, the man responsible for the free trade negotiations in the 1940s. Nitze subsequently went on to establish, in the 1970s, a group called the Committee for the Present Danger (CPD), which advocated an end to MAD by seeking to give the United States a military advantage over the Soviet Union. Key components of the CPD's policy suggestions included North American defence, as well as various other ideas that found their way into the SDI program. When Ronald Reagan became president, forty members of his foreign policy staff were members of the CPD, including Anderson, Shultz, Allen, and Reagan himself. For more on the CPD, see FitzGerald (2000).

107 William Brock (pers. comm.).

108 George Shultz (pers. comm.).

109 Ibid. Also, Doern and Tomlin (1992, 21–2).

110 "Canada's New Prime Minister Woos Reagan" (1984). For further detail on this meeting, see Mulroney (2007, 289).
111 Mulroney (2007, 326–8).
112 "US Conducts Second Cruise Missile Test over Canada" (1985). These tests were part of a larger series of tests, agreed to by the Trudeau administration in 1982, in the context of US-Canadian negotiations for responding to the new threat posed by Soviet cruise missiles.
113 See, for instance, McDonald (1985) and Wren (1985).
114 Doern and Tomlin (1992, 26).
115 Cameron and Tomlin (2000, 47–8).
116 "Shamrock Summit" (2000).
117 Mulroney (pers. comm.). See also Mulroney (2007, 228–31).
118 Ibid.
119 Mulroney (2000, 574).
120 Derek Burney (pers. comm.). On Burney's appointment, see Mulroney (2007, 266).
121 On this point, see Mulroney (2007, 336–8).
122 Burney (pers. comm.).
123 See Inwood (2004).
124 Burney (pers. comm.).
125 Reagan (1988).
126 Reagan (1979).

3. NAFTA

1 Meyer and Sherman (1995, 315–16).
2 Ibid. (322–5). In 1829 Spain tried to retake Mexico by force, but was repelled by the Mexicans, led by Santa Anna (ibid., 320–1).
3 On Jackson's motivations regarding Texas and the commercial treaty with Mexico, see Remini (1981, 202, 218–20, 289–90; 1984, 197, 352–6).
4 Meyer and Sherman (1995, 335–6).
5 See, for instance, James (1938, 705, 716). See also Wilson (1984, 151).
6 See James (1938, 762, 764–5) regarding Houston's acting for Texas's security.
7 US president John Tyler, fearing the establishment of a British hold on Texas, sent a treaty to Congress for the annexation of Texas, but Congress, divided by sectional rivalries, refused to ratify it (Peterson 1989, 194–5). In response, Houston added further vigour to his courtship of Britain. At this point, former US president Andrew Jackson became extremely concerned. Jackson feared not only the prospect of British control of

Canada and Texas but also the prospect of Britain attempting to connect up its Texas and Oregon territories, thereby forming "an iron hoop about us." The United States, he declared, would "burst asunder that iron hoop though it cost oceans of blood and millions of money" (James 1938, 766, 769). Following the election of James Polk in 1844, therefore, the outgoing president, John Tyler, along with Polk and former president Jackson, teamed up to successfully pressure Congress to admit Texas as a US state, so as to preclude its close association with Britain. A year later Texas was officially incorporated into the United States (ibid., 774–7).

8 See Gara (1991, 129–33), regarding the Gadsden Purchase, and William Walker's expedition to Baha California.

9 France's engagement in the Caribbean region received its most prominent expression, of course, in the form of French efforts to construct the Panama Canal, prior to the US assumption of the task.

10 Curtis (1883, 219–20).

11 Ibid. (220–2).

12 Ibid. (222).

13 Pletcher (1962, 170).

14 On Frelinghuysen's desire to use reciprocity to achieve the aims of the Monroe Doctrine, and hence to use trade for security purposes, see, for instance, Pletcher (1962, 180, 191). Regarding Frelinghuysen's perspective on the incompatibility of US and Latin American cultures, see Reeves (1975, 407).

15 Pletcher (1962, 286–7).

16 Ibid. (180).

17 Pletcher (1998, 108–9).

18 Pletcher (1962, 183).

19 Coerver (1979, 144). Also, see Pletcher (1962, 188).

20 Blaine's first attempt at hemispheric cooperation occurred in 1881, when, as James Garfield's secretary of state, he sought to organize a Pan-American conference. The immediate inspiration for this conference was the outbreak of war between Peru, Bolivia, and Chile, and Blaine's fears that this and other conflicts might be used by European powers as a pretext to establish strategic influence in the region (Crapol 2000, 71–3). Garfield's assassination, however, resulted in this conference not taking place. When Blaine returned in 1889 as Benjamin Harrison's secretary of state, he picked up where he left off by hosting the First International Conference of the American States in December 1889 (ibid., 118).

21 Socolofsky and Spetter (1987, 121).

22 Coletta (1973, 179–91).

23 Ibid. (175).

24 Nonetheless, Wilson preferred Carranza to the other options, even lending Carranza vital support at times to assist him in his power-consolidation struggles. Such support included sending the US navy to blockade – unsuccessfully – Mexican ports in order to prevent arms shipments from reaching Carranza's enemies.

25 Link (1947d, 469).

26 See, for example, ibid. (471), regarding the sinking of the Lusitania, and p. 534 regarding US efforts in Haiti, in light of the German threat.

27 The effort to promote discord between the United States and Mexico was undertaken by an extensive German spy network, operating in the United States and Mexico (ibid., 554–63).

28 See Link (1947b, 215), regarding General Pershing entering Mexico. Regarding Pershing's push south and fighting Mexican soldiers, see pp. 284–5. Regarding Carranza preparing for war, see pp. 293–5. See Link (1947a, 53–5, 120) regarding Wilson's accepting the idea of Joint High Commission.

29 Ibid. (336).

30 On US fears regarding Germany in the western hemisphere, see Link (1947d, 469, 471, 534, 554–63, 636). See also Link (1947a, 337).

31 Link (1947a, 343–5).

32 The United States was seeking to ensure that a pro-US regime was in place in Nicaragua, given that Nicaraguan territory played a key role in securing the Panama Canal, while Mexico supported the opposing Nicaraguan forces, in an effort to prevent US hegemony in the region. This Mexican policy of preventing US dominance in Central America was known as the "Carranza Doctrine" (Ferrell 1998, 126).

33 This policy orientation was set in place by Herbert Hoover. See De Conde (1951, 14, 45–64).

34 Ibid. (125).

35 Guerrant (1950, 73–4).

36 See, for instance, Hull (1948, 81). Hull accepted the position of secretary of state under Roosevelt precisely because it offered him an ideal position for promoting his ideas of international economic peace, and therefore political peace, which he had championed for much of his political career (ibid., 157).

37 Schuler (1998, 94–5).

38 Not wanting tensions over the issue to spoil US-Mexican relations, and US-Latin American relations more generally, the United States reacted relatively passively to this course of action. When meeting with American oil

representatives over the issue, Hull stressed the world security situation and the importance of Mexico in that regard. Hull claims that "the broad settlement reached with Mexico was a large factor in having our neighbor to the South in full accord with us at the moment of Pearl Harbor" (1948, 1142). On the day the Germans invaded Poland, FDR went out of his way to inform the Mexican ambassador that the two regimes would find a satisfactory solution to the oil problem. This was a major departure from previous diplomatic positions of the White House (Schuler 1998, 104).

39 Ibid. (161–203). In various texts the point is made that settlement of the oil issue needed to be attained before all other issues could be handled satisfactorily. For instance, see B. Wood (1961, 250). After the Mexican election in July 1940, bilateral US-Mexican military talks resumed. Throughout the first half of 1941, the two states moved towards an understanding on important defence and economic matters. By the summer of 1941 the oil dispute was the chief remaining obstacle to a general settlement with Mexico, and hence to closer US-Mexican defence cooperation (Cronon 1960, 260).

40 Indeed, with war looming, the purely economic rationale for reciprocity was problematized by the fact that wartime restrictions on trade would be put into effect, which is precisely what occurred. In fact, during the war the terms of all the reciprocity agreements were suspended. Also worth noting is the fact that between 1934 and 1940 the United States concluded trade agreements with several Latin American states. Although trade between the United States and these states increased 79 per cent over previous levels, between 1934 and 1940 the total trade between United States and nontrade agreement Latin American states – Mexico, Peru, Panama, others – increased 89 per cent (Guerrant 1950, 96–8).

41 B. Wood (1985, x).

42 Rabe (1988, 165). When Mexico, prior to the overthrow of Arbenz, resisted calls by Eisenhower's secretary of state, John Foster Dulles, for a Latin American anti-communist manifesto aimed at Guatemala, Dulles determined that this reflected "a real infiltration of communist, or fellow traveler influence into the Mexican government itself" (ibid., 52).

43 This middle-of-the-road approach was set in place by Adolfo Lopez Mateos, who assumed the Mexican presidency in 1958 (Meyer and Sherman 1995, 658–9). Also see A. Smith (1970, 180–1). As Smith also explains, the degree to which Lopez Mateos leaned towards one side or the other was also due in part to domestic political dynamics (85–146).

44 Even Luis Echeverria, who enjoyed fairly cordial relations with President Nixon, took various actions designed to demonstrate Mexican independence from the United States (Kissinger 1999, 719–20).

45 Meyer and Sherman (1995, 681).

46 Jauberth (1992, 59–61).

47 Carlos Salinas (pers. comm.).

48 Ibid.

49 Ibid.

50 On the manner in which the Caribbean integration movement was rein-
    vigorated when pro-communist Michael Manley came to office in Jamaica,
    see Payne (1980, 140). For the CIA's probable involvement in Manley
    losing the 1980 election, see Kaufman (1985, 187–9) and Payne (1988, 50–9).
    For the manner in which Manley's foreign policy was fundamentally
    focused on resisting US hegemony, see Persaud (2001, 154–5, 181). Al-
    though Manley often promoted CARICOM by noting economic concerns –
    see, for instance, Manley (1970, 1974) – his first priority was apparently
    not economic, but rather to assert and protect Jamaica's sovereign inde-
    pendence vis-à-vis the United States. This is suggested by the fact that in
    1979, when Jamaica's economy was in serious trouble and badly needed
    economic assistance from the United States – both in terms of direct aid
    and through US support in the IMF – Manley travelled to Cuba and gave a
    speech praising Lenin, and also called for the full independence of Puerto
    Rico, where – according to Persaud (2001, 185) – Manley knew Marxists
    were at the forefront of the independence campaign. Manley must have
    anticipated that this behaviour would prompt the United States to cut off
    economic support to Jamaica, and indeed it did.

51 Clines (1984). Also, for typical Reagan comments on the topic, see, for
    instance, "Mexican President, Reagan" (1984).

52 Goshko (1984).

53 Johnson (1984).

54 Kirkpatrick (1984).

55 Lustig (1992, 2).

56 Meyer and Sherman (1995, 686–8).

57 Lustig (1992, 130–1).

58 Ibid. (131).

59 Ibid. (133).

60 Salinas (2002, 38).

61 Ibid.

62 Carlos Salinas (pers. comm.).

63 Salinas (2002, 38).

64 Ibid. (38–9).

65 Ibid. (39).

66 Ingwerson (1990).

67 Bush (1991, 1).

68 Bush (1990, 1).
69 Bush (1991, 1).
70 Russell (1994, 177–82).
71 Salinas (2002, 9–36).
72 Ibid. (12).
73 George H.W. Bush (pers. comm.).
74 James Baker (pers. comm.).
75 Petras and Vieux (1992, 43).
76 Ibid.
77 This is by no means to suggest that the Bush administration did not
   play a centrally important role in the overall FTA negotiating process.
   Indeed, Bush took a substantial risk when he decided to push forward
   with NAFTA, and his decision to do so arguably cost him his re-election.
   Ross Perot, who entered the election contest as a third-party candidate,
   ran largely on an anti-NAFTA platform, memorably describing the "giant
   sucking sound" that would result from NAFTA's creation, as American
   jobs were shipped south of the border. Obliged to run against both Perot
   and Bill Clinton, Bush ultimately lost the race.
78 Salinas (2002, 12).
79 "Joint Communiqué on Trade and Investment" (1989).
80 Branigin (1989).
81 Robert Mosbacher (pers. comm.).
82 Salinas (2002, 37).
83 Ibid. (40–1).
84 Ibid. (39–41).
85 Ibid. (38).
86 Ibid. (45).
87 Ibid. (45–6).
88 Ibid. (47).
89 Ibid. (47–9).
90 Jaime Serra Puche (pers. comm.).
91 Salinas (2002, 43–9); Jaime Serra Puche (pers. comm.); Pedro Aspe (pers.
   comm.).
92 In the words of Jorge Castaneda, a prominent Mexican political scientist
   and periodic political figure, "They [the Salinas team] knew – certainly
   from mid-1989, when Salinas went off to Paris for the two hundredth anni-
   versary of the French Revolution – that this whole idea that the Europeans
   were going to start investing in Mexico was false. You didn't have to go to
   Davos for that. Any reasonable official or economist knows that Western
   Europe stopped being interested in Mexico around 1895. The United States
   became Mexico's leading trading partner, leading source of investment,

in the 1890s. There was never any sense that the British or the Germans or the French were going to invest massively in Mexico or lend Mexico money massively" (MacArthur 2000, 92).

93 Gatz (1997, 55). For more on the topic of FDI in Mexico, see, for instance, Middlebrook and Zepeda (2003); Narula (2006); and Haber, Klein, Maurer, and Middlebrook (2008).

94 Gatz (1997, 55).

95 James Baker (pers. comm.).

96 Cameron and Tomlin (2000, 33).

97 Gruber (2000, 96).

98 Ibid. As Cameron and Tomlin further explain, this system built upon the dispute resolution mechanism that was part of the US-Canadian FTA (2000, 47–8).

99 Clarkson (2008, 83–5).

100 Ibid. (chaps. 8–10).

101 Ibid. (392–405).

102 The analytical process was spearheaded by the US-based Council on Foreign Relations. See Council on Foreign Relations (2005).

103 US Department of State (2005).

104 Ibid.

105 Ibid.

106 One further element of the SPP story is the creation of the North American Competitiveness Council, a forum for trilateral discussions among business and political figures, which was established in 2006 at the advocacy of the three states' business communities, in reaction to the SPP's public sector–driven nature (Clarkson 2008, 439).

107 Burney (pers. comm.).

108 See, for instance, R. Pastor (2008, 84–98).

109 Clarkson (2008, 437).

110 Borgerson (2008, 63–77).

111 Borgerson (2013, 76–89).

112 "Bush Signs CAFTA into Law" (2005).

113 Raum (2005).

114 Thompson (2011, 1).

4. The Broader Context

1 This project is part of a small but burgeoning trend in IR studies, which takes seriously the security motivations for regional integration. In this regard, see, for example, Sheetz (1999); Ikenberry (2000); Craig (2003);

and Rosato (2006). Furthermore, Rosato (2003) serves as something of a prelude to the analytical approach used in his 2006 dissertation.

2 Schuman (1954, 13–19).

3 Fontaine (2000, 14).

4 Ibid.

5 See, for instance, Schuman (1954, 1963).

6 Adenauer (1966, 257).

7 Despite the clarity of Schuman's and Adenauer's statements, and despite the legitimate nature of the security concerns being expressed at the time, many prominent scholars of European integration have focused primarily on the economic incentives of the relevant states involved, while largely ignoring or diminishing the importance of the security issues cited by Schuman, Adenauer, and others. The tendency of such scholars to focus primarily on economic factors rather than on security concerns can be explained, in part, by the previously noted bifurcation of IR studies into contending camps of realist and liberal scholarship. For the liberal, economics-focused scholars of European integration, in particular, the tendency was set in place by Haas (1958), who sought a certain scientific precision for his argument, and who wrote, "The most inviting index of integration – because it can be verified statistically – is the economic one" (ibid., 283). Indeed, the socially *scientific* aspirations of Haas's approach come out with even more clarity in another instance, when he writes, "For the political scientist the unification of Europe has a peculiar attraction quite irrespective of merits and types. He may see in it, as I do, an instance of voluntary 'integration' taking place before his eyes, as it were under laboratory conditions. He will wish to study it primarily because it is one of the very few current situations in which the decomposition of old nations can be systematically analyzed within the framework of the evolution of a larger polity – a polity destined, perhaps, to develop into a nation of its own" (ibid., xi–xii).

8 Despite the very clear nature of the security threat facing these states, and the equally clear statements regarding security threats – and the use of trade techniques to address such – which were made by the key actors involved in the EEC's creation, the most prominent scholarship on the topic, has, as with the creation of the ECSC, emphasized primarily the economic incentives for integration. See, for instance, Haas (1958, 299–301) and Moravcsik (1998, 135–6).

9 For one of many treatments on this topic, see, for instance, Zurcher (1958, 83).

10 Beyen (1953a, 234). In its French formulation his statement reads, "Le premiere but de l'intégration européenne devrait être, semble-t-il, l'élévation

du niveau de vie général des peoples européennes, á part le renforcement de la défense par une coopréation plus étroite dans la domaine militaire, tel qu'il est prévue dans le Traité instituant la Communauté Européenne de la Défense."

11 Ibid.

12 Ibid. (237).

13 Ibid.

14 Ibid. (238).

15 Beyen (1953b). Beyen continued to focus on these points after he left public office as well. See, for instance, Beyen (1968, 223).

16 Edmund Wellenstein (pers. comm.). It is worth noting that the man who preceded Beyen in the job of Dutch foreign minister – Dirk Stikker – was equally clear regarding the fundamental security rationale for European integration (Stikker 1966, 162). So too, Paul-Henri Spaak, the Belgian foreign minister who ultimately led the diplomatic push for both Beyen's idea of a customs union and Spaak's idea for European nuclear industry integration – the twin-pronged approach that resulted in the Treaties of Rome in 1957 – repeatedly points out in his memoirs how the security and economic rationales for integration were linked (1971, 76–81, 200–7). For the record, on the other hand, Charles Rutten, who was a member of the Netherlands's delegations to the negotiations regarding the EDC and the Treaties of Rome, informed the author (pers. comm.) that he viewed Beyen's motivations as being primarily economics policy–focused.

17 For a comprehensive analysis of this strategic situation, see Cartwright and Critchley (1985); Haslam (1990); and Hert (1991).

18 For a sampling of his comments on this topic, as well as his long-standing, security-focused support of the integration effort, see Mitterrand (1986).

19 Mitterrand (May 1984, 2).

20 Ibid.

21 Ibid. (3).

22 I was first made aware of these meetings during my interviews of Lord David Hannay, a key foreign policy official in the Thatcher government, whom I interviewed on 1 February 2006.

23 Roland Dumas (pers. comm.).

24 Guy Legras (pers. comm.). As is the case with the analysis of previous episodes of European integrative advancement, and despite strong evidence pointing in the opposite direction, the most prominent EU scholars have argued that security motivations were of relatively little relevance to this particular integrative moment. See, in particular, Moravcsik (1998, 317).

25 Lord David Hannay (pers. comm.). According to Lord Hannay, the French
    ultimately gave the British essentially what the British had been asking
    for all along. Hannay, who was close to the negotiations, claims that this
    French conciliatoriness was also aided by Legras's considerable negotiat-
    ing skill.

26 For examples; see Attali (1995, 354); Sturmer (2001, 25–6); Moravcsik (1998,
    407); S. Wood (1998, 212); and Thatcher (2002, 2).

27 Dinan (1999, 133).

28 A useful, concise explanation of this history is provided by Fournier (1999,
    39–75).

29 It was also during the 1990s that another notable free trade initiative was
    undertaken in the region: the Free Trade Area of the Americas (FTAA),
    which was championed by the United States as an hemisphere-wide
    extension of NAFTA, was essentially a repackaged version of George H.W.
    Bush's Enterprise for the America's Initiative, and served as a competitor
    concept of sorts to Mercosur in South America. By the middle of the first
    decade of the twenty-first century, however, the FTAA idea had lost much
    of its momentum, although there are, as of this writing, still some indica-
    tions that the idea might be revived.

30 For a detailed history of ASEAN's first few decades of development, see
    Acharya (2001).

31 See Nyerere (1967, 188–9). According to Nyerere, mere economic integra-
    tion was not enough to meet Africa's most pressing needs, and thus full
    political integration was required (ibid., 190). When pan-African unity
    appeared unattainable, Nyerere focused his policies on the East African
    region.

32 On the history of this integration effort, and the motivations behind it, see
    Nyerere (1967, 348) and Smith (1974, 96, 122–9, 201). On the resistance to
    integration by the Zanzibar regime specifically, see Smith (1974, 131–7).

33 Jankowski (2002, 28, 32–4, 59, 71–2, 116–26).

34 For a history of Yemen-Saudi relations prior up to 1990, see Cause (1990).
    See also Almadhagi (1996, 115–19, 136–8) and Wenner (1991, 164–6).

35 For the founding of the UAE, see Khalifa (1979, 24–35). On the institutional
    structure of the UAE, see Khalifa (1979, 37–56, 82–3) and Anthony (1975,
    104–12).

36 The most notable articulation of these security motivations can be found
    in Hamilton, Madison, and Jay (1979). See specifically Federalist Nos. III–
    VIII. Of course, between the founding of the United States in the late 1700s
    and the democracy-dominant integration schemes that began in the twen-
    tieth century, there were various examples of apparent peaceful integration

involving nondemocracies, particularly in Europe. Upon closer inspection, however, in general the evidence does tend to support the democracy/ integration correlation. For example, the formation of Germany in the 1800s, while seemingly a peaceful – at least in part – integrative enterprise, nonetheless required that Bismarck make use of threats relating to the 1870 war with France, and diplomatic trickery with regard to Bavaria, in order to bring about a union of the Germanic states. For Bismarck's behaviour around the time of the 1870 war, see Pflanze (1990, 445–57). For the diplomatic intrigue used to gain control of Bavaria, see Richter (1954, 176–87).

37 On the Hapsburg threat, see Thurer (1971, 23–6). The Swiss, being partially democratized, achieved partial integration. On this point, see McCrackan (1901, 281) and Luck (1985, 65).

38 The role of democracy in Athens's alliance/imperial structure is treated in numerous instances in Thucydides's *The Peloponnesian War*. For the tendency of democracies and nondemocracies to align with similar such regimes, see Strassler (1996, 199). For the way in which democratic sympathies kept many states quiescent within the Athenian structure, see, for example, p. 182. For further treatment, see Appendix B in the same text, pp. 583–8.

39 Granted, Napoleon did make certain attempts at establishing a system of rule based on membership in his family, but none of these attempts got very far or lasted for very long, and thus, fundamentally, his rule was a one-man show.

40 It is true that in certain cases of family groups–based oligarchy we find that it is the rich who rule, and wealth is not necessarily a person-specific characteristic. Over time, however, those associated with both wealth and power also tend to become specified in terms of identity, such that, before long, what began as a wealth-based privilege to wield power transforms itself into an identity-based privilege as well. An added point regarding oligarchies: although certain theocratic oligarchies do not have person-specific rules regarding who is allowed to rule, nonetheless regime-running priesthoods do not typically lend themselves easily to integrating with other regimes, for fairly obvious reasons.

41 Given the prominence of the Mexican case in the context of this study, it is useful to explain why the Mexican president who succeeded Salinas – Ernesto Zedillo – was willing to allow his state to transition to democracy, given that regime leaders are presumed to resist such changes. The answer lies in the well-known designation of the Mexican regime prior to 2000 as "the perfect dictatorship." Mexico's pre-2000 regime rules were established in the early twentieth century in such a way that every president was

essentially a king in all but name. Nonetheless, the Mexican constitution allows these monarchs to serve only one six-year term. That constitution, in turn, was arrived at via massive revolutionary violence, and no Mexican president has been willing to risk dissolving the constitution-based peace in order to extend his stay in power. In lieu of perpetuating his own reign, therefore, at the end of his presidency each president – prior to 2000 – would designate who he specifically wanted to succeed him in office. In essence, what this meant is that each outgoing president chose the subsequent theory of justice for the state. Thus, when Zedillo chose democracy in 2000 – after Salinas began pointing the regime in that general direction during the 1990s – he was in fact acting in a manner similar to that of previous presidents, although his choice produced a significantly different outcome.

42 Aristotle (1992, 59–61). Of course, Aristotle was not particularly in favour of democracy, or at least, of "pure" democracy.

43 While history demonstrates that regimes are typically reluctant to change their rules regarding who is allowed to rule, that does not mean that such things never transpire. For instance, certain states have periodically surrendered peacefully to other, far more powerful states when the weaker states knew that they were no match for the massive military forces that they were facing.

44 The scholarly literature pertaining to the concept of "democratic peace" is vast. Some of the foundational essays of this literature can be found in Brown, Lynn-Jones, and Miller (1996).

45 Acharya (2001, 81, 128).

46 My (1992, 141–2).

47 Rene Pastor (1997).

48 The idea of a global polity is, of course, nothing new. In the contemporary era, we find the "founding father" of IR studies, Hans Morgenthau, concluding that a world of independent sovereign states is so dangerous that, in order for the human race to survive, a global state must be created (Morgenthau [1948] 1985, 525–94). The most notable recent treatment of the subject is Wendt (2003).

49 In contemporary IR studies, a famous questioning of global democratic order is offered by Francis Fukuyama, with his "end of history" thesis. Drawing on concepts from Hegel, Fukuyama posits that the global triumph of liberalism will lead to the end of meaningful political struggle and thus give rise to a certain sort of peaceful, global arrangement of states, thereby potentially resulting in centuries of boredom. See Fukuyama (1993). Fukuyama's claims thus provided a context for Samuel

Huntington to develop his equally famous "clash of civilizations" thesis, Huntington's argument being that western liberalism has not won a
permanent victory, that history has therefore not necessarily "ended," and
that the coming political conflicts will play out among noncombinable,
civilization-based groupings of states (1996). Huntington followed up this
point by specifically considering the intercivilizational tensions within
North America – in particular, relations between the United States and its
Hispanic neighbours – and the problems that he thinks might potentially
arise from too-close association between these groups (2005).

Bibliography

Acharya, Amitav. 2001. *Constructing a Security Community in Southeast Asia: ASEAN and the Problem of Regional Order.* New York: Routledge.

Adenauer, Konrad. 1966. *Memoirs 1945–1953.* Chicago, IL: Henry Regnery.

Almadhagi, Ahmed Noman Kassim. 1996. *Yemen and the United States: A Study of a Small Power and Super-State Relationship: 1962–1994.* New York: I.B. Tauris.

Anderson, Donald. 1973. *William Howard Taft: A Conservative's Conception of the Presidency.* Ithaca, NY: Cornell University Press.

Anderson, Jeffrey. 1999. *Regional Integration and Democracy.* New York: Rowman and Littlefield.

Anthony, John Duke. 1975. *Arab States of the Lower Gulf: People, Politics, Petroleum.* Washington, DC: Middle East Institute.

Aristotle. 1992. *The Politics.* New York: Penguin.

Attali, Jacques. 1995. *Verbatim: Tome III.* Paris: Fayard.

Axelrod, Robert. 1984. *The Evolution of Cooperation.* New York: Basic Books.

Barry, Donald, Mark Dickerson, and James Gaisford, eds. 1995. *Toward a North American Community? Canada, the United States and Mexico.* Boulder, CO: Westview.

Bemis, Samuel. 1949. *John Quincy Adams and the Foundations of American Foreign Policy.* New York: A.A. Knopf.

Bergeron, Paul. 1987. *The Presidency of James K. Polk.* Lawrence: University Press of Kansas.

Beyen, Johann. 1953a. *Jaarboek, Van Het Ministerie, Van Buitenlandse Zaken, 1952–53.* The Hague, Netherlands: Netherlands Foreign Ministry Archives.
———. 1953b. "L'idee Europeene Dans La Tempete." The Hague, Netherlands: Netherlands Foreign Ministry Archives, file 6262 (g), ABZ913.10 Europese Integratie. Deel. 28 September.

————. 1968. *Het Spel en de Knikkers*. Rotterdam, Netherlands: AD Donker.

Bland, Douglas, ed. 1997. *Canada's National Defense*. Vol. 1, *Defense Policy*. Kingston, Canada: School of Policy Studies.

Bognanno, Mario, and Kathryn Ready, eds. 1993. *The North American Free Trade Agreement*. Westport, CT: Quorum Books.

Borgerson, Scott. 2008. "Arctic Meltdown: The Economic and Security implications of Global Warming." *Foreign Affairs* 87 (March–April): 63–77.

————. 2013. "The Coming Arctic Boom: As the Ice Melts, the Region Heats Up." *Foreign Affairs* 92 (July–August): 76–89.

Bow, Brian. 2009. *The Politics of Linkage: Power, Interdependence and Ideas in Canada-US Relations*. Vancouver: University of British Columbia Press.

Branigin, William. 1989. "Mosbacher Says U.S. Encouraged by Economic Changes in Mexico." *Washington Post*, 23 November. Accessed 17 January 2007. http://www.lexisnexis.com.

Brant, Irving. 1941. *James Madison*. Indianapolis, IN: Bobbs-Merrill.

Brown, Michael, Sean Lynn-Jones, and Steven Miller, eds. 1996. *Debating the Democratic Peace*. Cambridge, MA: MIT.

Bush, George. 1990. "To the Congress of the United States." *The White House: Office of the Press Secretary*. College Station, TX: George H.W. Bush Presidential Library Archives. 14 September.

————. 1991. "One Year Ago Today ..." *United States Department of State*. College Station, TX: George H.W. Bush Presidential Library Archives. 24 June.

"Bush Signs CAFTA into Law." 2005. *United Press International*, 2 August. Accessed 7 December 2006. http://www.lexisnexis.com.

Byers, R.B., and Michael Slack, eds. 1986. *Strategy and the Arctic*. Toronto: Canadian Institute of Strategic Studies.

Cameron, Max, and Brian Tomlin. 2000. *The Making of NAFTA: How the Deal Was Done*. Ithaca, NY: Cornell University Press.

"Canada's New Prime Minister Woos Reagan / Mulroney Meets US President in Washington." 1984. *Guardian*, 27 September. Accessed 17 January 2007. http://www.lexisnexis.com.

Carlson, Peter. 2005. "Raiding the Icebox." *Washington Post*, 30 December. Accessed 30 September 2010. http://www.washingtonpost.com/wp-dyn/content/article/2005/12/29/AR2005122901412.html.

Carroll, John, and Mary Ashworth. 1948. "First in Peace." Vol. 7 of *George Washington: A Biography*, by Douglas Freeman. New York: Scribner.

Cartwright, John, and Julian Critchley. 1985. *Cruise, Pershing and SS-20: The Search for Consensus: Nuclear Weapons in Europe*. New York: Pergamon.

Cause, F. Gregory. 1990. *Saudi-Yemeni Relations: Domestic Structures and Foreign Influence*. New York: Columbia University Press.

Clarkson, Stephen. 2002. *Uncle Sam and Us: Globalization, Neoconservatism, and the Canadian State*. Toronto: University of Toronto Press.

———. 2008. *Does North America Exist?: Governing the Continent after NAFTA and 9/11*. Toronto: University of Toronto Press.

Clarkson, Stephen, and Matto Mildenberger. 2011. *Dependent America?: How Canada and Mexico Construct US Power*. Toronto: University of Toronto Press.

Clines, Francis. 1984. "Blunt Talk Marks Reagan's Welcome for Mexico's Chief." *New York Times*, 16 May. Accessed 21 May 2008. http://www .lexisnexis.com.

Coerver, Dan. 1979. *The Porfirian Interregnum: The Presidency of Manuel Gonzalez of Mexico, 1880–1884*. Fort Worth: Texas Christian University Press.

Coffey, Peter J., Colin Dods, Enrique Lazcano, and Robert Riley, eds. 1999. *NAFTA: Past, Present and Future*. Boston, MA: Kluwer Academic.

Coletta, Paolo. 1973. *The Presidency of William Howard Taft*. Lawrence: University Press of Kansas.

Council on Foreign Relations. 2005. *Building a North American Community: Report of an Independent Task Force*. Washington, DC.

Craig, Campbell. 2003. *Glimmer of the New Leviathan: Total War in the Realism of Niebuhr, Morgenthau, and Waltz*. New York: Columbia University Press.

Crapol, Edward. 2000. *James G. Blaine: Architect of Empire*. Wilmington, DE: Scholarly Resources.

Creighton, Donald. 1998. *John A. Macdonald: The Old Chieftain*. Toronto: University of Toronto Press.

Cronon, Edmund. 1960. *Josephus Daniels in Mexico*. Madison: University of Wisconsin Press.

Curtis, George. 1883. *The Life of James Buchanan*. New York: Harper and Bros.

De Conde, Alexander. 1951. *Herbert Hoover's Latin-American Policy*. Stanford, CA: Stanford University Press.

Dinan, Desmond. 1999. *Ever Closer Union*. Boulder, CO: Lynne Rienner.

Dobson, John. 1988. *Reticent Expansionism: The Foreign Policy of William McKinley*. Pittsburgh, PA: Duquesne University Press.

Doern, G. Bruce, and Brian Tomlin. 1992. *Faith and Fear: The Free Trade Story*. Toronto: Stoddart.

Dowty, Allen. 1971. *The Limits of American Isolationism: The United States and the Crimean War*. New York: New York University Press.

Ferrell, Robert. 1998. *The Presidency of Calvin Coolidge*. Lawrence: University Press of Kansas.

FitzGerald, Frances. 2000. *Way Out There in the Blue: Reagan, Star Wars and the End of the Cold War*. New York: Simon and Schuster.

Fleeman, Eugene. 2001. *Tactical Missile Design*. Reston, VA: American Institute of Aeronautics and Astronautics.

Fontaine, Pascale. 2000. *A New Idea for Europe: The Schumann Declaration – 1950–2000*. Brussels, Belgium: European Communities.

Fournier, Dominique. 1999. "The Alfonsin Administration and the Promotion of Democratic Values in the Southern Cone and the Andes." *Journal of Latin American Studies* 31 (February): 39–75.

Fukuyama, Francis. 1993. *The End of History and the Last Man*. New York: Harper.

Gara, Larry. 1991. *The Presidency of Franklin Pierce*. Lawrence: University Press of Kansas.

Garber, Peter. 1993. *The Mexico-US Free Trade Agreement*. Cambridge, MA: MIT Press.

Gatz, Jurgen. 1997. *The Socio-economic Impact of NAFTA's FDI Potential for Mexico*. Frankfurt: Peter Lang.

Gellner, John. 1986. "The Arctic as Strategic Forefield." In *Strategy and the Arctic*, edited by R.B. Byers and Michael Slack, 47–52. Toronto: Canadian Institute of Strategic Studies.

George, Alexander, and Andrew Bennett. 2005. *Case Studies and Theory Development in the Social Sciences*. Cambridge, MA: MIT Press.

Goshko, John. 1984. "Reagan Raps Mexico's Latin Policy; Leader Welcomed to White House." *Washington Post*, 16 May. Accessed 21 May 2008. http://www.lexisnexis.com.

Granatstein, J.L., and Robert Bothwel. 1991. *Pirouette: Pierre Trudeau and Canadian Foreign Policy*. Toronto: University of Toronto Press.

Grayson, George. 1995. *The North American Free Trade Agreement: Regional Community and the New World Order*. Lanham, MD: University Press of America.

Grieco, Joseph. 1988. "Anarchy and the Limits of Cooperation: A Realist Critique of the Newest Liberal Institutionalism." *International Organization* 42 (Summer): 498–500.

———. 1995. "The Maastricht Treaty: Economic and Monetary Union and the Neo-realist Research Programme." *Review of International Studies* 21 (1): 21–40.

———. 1996. "States' Interests and Institutional Rule Trajectories: A Neorealist Reinterpretation of the Maastricht Treaty and European Economic and Monetary Union." In *Realism: Restatement and Renewal*, edited by Benjamin Frankel, 262–305. London: Frank Cass.

Gruber, Lloyd. 2000. *Ruling the World: Power Politics and the Rise of Supranational Institutions*. Princeton, NJ: Princeton University Press.

Guerrant, Edward. 1950. *Roosevelt's Good Neighbor Policy*. Albuquerque: University of New Mexico Press.

Haas, Ernest. 1958. *The Uniting of Europe: Political Social and Economic Forces 1950–1957*. Stanford, CA: Stanford University Press.

———. 1964. *Beyond the Nation-State*. Stanford, CA: Stanford University Press.

Haber, Stephen, Herbert Klein, Noel Maurer, and Kevin Middlebrook. 2008. *Mexico since 1980*. Cambridge, UK: Cambridge University Press.

Hakim, Peter, and Robert Litan. 2002. *The Future of North American Integration: Beyond NAFTA*. Washington, DC: Brookings Institution Press.

Hamilton, Alexander, James Madison, and John Jay. 1979. *The Federalist Papers*. Norwalk, CT: Easton Press.

Hart, Michael, with Bill Dymond and Colin Robertson. 1994. *Decision at Midnight: Inside the Canada-US Free Trade Negotiations*. Vancouver: UBC Press.

Haslam, Jonathon. 1990. *The Soviet Union and the Politics of Nuclear Weapons in Europe, 1968–87*. Ithaca, NY: Cornell University Press.

Hayden, Peter. 1993. *The 1962 Cuban Missile Crisis: Canadian Involvement Reconsidered*. Toronto: Canadian Institute of Strategic Studies.

Hert, Jeffrey. 1991. *War by Other Means: Soviet Power, West German Resistance, and the Battle of the Euromissiles*. New York: Free Press.

Honderich, John. 1985. "Why Canada May Star in Star Wars." *Toronto Star*, 10 November. Accessed 11 June 2008. http://www.lexisnexis.com.

Huisken, Ronald. 1981. *The Origin of the Strategic Cruise Missile*. New York: Praeger.

Hull, Cordell. 1948. *The Memoirs of Cordell Hull*. New York: Macmillan.

Huntington, Samuel. 1996. *The Clash of Civilizations and the Re-making of World Order*. New York: Simon and Schuster.

———. 2005. *Who Are We?: The Challenges to America's National Identity*. New York: Simon and Schuster.

Ikenberry, John. 2000. *After Victory*. Princeton, NJ: Princeton University Press.

Ingwerson, Marshall. 1990. "Bush Speech Calls for New World Order." *Christian Science Monitor*, 13 September. Accessed 21 May 2008. http://www.lexisnexis.com.

Inwood, Greg. 2004. *Continentalizing Canada: The Politics and Legacy of the Macdonald Royal Commission*. Toronto: University of Toronto Press.

James, Marquis. 1938. *The Life of Andrew Jackson*. Indianapolis, IN: Bobbs-Merrill.

Jankowski, James. 2002. *Nasser's Egypt, Arab Nationalism, and the United Arab Republic*. Boulder, CO: Lynne Rienner.

Jauberth, H. Rodrigo. 1992. "The Mexico-Central America-United States Triangle and the Negotiations Process." In *The Difficult Triangle: Mexico, Central America, and the United States*, edited by H. Rodrigo Jauberth, Gilberto Castaneda, Jesus Hernandez, and Pedro Vuskovic, 59–61. Boulder, CO: Westview.

Jockel, Joseph, and Joel Sokolsky. 1986. *Canada and Collective Security: Odd Man Out*. New York: Praeger.

Johnson, William. 1984. "Force Won't Cure Latin American Unrest, Mexican Leader Tells Congress." *Globe and Mail*, 17 May. Accessed 21 May 2008. http://www.lexisnexis.com.

"Joint Communiqué on Trade and Investment Issued by Ambassador Hills and Secretary Serra on the Occasion of the U.S.-Mexican Presidential Summit." 1989. *Federal News Service*, 3 October. Accessed 17 January 2007. http://www.lexisnexis.com.

Jones, Clayton. 1980. "Reagan's 'North American Accord' Has Support, but Faces Obstacles." *Christian Science Monitor*, 26 December. Accessed 17 January 2007. http://www.lexisnexis.com.

Jones, Howard. 1977. *The Webster-Ashburton Treaty*. Chapel Hill: University of North Carolina Press.

———. 1990. "Daniel Webster: The Diplomatist." In *Daniel Webster: The Completest Man*, edited by Ken Shewmaker, 203–17. Hanover, NH: University Press of New England.

Kaufman, Michael. 1985. *Jamaica under Manley: Dilemmas of Socialism and Democracy*. Westport, CT: L. Hill.

Kaufman, Stuart, Richard Little, and William Wohlforth, eds. 2007. *The Balance of Power in World History*. New York: Palgrave Macmillan.

Keohane, Robert. 1984. *After Hegemony: Cooperation and Discord in the World Political Economy*. Princeton, NJ: Princeton University Press.

Keohane, Robert, and Joseph Nye. 1979. *Power and Interdependence*. New York: Longman.

Khalifa, Ali Mohammed. 1979. *The United Arab Emirates: Unity in Fragmentation*. Boulder, CO: Westview.

King, Gary, Robert Keohane, and Sydney Verba. 1994. *Designing Social Inquiry*. Princeton, NJ: Princeton University Press.

Kirkpatrick, Jeane. 1984. Address to the Republican National Convention. 20 August. Accessed 18 January 2007. http://www.cnn.com/ALLPOLITICS/1996/conventions/san.diego/facts/GOP.speeches.past/84.kirkpatrick.shtml.

Kissinger, Henry. 1999. *Years of Renewal*. New York: Simon and Schuster.

Krasner, Stephen. 1983. *International Regimes*. Ithaca, NY: Cornell University Press.

Kupchan, Charles, and Clifford Kupchan. 1991. "Concerts, Collective Security, and the Future of Europe." *International Security* 16 (1); 114–61.

Lange, Thomas, and J.R. Shackleton. 1998. *The Political Economy of German Unification*. London: Berghahn Books.

Lawrence, Robert. 1993. "International Competition and the Evolution of a North American Free Trade Area." In *The North American Free Trade Agreement*, edited by Mario Bognanno and Kathryn Ready, 151–2. Westport, CT: Quroum Books.

Legro, Jeffrey, and Andrew Moravcsik. 1999. "Is Anybody Still a Realist?" *International Security* 24 (2): 5–55.

Lindberg, Leon. 1963. *The Political Dynamics of European Economic Integration*. Stanford, CA: Stanford University Press.

Link, Arthur. 1947a. *Wilson: Campaigns for Progressivism and Peace*. Princeton, NJ: Princeton University Press.

———. 1947b. *Wilson: Confusions and Crises*. Princeton, NJ: Princeton University Press.

———. 1947c. *Wilson: The New Freedom*. Princeton, NJ: Princeton University Press.

———. 1947d. *Wilson: The Struggle for Neutrality*. Princeton, NJ: Princeton University Press.

Lipson, Charles. 1984. "International Cooperation in Economic and Security Affairs." *World Politics* 37 (1): 1–23.

Luck, James. 1985. *A History of Switzerland*. Palo Alto, CA: SPOSS.

Lustig, Nora. 1992. *Mexico: The Remaking of an Economy*. Washington, DC: Brookings Institution Press.

MacArthur, John. 2000. *The Selling of "Free Trade:" NAFTA, Washington and the Subversion of American Democracy*. New York: Hill and Wang.

Mahant, Edelgard, and Graeme Mount. 1999. *Invisible and Inaudible in Washington: American Policies toward Canada*. Vancouver: UBC Press.

Malone, Dumas. 1974. *Jefferson and His Time*. Vol. 7, *Jefferson the President: Second Term, 1805–1809*. Boston, MA: Little, Brown.

Maloney, Sean. 2007. *Learning to Love the Bomb: Canada's Nuclear Weapons during the Cold War*. Washington, DC: Potomac Books.

Manley, Michael. 1970. "Overcoming Insularity in Jamaica." *Foreign Affairs* 49 (1): 100–10.

———. 1974. *Politics of Change: A Jamaican Testament*. London: Deutsch.

Martin, Lisa. 1992. *Coercive Cooperation: Explaining Multilateral Economic Sanctions*. Princeton, NJ: Princeton University Press.

Mayer, Frederick. 1998. *Interpreting NAFTA: The Science and Art of Political Analysis*. New York: Columbia University Press.

McCrackan, W.D. 1901. *The Rise of the Swiss Republic*. New York: Henry Holt.

McDonald, Marci. 1985. "After the Eyes Have Stopped Smiling." *Maclean's*, 1 April. Accessed 17 January 2007. http://www.lexisnexis.com.

Mearsheimer, John. 1994–5. "The False Promise of International Institutions." *International Security* 19 (Winter): 5–49.

———. 2001. *The Tragedy of Great Power Politics*. New York: W.W. Norton.

"Mexican President, Reagan; Differ on Central America." 1984. *Facts on File*, 18 May. Accessed 18 January 2007. http://www.lexisnexis.com.

Meyer, Michael, and William Sherman. 1995. *The Course of Mexican History*. New York: Oxford University Press.

Middlebrook, Kevin, and Eduardo Zepeda. 2003. *Confronting Development: Assessing Mexico's Economic and Social Policy Challenges*. Stanford, CA: Stanford University Press.

Milner, Helen. 1997. *Interests, Institutions, and Information: Domestic Politics and International Relations*. Princeton, NJ: Princeton University Press.

Mitterrand, François. 1984. "Speech by François Mitterrand to the European Parliament," 24 May, *Centre Virtuel de la Connaissance sur l'Europe*. 2 October 2012. Accessed 15 September 2013. http://www.cvce.eu/content/publication/2001/10/19/cdd42d22-fe8e-41bb-bfb7-9b655113ebcf/publishable_en.pdf.

———. 1986. *Réflexions sur la Politique Extérieure de la France*. Paris: Fayard.

Moravcsik, Andrew. 1998. *The Choice for Europe: Social Purpose and State Power from Messina to Maastricht*. Ithaca, NY: Cornell University Press.

Morgenthau, Hans. (1948) 1985. *Politics among Nations*. New York: McGraw-Hill.

Morton, Desmond. 1983. *A Short History of Canada*. Edmonton, Canada: Hurtig.

———. 1999. *A Military History of Canada*. Toronto: McClelland and Stewart.

Mulroney, Brian. 2007. *Memoirs: 1939–1993*. Toronto: McClelland and Stewart.

My, Thu. 1992. "Renovation in Vietnam and Its Effects on Peace, Friendship and Cooperation in Southeast Asia." In *Unity in Diversity: Cooperation between Vietnam and Other Southeast Asian Countries*, edited by Nguen Duy Quy, 141–2. Hanoi, Vietnam: Science Publishing House.

Narula, R. 2006. *Understanding FDI-Assisted Economic Development*. London: Routledge.

Nevins, Allan. 1932. *Grover Cleveland: A Study in Courage*. New York: Dodd, Mead.

———.1957. *Hamilton Fish: The Inner History of the Grant Administration*. New York: F. Ungar.

Nyerere, Julius. 1967. *Freedom and Unity*. London: Oxford University Press.

Orchard, David. 1993. *The Fight for Canada: Four Centuries of Resistance to American Expansionism*. Toronto: Stoddart.

Orme, William. 1996. *Understanding NAFTA: Mexico, Free Trade and the New North America*. Austin: University of Texas Press.

Oye, Kenneth. 1986. *Cooperation under Anarchy*. Princeton, NJ: Princeton University Press.

Paolino, Ernest. 1973. *The Foundations of the American Empire: William Seward and United States Foreign Policy*. Ithaca, NY: Cornell University Press.

Parsons, Lynne Hudson. 1998. *John Quincy Adams*. Madison, WI: Madison House.

Pastor, Rene. 1997. "ASEAN Expands Due to Worries over China." *Reuters*, 4 June.

Pastor, Robert. 2001. *Toward a North American Community*. Washington, DC: Peterson Institute Press.

———. 2008. "The Future of North America: Replacing a Bad Neighbor Policy." *Foreign Affairs* 87 (4): 84–98.

Payne, Anthony. 1980. *The Politics of the Caribbean Community, 1961–1979: Regional Integration amongst New States*. New York: St Martin's Press.

———. 1988. *Politics in Jamaica*. New York: St Martin's Press.

Pearson, Lester. 1973. *Mike: The Memoirs of the Right Honourable Lester B. Pearson*. Vol. 2, *1948–1957*. New York: Quadrangle.

Persaud, Randolph. 2001. *Counter-Hegemony and Foreign Policy: The Dialectics of Marginalized and Global Forces in Jamaica*. Albany: State University of New York Press.

Peterson, Norma. 1989. *The Presidencies of William Henry Harrison and John Tyler*. Lawrence: University Press of Kansas.

Petras, James, and Steve Vieux. 1992. "Twentieth Century Neoliberals: Inheritors of the Exploits of Columbus." *Latin American Perspectives* 19 (Summer): 25–46.

Pflanze, Otto. 1990. *Bismarck and the Development of Germany*. Vol. 1, *The Period of Unification: 1815–1871*. Princeton, NJ: Princeton University Press.

Pletcher, David. 1962. *The Awkward Years: American Foreign Relations under Garfield and Arthur*. Columbia: University of Missouri Press.

———. 1998. *The Diplomacy of Trade and Investment*. Columbia: University of Missouri Press.

Powell, Robert. 1991. "Absolute and Relative Gains in International Relations Theory." *American Political Science Review* 85 (4): 1303–20.

Purver, Ron. 1986. "The Strategic Importance of the Arctic Region." In *Strategy and the Arctic*, edited by R. B. Byers and Michael Slack, 30–8. Toronto: Canadian Institute of Strategic Studies.

Rabe, Stephen. 1988. *Eisenhower and Latin America: The Foreign Policy of Anticommunism*. Chapel Hill: University of North Carolina Press.

Raum, Tom. 2005. "Bush Signs Trade Bill, but Bruising Battle Casts Doubt on Future Pacts." *Associated Press*, 2 August. Accessed 7 December 2006. http://www.lexisnexis.com.

Reagan, Ronald. 1979. *Official Announcement*. 13 November. Accessed 31 August 2007. http://www.4president.org/speeches/reagan1980announcement.htm.

———. 1988. *Remarks on Canada-United States Free Trade Agreement*. 25 July. Accessed 23 November 2013. http://www.reaganlibrary.gov/archives/speeches/36-archives/speeches/1988/8323-072588c.

Reeves, Thomas. 1975. *Gentleman Boss: The Life of Chester A. Arthur*. New York: Knopf.

Reisman, Simon. 1984. "The Issue of Free Trade." Address to the Brookings Institution. Library and Archives Canada. Vol. 4. File 13. Washington, DC, 16 April.

———. 1985. "Canadian Trade at the Crossroads: Options for New International Agreements, Trade Policy Options in Perspective." Ontario Economic Council Conference. Library and Archives Canada. Vol. 4. File 14. Toronto, 16–17 April.

Remini, Robert. 1981. *Andrew Jackson and the Course of American Freedom, 1822–1832*. New York: Harper and Row.

———. 1984. *Andrew Jackson and the Course of American Democracy, 1833–1845*. New York: Harper and Row.

———. 2000. *John Quincy Adams*. New York: Times Books.

Richter, Werner. 1954. *The Mad Monarch: The Life and Times of Ludwig II of Bavaria*. Chicago, IL: H. Regnery.

Rosato, Sebastian. 2003. "The Flawed Logic of Democratic Peace Theory." *American Political Science Review* 97 (4): 585–602.

———. 2006. "The Strategic Logic of European Integration." PhD diss. University of Chicago, Chicago, IL.

Russell, Phillip. 1994. *Mexico under Salinas*. Austin, TX: Mexico Resource Center.

Salinas de Gortari, Carlos. 2002. *Mexico: The Policy and Politics of Modernization*. Barcelona, Spain: Plaza & Janés Editores.

Scarry, Robert. 2001. *Millard Fillmore*. Jefferson, NC: McFarland.

Schuler, Friedrich. 1998. *Mexico between Hitler and Roosevelt: Mexican Foreign Relations in the Age of Lazaro Cardenas, 1934–1940*. Albuquerque: University of New Mexico Press.

Schull, Joseph. 1966. *Laurier: The First Canadian*. Toronto: Macmillan.

Schuman, Robert. 1954. *French Policy towards Germany since the War*. London: Oxford University Press.

———. 1963. *Pour L'Europe*. Paris: Nagel.

Schweller, Randall. 1994. "Bandwagoning for Profit: Bringing the Revisionist State Back In." *International Security* 19 (1): 72–107.

Setser, Vernon. 1937. *The Commercial Reciprocity Policy of the United States, 1774–1829*. Philadelphia: University of Pennsylvania Press.

"Shamrock Summit Seen as 'Turning Point' for U.S.-Canada Relations." 2000. *Canada Broadcasting Corporation*, 10 November. Accessed 15 September 2013. http://www.cbc.ca/news/world/shamrock-summit-seen-as-turning-point-for-u-s-canada-relations-1.171924

Sheetz, Mark. 1999. "Exit Strategies: American Grand Designs for Postwar European Security." *Security Studies* 8 (Summer): 1–43.

Smith, Arthur. 1970. *Mexico and the Cuban Revolution: Foreign Policy-Making in Mexico under President Adolfo Lopez Mateos, 1950–1964*. Ithaca, NY: Cornell University Press.

Smith, William. 1974. *Nyerere of Tanzania*. Nairobi, Kenya: Transafrica.

Snidal, Duncan. 1985. "The Limits of Hegemonic Stability Theory." *International Organization* 39 (4): 579–614.

———. 1991. "Relative Gains and the Pattern of International Cooperation." *American Political Science Review* 85 (3): 702–26.

Socolofsky, Homer, and Allan Spetter. 1987. *The Presidency of Benjamin Harrison*. Lawrence: University Press of Kansas.

Sokolsky, Joel. 1989. *Defending Canada*. New York: Priority Press.

Spaak, Paul-Henri. 1971. *The Continuing Battle*. New York: Little Brown.

Stikker, Dirk. 1966. *Men of Responsibility*. New York: Harper and Row.

Strassler, Robert, ed. 1996. *The Landmark Thucydides*. New York: Touchstone.

Sturmer, Michael. 2001. "France and Germany: An Unlikely Couple." In *France-Germany in the Twenty-First Century*, edited by Patrick McCarthy, 21–34. New York: Palgrave.

Thatcher, Margaret. 2002. *Statecraft: Strategies for a Changing World*. New York: Harper Collins.

Thompson, Ginger. 2011. "US Widening Its Role in Mexico's Drug War." *New York Times*, 7 August.

Thompson, John, and Stephen Randall. 2002. *Canada and the United States: Ambivalent Allies*. Athens: University of Georgia Press.

Thomson, Dale. 1960. *Alexander Mackenzie: Clear Grit*. Toronto: Macmillan.

Thurer, Greg. 1971. *Free and Swiss*. Translated by R.P. Heller and E. Long. Coral Gables, FL: University of Miami Press.

"US Conducts Second Cruise Missile Test over Canada." 1985. *Xinhua General News Service*, 6 January. Accessed 17 January 2007. http://www.lexisnexis.com.

US Department of State. 2005. "North American Leaders Unveil Security and Prosperity Partnership." 23 March. Accessed 15 September 2013. http://

iipdigital.usembassy.gov/st/english/texttrans/2005/03/20050323130436as
rellim0.1463282.html#axzz2ezYk2X1U.

Vasquez, John A., and Colin Elman, eds. 2003. *Realism and the Balancing of Power*. Upper Saddle River, NJ: Prentice Hall.

Walt, Stephen. 1987. *The Origins of Alliances*. Ithaca, NY: Cornell University Press.

Waltz, Kenneth. 1979. *Theory of International Politics*. New York: McGraw-Hill.

Weisman, Steven. 1981. "Reagan Will Meet Mexico Chief Today." *New York Times*, 5 January. Accessed 17 January 2007. http://www.lexisnexis.com.

Wendt, Alex. 2003. "Why a World State Is Inevitable." *European Journal of International Relations* 9 (4): 491–542.

Wenner, Manfred. 1991. *The Yemen Arab Republic*. Boulder, CO: Westview Press.

Werrell, Kenneth. 1985. *The Evolution of the Cruise Missile*. Maxwell Air Force Base, AL: Air University Press.

Wilson, Major. 1984. *The Presidency of Martin Van Buren*. Lawrence: University Press of Kansas.

Wood, Bryce. 1961. *The Making of the Good Neighbor Policy*. New York: Columbia University Press.

———. 1985. *The Dismantling of the Good Neighbor Policy*. Austin: University of Texas Press.

Wood, Stephen. 1998. *Germany, Europe and the Persistence of the Nation State*. Brookfield, VT: Ashgate.

Wren, Christopher. 1985. "US Weapons Ties Have Mulroney on the Defensive." *New York Times*, 24 March. Accessed 17 January 2007. http://www.lexisnexis.com.

Yarbrough, Beth, and Robert Yarbrough. 1992. "International Institutions and the New Economics of Organization." *International Organization* 44 (2): 235–59.

Young, Oran. 1985–6. "The Age of the Arctic." *Foreign Policy* 61 (Winter): 160–79.

Zurcher, Arnold. 1958. *The Struggle to Unite Europe*. Westport, CT: Greenwood Press.

Index